THE KEY

STUDENT STUDY GUIDE

THE KEY

THE KEY series of student study guides is specifically designed to assist students in preparing for unit tests, provincial achievement tests, and diploma examinations. Each *KEY* includes questions, answers, detailed solutions, and practice tests. The complete solutions show problem-solving methods, explain key concepts, and highlight potential errors.

TABLE OF CORRELATIONS

Castle Rock Research has designed *THE KEY* by correlating every question and its solution to Alberta Education's curriculum outcomes. Each unit of review begins with a Table of Correlations that lists the General and Specific Outcomes from the Alberta curriculum along with Related Questions that correspond to the outcomes. Usually the emphasis placed on outcomes, concepts, and skills within each unit varies. Students and teachers can quickly identify the relevant importance of each outcome and concept in the unit as determined by the number of related questions provided in *THE KEY*.

For grades 3, 6, 9, and 12, the weighting of each unit and concept is determined by analyzing the blueprint for the respective provincial achievement tests and diploma examinations. Based on this analysis, the Related Questions for outcomes and concepts are organized on a proportionate basis. For grades other than 3, 6, 9, and 12, the breakdown of each course is determined by consulting with experienced teachers and by reviewing curriculum guides and textbooks.

The Table of Correlations is a critical component of *THE KEY*. For students, it offers a visual cue for effectively organizing study time. For teachers, the Table of Correlations indicates the instructional focus for each content strand, serves as a curriculum checklist, and focuses on the outcomes and concepts that are the most important in the unit and the particular course of study. Students become "test wise" by becoming familiar with exam and question formats used most often in provincial examinations.

Canadian Cataloguing in Publication Data

Rao, Gautam, 1961 –
THE KEY – Chemistry 20 (AB)

1.   Chemistry – Juvenile Literature. I. Title

Published by
Castle Rock Research Corp.
2340 Manulife Place
10180 – 101 Street
Edmonton, AB T5J 3S4

5 6 7 FP 07 06 05

Printed in Canada

Publisher
Gautam Rao

Contributors
Chris Dambrowitz
Christine Faraq
Rob Hill
Karen Kline
Simonne Longerich
Vik Maraj
Rob Schultz
Sanjay K. Sharma

Dedicated to the memory of Dr. V. S. Rao

THE KEY – CHEMISTRY 20

THE KEY is a study guide specifically designed to complement classroom instruction and assist students in preparing for unit tests and final exams. It is a compilation of teacher-generated questions and answers that are correlated to the Chemistry 20 curriculum and that have been written to model the rigour and format of the Grade 12 diploma examinations. Questions have been grouped by concepts so that students can use the resource to study throughout the year. **Detailed solutions are provided for all questions.** An overview of the main sections of *THE KEY* follows.

I.   **Key Factors Contributing to School Success** provides students with examples of study and review strategies. Information is included on learning styles, study schedules, and developing review notes.

II.   *Unit Review* includes questions related to the four units that comprise the Chemistry 20 curriculum. Each unit begins with a Table of Correlations in which the questions are classified according to the specific learner outcomes of the curriculum. In *Unit Review*, questions considered to be more difficult are labelled as *Challenger* questions. By emphasizing questions of a more challenging nature, it is hoped that students will become more familiar with the depth of knowledge required to achieve at the standard of excellence. *THE KEY* **provides detailed solutions for all questions.**

III. **Key Strategies for Success on Exams** explores topics such as common exam question formats and strategies for responding, directing words most commonly used, how to begin the exam, and managing test anxiety.

IV.   The ***Practice Exam*** section contains two complete practice examinations. The questions presented here are distinct from the questions in the previous section. It is **recommended** that students work through the exams carefully because they are reflective of the exam format and level of difficulty that students are likely to encounter on final exams. **Complete solutions are provided for all questions in this section.**

THE KEY *Study Guides* are available for Biology 20, Chemistry 20, English 20-1, Physics 20, Mathematics 20 (Pure), and Social Studies 20. A complete list of *THE KEY* *Study Guides* available for grades 3 to 12 is included at the back of this book.

For information about any of our resources or services, please call Castle Rock Research Corp at 780.448.9619 or visit our web site at http://www.castlerockresearch.com.

At Castle Rock Research, we strive to produce a resource that is error-free. If you should find an error, please contact us so that future editions can be corrected.

CONTENTS

KEY FACTORS CONTRIBUTING TO SCHOOL SUCCESS

KEY FACTORS CONTRIBUTING TO SCHOOL SUCCESS

In addition to learning the contents of your courses, there are some other things that you can do to help you do your best at school. Some of these strategies are listed below.

- **ATTEND SCHOOL REGULARLY** so that you do not miss any classes, notes, and important activities that help you learn.

- **KEEP A POSITIVE ATTITUDE.** Always reflect on what you can already do and what you already know.

- **BE PREPARED TO LEARN.** Have ready the necessary pencils, pens, notebooks, and other required materials in class.

- **COMPLETE ALL OF YOUR ASSIGNMENTS.** Do your best to finish all of your assignments. Even if you know the material well, practice will reinforce your knowledge. If an assignment or question is difficult for you, work through it as far as you can so that your teacher can see exactly where you are having difficulty.

- **SET SMALL GOALS** for yourself when you are learning new material. For example, when learning the names of minerals, do not try to learn everything in one night. Work on only one set of names each study session. When you have memorized one particular set, move on to another one. Continue this process until you have memorized all of the minerals that you have to know.

- **REVIEW YOUR CLASSROOM WORK** regularly at home to be sure that you understand the material that you learned in class.

- **ASK YOUR TEACHER FOR HELP** when you do not understand something or when you are having a difficult time completing your assignments.

- **GET PLENTY OF REST AND EXERCISE.** Concentrating in class is hard work. It is important to be well-rested and have time to relax and socialize with your friends. This helps you to keep your positive attitude about your school work.

- **EAT HEALTHY MEALS.** A balanced diet keeps you healthy and gives you the energy that you need for studying at school and at home.

HOW TO FIND YOUR LEARNING STYLE

Every student has a certain manner in which it seems easier for him or her to learn. The manner in which you learn best is called your learning style. By knowing your learning style, you can increase your success at school. Most students use a combination of learning styles. Do you know what type of learner you are? Read the following descriptions. Which of these common learning styles do you use most often?

- **Do you need to say things out loud?** You may learn best by saying, hearing, and seeing words. You are probably really good at memorizing things such as dates, places, names, and facts. You may need **to write and then say out loud** the steps in a process, a formula, or the actions that lead up to a significant event.

- **Do you need to read or see things?** You may be a learner who learns best by seeing and working with pictures. You are probably really good at puzzles, imagining things, and reading maps and charts. You may need to use strategies like **mind mapping and webbing** to organize your information and study notes.

- **Do you need to draw or write things down?** You may learn best by touching, moving, and figuring things out using manipulatives. You are probably really good at physical activities and learning through movement. You may need to **draw your finger over a diagram** to remember it, **"tap out" the steps** needed to solve a problem, or **"feel" yourself writing** or typing a formula.

SCHEDULING STUDY TIME

Effective time management skills are an essential component to your academic success. The more effectively you manage your time, the more likely you are to achieve goals such as completing all of your assignments on time or finishing all of the questions on a unit test or year-end test. Developing a study schedule helps to ensure you have adequate time to review the subject content and prepare for the test.

You should review your class notes regularly to ensure that you have a clear understanding of all new material. Reviewing your lessons on a regular basis helps you to learn and remember the ideas and concepts taught to you in class. It also reduces the quantity of material that you need to study prior to a unit or year-end test. Establishing a study schedule will help you to make the best use of your time. The following brief descriptions are three types of study schedules.

- **LONG-TERM STUDY SCHEDULE**—begins early in the school year or semester and well in advance of a test; is the **most effective** method for improving your understanding and retention of concepts, as well as increasing your self-confidence; involves regular, nightly review of class notes, handouts, and textbook material

- **SHORT-TERM STUDY SCHEDULE**—begins five to seven days prior to a test; the volume of material to be covered should be reorganized so that the most difficult concepts come first; each study session starts with a brief review of what was studied the day before

- **CRAMMING**—occurs the night before a test; is the **least effective** method for studying or test preparation; focuses on memorizing and reviewing critical information such as facts, dates, and formulas; does not introduce new material; has the potential to increase test anxiety by revealing something you do not know

Regardless of the type of study schedule you use, you may want to consider the following strategies for maximizing your study time and effort:

➤ Establish a regular time and place for doing your studying.

➤ Minimize distractions and interruptions during your study time.

➤ Plan a ten-minute break for every hour that you study.

➤ Organize the material so that you begin with the most challenging content first.

➤ Divide the subject content into small, manageable "chunks" to review.

➤ Develop a marking system using symbols or highlighting for your study notes in order to identify key and secondary concepts, concepts that you are confident about, and concepts that require additional attention, or those about which you still have questions.

➤ Reward yourself for sticking to your schedule and/or completing each review section.

➤ Alternate the subjects that you are studying and types of study activities to maintain your interest and motivation.

➤ Make a daily list with the headings "must do," "should do," and "could do."

➤ Begin each study session by quickly reviewing what you studied the day before.

➤ Maintain your usual routine of eating, sleeping, and exercising so that you are able to concentrate for extended periods of time.

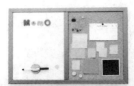

CREATING STUDY NOTES

MIND-MAPPING OR WEBBING

- Use the key words, ideas, or concepts from your reading or class notes to create a *mind map* or *web* (a diagram or visual representation of the given information). A mind map or web is sometimes referred to as a *knowledge map*.
- Write the key word, concept, theory, or formula in the centre of your page.
- Write down related facts, ideas, events, and information and link them to the central concept with lines.
- Use coloured markers, underlining, or other symbols to emphasize things such as relationships, timelines, and information of primary and secondary importance.
- The following example of a mind map or web illustrates how this technique can be used to learn a new term.

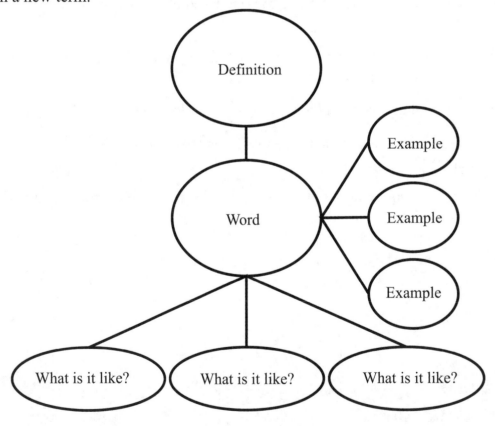

INDEX CARDS

To use index cards while studying, follow these steps:

- Write a key word or question on one side of an index card.
- On the reverse side, write the definition of the word, answer to the question, or any other important information that you want to remember.

> # What is an
> # organism?

> **What is an organism?**
>
> An organism is a living thing
> E.g., a plant or an animal

SYMBOLS AND STICKY NOTES—IDENTIFYING IMPORTANT INFORMATION

- Use symbols to mark your class notes. For example, an exclamation mark (!) might be used to point out something that must be learned well because it is a very important idea. A question mark (?) may highlight something that you are not certain about, and a diamond (◊) or asterisk (*) could mark interesting information that you want to remember.
- Use sticky notes when you are not allowed to put marks in books.
- Use sticky notes to mark a page in a book that contains an important diagram, formula, explanation, etc.
- Use sticky notes to mark important facts in research books.

MEMORIZATION TECHNIQUES

- **ASSOCIATION** relates new learning to something you already know. For example, to remember the spelling difference between *dessert* and *desert*, recall that the word *sand* has only one *s*. So, because there is sand in a desert, the word *desert* only has one *s*.

- **MNEMONIC DEVICES** are sentences that you create to remember a list or group of items. For example, the first letter of each word in the phrase "**E**very **G**ood **B**oy **D**eserves **F**udge" helps you to remember the names of the lines on the treble clef staff (E, G, B, D, and F) in music.

- **ACRONYMS** are words that are formed from the first letters or parts of the words in a group. For example, *radar* is actually an acronym for <u>ra</u>dio <u>d</u>etecting <u>a</u>nd <u>r</u>anging, and *MASH* is an acronym for <u>m</u>obile <u>a</u>rmy <u>s</u>urgical <u>h</u>ospital.

- **VISUALIZING** requires you to use your mind's eye to "see" a chart, list, map, diagram, or sentence as it is in your textbook or notes, on the chalkboard or computer screen, or in a display.

- **INITIALISMS** are abbreviations that are formed from the first letters or parts of the words in a group. Unlike acronyms, initialisms cannot be pronounced as a word themselves. For example, IBM is an initialism for International Business Machines, and **HOMES** helps you to remember the names of the five Great Lakes (**H**uron, **O**ntario, **M**ichigan, **E**rie, and **S**uperior)

KEY STRATEGIES FOR REVIEWING

Reviewing textbook material, class notes, and handouts should be an ongoing activity. Spending time reviewing becomes more critical when you are preparing for tests. You may find some of the following review strategies useful when studying during your scheduled study time.

• Before reading a selection, preview it by noting the headings, charts, graphs, and chapter questions.

• Read the complete introduction to identify the key information that is addressed in the selection.

• Read the first sentence of the next paragraph for the main idea.

• Skim the paragraph and note key words, phrases, and information.

• Read the last sentence of the paragraph.

• Repeat the process for each paragraph and section until you have skimmed the entire selection.

KEY STRATEGIES FOR SUCCESS—A CHECKLIST

Review, review, review: that is a huge part of doing well at school and preparing for tests. Here is a checklist for you to keep track of how many suggested strategies for success you are using. Read each question and then put a check mark (✓) in the correct column. Look at the questions where you have checked the "No" column. Think about how you might try using some of these strategies to help you do your best at school.

KEY Strategies for Success	Yes	No
Are you going to school regularly?		
Do you know your personal learning style—how you learn best?		
Do you spend 15 to 30 minutes a day reviewing your notes?		
Do you study in a quiet place at home?		
Do you clearly mark the most important ideas in your study notes?		
Do you use sticky notes to mark texts and research books?		
Do you practice answering multiple-choice and written-response questions?		
Do you ask your teacher for help when you need it?		
Are you maintaining a healthy diet and sleep routine?		
Are you participating in regular physical activity?		

The Diversity of Matter and Chemical Bonding

THE DIVERSITY OF MATTER AND BONDING

TABLE OF CORRELATIONS		
General Outcome	**Specific Outcome**	**Related Questions**
	Students are expected to:	
1. Students will describe the role of modelling, evidence, and theory in explaining and understanding the structure, chemical bonding, and properties of ionic compounds.	1.1 recall principles for assigning names to ionic compounds	29, 29
	1.2. explain why formulas for ionic compounds refer to the simplest whole-number ratio of ions that result in a net charge of zero	26, 27
	1.3. define valence electron, electronegativity, ionic bond, and intramolecular force	2, 3, 4, 30, 31
	1.4 use the periodic table and electron dot diagrams to support and explain ionic bonding theory	24
	1.5 explain how an ionic bond results from the simultaneous attraction of oppositely charged ions	5, 9
	1.6 explain that ionic compounds form lattices and that these structures relate to the compounds' properties; *e.g., melting point, solubility, reactivity*	13, WR2
2. Students will describe the role of modelling, evidence, and theory in explaining and understanding the structure, chemical bonding, and properties of molecular substances.	2.1. recall principles for assigning names to molecular substances	32, 33
	2.2 explain why formulas for molecular substances refer to the number of atoms of each constituent element	34
	2.3. relate electron pairing to multiple and covalent bonds	35, 36
	2.4 draw electron dot diagrams of atoms and molecules, writing structural formulas for molecular substances and using Lewis structures to predict bonding in simple molecules	37
	2.5 apply VSEPR theory to predict molecular shapes for linear, angular (V-shaped, bent), tetrahedral, trigonal pyramidal and trigonal planar molecules	38, 39
	2.6 illustrate, by drawing or by building models, the structure of simple molecular substances	40
	2.7 explain intermolecular forces, London (dispersion) forces, dipole-dipole forces and hydrogen bonding	11, 12, 14, 15, 19, 20, 21, NR1, NR2
	2.8 relate properties of substances (*e.g. melting and boiling points, enthalpies of fusion and vapourization*) to the predicted intermolecular bonding in the substances	16, 17
	2.9 determine the polarity of a molecule based on simple structural shapes and unequal charge distribution	WR1
	2.10 describe bonding as a continuum ranging from complete electron transfer to equal sharing of electrons	6, 8, 10

IONIC COMPOUNDS

Students will describe the role of modelling, evidence, and theory in explaining and understanding the structure, chemical bonding, and properties of ionic compounds.

20-A1.1k   recall principles for assigning names to ionic compounds

To assign a name for an ionic compound, look at the formula and pick out the anion and cation present. The compound name is the name of the cation, followed by the name of the anion.

Examples:

$MgCl_2$ cation: Mg^{2+}, magnesium;
anion: Cl^-, chloride (monatomic anions always have an *ide* ending)
Compound name: magnesium chloride

ZnS cation: Zn^{2+}, zinc;
anion: S^{2-}, sulfide.
Compound name: zinc sulfide

$(NH_4)_2SO_4$ cation: NH_4^+, ammonium;
anion: SO_4^2, sulfate.
Compound name: ammonium sulfate

$Cr_2(CO_3)_3$ cation: Cr^{3+}, chromium (III);
anion: CO_3^{2-}, carbonate.
Compound name: chromium (III) carbonate

For elements like chromium that have more than 1 ion charge, it is necessary to first determine the ion charge by working backwards from the balanced formula, and then state the name of the ion by using a roman numeral to indicate the charge.

Related Questions: 28, 29

20-A1.2k   explain why formulas for ionic compounds refer to the simplest whole-number ratio of ions that result in a net charge of zero

When writing formulas for ionic compounds, it is necessary to balance ion charges so that the total charge of the anions and cations (each multiplied by their balancing coefficients) adds to zero.

Examples:

sodium chloride: ions: Na^+ and Cl^-
The total charge of these ions already zero, so the balanced formula is $NaCl$

aluminium sulfide: ions: Al^{3+} and S^{2-}.
The total charge of these ions does not add to zero, so balancing coefficients must be added to make them add to zero. To balance, multiply Al^{3+} by 2 to make 6^+ and multiply S^{2-} by 3 to make 6^-. This now adds to zero so that the balanced formula is Al_2S_3

Some of you will have been taught to balance ionic formulas by trading numbers.
For aluminium sulfide,

$$Al^{3+} \quad S^{2-}$$

leading to Al_2S_3. Use this method with caution. It is dangerous.

magnesium nitrate: ions: Mg^{2+} and NO_3^-.
Multiply NO_3^- by 2; leave Mg^{2+} to get the balanced formula: $Mg(NO_3)_2$

In ionic compounds, the formula is written in this manner. It is the formula made up of the lowest whole number ratio of cations to anions in the crystal lattice. See sections 20-A1.5k and 6k for the reason why.

Related Questions: 26, 27

20-A1.3k   define valence electron, electronegativity, ionic bond, and intramolecular force

Valence electrons are electrons in the highest or outermost energy level of the atom.
These electrons are the ones involved in chemical reactions and bonding.

Electronegativity is a number that describes the relative ability of an element to attract shared electrons in a covalent bond.
A large electronegativity means strong attraction; a small electronegativity means weak attraction.

An *ionic bond* is an electrostatic attraction between a cation and an anion in an ionic crystal lattice.

An *intramolecular force* is a force or bond between atoms in the same molecule or polyatomic ion. Covalent bonds are intramolecular forces.

Related Questions: 2, 3, 4, 30, 31

20-A1.4k   use the periodic table and electron dot diagrams to support and explain ionic bonding theory

Metals have small electronegativities and thus weak attraction for their valence electrons. Non-metals have large electronegativities and thus strong attraction for their valence electrons. When metal and non-metal elements react, rather than sharing electrons to achieve stability, metals will tend to give up 1 or more valence electrons and form cations, while non-metals will take 1 or more electrons to form anions. The *transfer* of valence electrons from metal to non-metal makes both the metal and non-metal atoms more stable. Because F has a much higher electronegativity (4.0) than K (0.8), when a K atom and an F atom collide, electrons will be transferred.

$$K\bullet + {}^{\circ}_{\circ}\overset{\circ\circ}{F}{}^{\circ}_{\circ} \longrightarrow K^+ + \left({}^{\bullet}_{\circ}\overset{\circ\circ}{F}{}^{\circ}_{\circ}\right)^-$$

When calcium reacts with fluorine, the result is

$$\overset{\frown}{Ca}\bullet + {}^{\circ}\overset{\circ\circ}{F}{}^{\circ}_{\circ} \longrightarrow Ca^{2+} + 2\left({}^{\bullet}_{\circ}\overset{\circ\circ}{F}{}^{\circ}_{\circ}\right)^-$$
$${}^{\circ}\overset{\circ\circ}{F}{}^{\circ}_{\circ}$$

As these ions form, they will cluster to form a crystal lattice of K^+ and F^- in the first case, and Ca^{2+} and F^- in the second. These crystals will each contain a gigantically large number of ions.

Related Questions: 24

20-A1.5k   explain how an ionic bond results from the simultaneous attraction of oppositely charged ions

In an ionic crystal lattice, there will be a large number of cations and anions. Because positive charge is attracted to negative charge, in every case anions will be in closest proximity to as many cations as possible. Cations will also be in closest proximity to as many anions as possible. The relative sizes of the ions and the ratio of anion to cation (1:1 in KF and 2:1 in CaF_2) determines the shape of the crystal lattice. The static electrical (or electrostatic) attraction between the cations and anions in the crystal lattice is the cause of ionic bonds.

Related Questions: 5, 9

20-A1.6k   explain that ionic compounds form lattices and that these structures relate to the compounds' properties; e.g., melting point, solubility, reactivity

The crystal lattices are described in section 20-A1.5k. The ionic bonding between ions is strong. Therefore, ionic compounds have high *melting points* as considerable energy is required to split the lattice. This means that ionic compounds will be solids at room temperature. Ionic compounds will dissolve and dissociate into individual ions in a water solution if they dissolve. Cations will be surrounded by water molecules, as will anions. This is because water, even though it is a molecular compound, has one very positive end and one very negative end in its molecule. The new bonds that form between the ions and water are stronger than the bonds that existed between the ions in the crystal lattice in many cases, and heat will be released as they dissolve.
Ionic compounds tend to react as individual ions. In crystalline form, ionic compounds do not react easily. In the dissolved or aqueous state the ionic compound exists as individual ions. Because of this, ionic compounds dissolved in water react much more easily, than solid ionics.

Related Questions: 13, WR2

MOLECULAR COMPOUNDS

20-A2.1k   recall principles for assigning names to molecular substances

Binary molecular compounds (containing 2 elements) are named using a system of prefixes: Prefixes are inserted in front of the element to indicate the number of the atom in each molecule. The second atom in the formula gets an *ide* ending. The prefix mono is only used on the second atom in the formula.

Number	Prefix
1	mono
2	di
3	tri
4	tetra
5	penta
6	hexa
7	hepta
8	octa
9	nona
10	deca

Examples:
CCl_4 – carbon tetrachloride
As_2O_3 – diarsenic trioxide

Many binary molecular compounds have common names and in these cases, the common names should be used.

Example:
H_2O is called water, not dihydrogen monoxide.

Most non-binary molecular compounds are organic. They have a different system of nomenclature that you will learn in Chemistry 30.

Related Questions: 32, 33

20-A2.2k   explain why formulas for molecular substances refer to the number of atoms of each constituent element

Molecular compounds exist in stable groups of atoms called molecules. A molecule like H_2O contains 2 atoms of hydrogen and 1 atom of oxygen. It is not a ratio based formula as it is for ionic compounds.

Related Questions: 34

20-A2.3k   relate electron pairing to multiple and covalent bonds

A *covalent bond* is the attraction of two nuclei for a pair (or pairs) of electrons that they share. Multiple covalent bonds are possible.

Number of Pairs Shared	Name of Bond
1	single covalent
2	double covalent
3	triple covalent

It is **not** possible to share more than 3 pairs of electrons.

Related Questions: 35, 36

20-A2.4k   draw electron dot diagrams of atoms and molecules, writing structural formulas for molecular substances and using Lewis structures to predict bonding in simple molecules

Electron pairing is important in understanding chemical bonds. Valence electrons (actually all electrons) occupy *orbitals* which are *areas of space* where an electron of a given energy is most often found. The following are rules and related information about orbitals.

1. An orbital can hold a maximum of 2 electrons.
2. Since electrons repel each other, orbitals are filled by parallel spin to minimize repulsion. This means electrons occupy **empty** valence orbitals before pairing up.
3. There are 4 valence orbitals in the valence level of all non-metals in this simplified analysis.

4. Paired electrons in an orbital are called *lone pairs*.
5. Unpaired electrons in an orbital are called *bonding electrons*.
6. The number of bonding electrons is called the *bonding capacity* of the atom.
7. Atoms with a stable bonding condition will have 2 electrons in each of their 4 valence orbitals, a situation called a *stable octet*.

Lewis or electron-dot diagrams are a method of keeping track of the valence electrons of atoms. In these diagrams:

1. The element symbol represents the nucleus and inner electrons of the atom.
2. Each side of the symbol represents a valence orbital.

Examples:
1. Carbon, 4 valence electrons
From the diagram, carbon has 4 bonding electrons and 0 lone pairs.

• C •

2. Nitrogen, 5 valence electrons
From the diagram, nitrogen has 3 bonding electrons and 1 lone pair.

Note: it is unimportant which side has the lone pair.

• N •

To make Lewis diagrams of molecules it is a matter of sharing electrons between atoms so that each atom (other than hydrogen) ends up with a *stable octet*.

Examples:

NH₃

H N H
H

Note: that nitrogen ends up with the *stable octet* and each hydrogen with 2 electrons.

OF₂

: F ° O ° F :

Note: that O and each F all have a *stable octet*

HCN

H ° C ::: N °

In this case, it was necessary for C and N to share 3 pairs of electrons for each to achieve the *stable octet*

Related Questions: 37

20-A2.5k apply VSEPR theory to predict molecular shapes for linear, angular (V-shaped, bent), tetrahedral, trigonal pyramidal and trigonal planar molecules

VSEPR, the "Valence Shell Electron Pair Repulsion" theory, allows prediction of the shape around a central atom using the following main ideas
• Lone pairs and bonding pairs around a central atom move as far apart as possible to minimize repulsion
• Multiple bonding pairs are treated as if they were single bonding pairs

Examples:

Formula	Lewis Diagram	around central atom:		shape name	shape diagram
		lone pairs	bonding pairs		
CH_4	H : C : H (with H above and below)	0	4	tetrahedral bond angle = 109°	
NH_3	H : N : H (with H below)	1	3	trigonal pyramidal bond angle = 109°	
H_2O	H : O : H	2	2	v-shaped bond angle = 109°	
CH_2O	H : C :: O (with H below)	0	3	trigonal planar bond angle = 120°	
HCN	H : C :: N	0	2	linear bond angle = 180°	

out of page

flat on page

behind page

Related Questions: 38, 39

20-A2.6k *illustrate, by drawing or by building models, the structure of simple molecular substances*

The principles of the VSEPR Theory can be used to determine the shape of molecules even if there is more than one central atom.

Example:
CH_3COOH
Lewis diagram

2 lone pairs
2 bonding pairs
v-shaped

0 lone pairs
4 bonding pairs
tetrahedral

0 lone pairs
3 bonding pairs
trigonal planar

Shape diagram

Making models is a good way of equating the diagrams with the molecular shape.

Related Questions: 40

---

*20-A2.7k   explain intermolecular forces,
London (dispersion) forces, dipole-
dipole forces and hydrogen bonding*

Intermolecular forces are the forces among molecules — the forces that attract one molecule to another. If there were none, all molecular substances would be gases at all temperatures, even absolute zero.

Dipole-dipole forces – present in polar molecular substances only. These forces are due to the attraction of the positive end or pole of one molecule to the negative end or pole of neighbouring molecules. There is more about polar and non-polar molecules in 20-A2.9k.

London (dispersion) forces – present in all molecular substances. The greater the total number of electrons in a molecule, the greater the strength of the London forces.

When comparing the strength of the London forces in 2 different molecules with the same number of electrons, one with a shape that does not allow close approach of the molecules will have weaker forces than one that does.

London forces are caused by the interactions of temporary dipoles in molecules with each other. Even though non-polar molecules do not have permanent dipoles, they have temporary ones that average out to zero. These temporary dipoles induce temporary dipoles in their neighbours and cause attractions.

The greater the number of electrons, the more easily the temporary dipoles are induced.

Hydrogen bonds – extra-strong dipole-dipole forces are present in molecular compounds with hydrogen covalently bonded to F, O, or N. (Think hydrogen FONding.) Since F, O, and N have such high electronegativities compared to H, the covalent bond between H and one of them, leaves H essentially electron-free.

This electron-free H is strongly attracted to the highly electronegative F, O, or N on neighbouring molecules, which in a sense has extra electrons.

Related Questions: 11, 12, 14, 15,19, 20, 21, NR1, NR2

*20-A2.8k   relate properties of substances
(e.g. melting and boiling points,
enthalpies of fusion and
vapourization) to the predicted
intermolecular bonding in the
substance*

As the strength of intermolecular forces increases, boiling and melting points, and enthalpies of fusion and vapourization all increase.

When comparing the strength of London forces compare the total number of electrons.

When deciding whether dipole-dipole forces are present, decide whether or not the molecule is polar (see 20-A2.9k)

When deciding whether or not hydrogen bonding is present, look for compounds containing OH, NH, or FH bonds.

Related Questions: 16, 17

*20-A2.9k   determine the polarity of a molecule
based on simple structural shapes
and unequal charge distribution*

When atoms do not share electrons equally, the bond becomes a polar covalent bond.

The atom with higher electronegativity is partially negative, $\delta-$, while the one with lower electronegativity is partially positive, $\delta+$.

For example, in the bond between C and H, C has the greater electronegativity and is $\delta-$, while H has the lower electronegativity and is $\delta+$. Draw it like this:

The arrow, represents a bond dipole, where the arrowhead is the negative end and the tail represents the positive end of the polar covalent bond.

Just as bonds may be polar or non-polar, molecules may be polar or non-polar and the answer to this will have a large effect on a number of different physical properties including solubility and melting and boiling points.

In order to determine whether or not a molecule is polar, it is necessary to predict the shape of the molecule, determine the dipoles present on the bonds and see whether they cancel each other out or add to produce a net dipole, when you consider both size and direction of the dipoles.

Some examples and generalizations are given in the following chart:

Formula and Lewis Diagram	Shape Diagram with bond dipoles	Polar or non-polar
CH_4 H ∴ H∴C∴H ∴ H	*tetrahedral*	non-polar
C_2F_4 xx x F x xx • x xx x F • C ∷ C ∘ F x xx ∘x xx x F x xx	*trigonal planar*	non-polar
C_2Cl_2 ∷Cl∷ C ∷∷ C ∷Cl∷	Cl – C ≡ C – Cl *linear*	non-polar
Br_2 ∷Br∷Br∷	Br – Br *linear*	non-polar
HCl H ∷Cl∷	H – Cl *linear*	polar
CO_2 O ∷∘ C ∷∘ O	O = C = O *linear*	non-polar
NH_3 H∷N∷H ∘∘ H	*trigonal pyramidal*	polar
H_2O H∷O∷H	*v-shaped*	polar

Related Questions: WR1

20-A2.10k describe bonding as a continuum ranging from complete electron transfer to equal sharing of electrons

When electrons are shared, they are not necessarily shared equally. It is conceivable that some atoms have a greater attraction for shared valence electrons than others.

This relative attraction is known as electronegativity.

Two hydrogen atoms with their equal electronegativies will share a pair of electrons equally between them and will possess what is called a non-polar covalent bond.

Carbon and hydrogen will not share their pair of electrons equally in a carbon-hydrogen bond. Carbon has an electronegativity of 2.5 or 2.6 depending on the periodic table you use, while hydrogen has an electronegativity of 2.1 or 2.2 depending again on the periodic table.

Since carbon has the higher electronegativity, it will have a stronger hold on the shared electron pair, making the covalent bond have one end that is partially negative, $\delta -$, and one end that is partially positive, $\delta +$. This is called a polar covalent bond since it will have positive and negative poles.

In an extreme case, sodium, with an electronegativity of 0.9 and fluorine, with an electronegativity of 4.0 could react.

In this case sharing would not occur at all. When they reacted sodium would simply donate an electron to fluorine forming a sodium ion, Na^+, and fluoride ion, F^-. The bond between Na^+ and F^- is an ionic bond.

Note: there is not a sharp dividing line between ionic bonding and covalent bonding. Bonding becomes more ionic and less covalent the greater the electronegativity difference. In general, bonding between non-metals is referred to as covalent bonding, and bonding between metals and non-metals is referred to as ionic bonding.

Related Questions: 6, 8, 10

Use the following information to answer the next question.

Salts of silver are notoriously insoluble and yet silver nitrate is a high solubility compound. Silver nitrate can react with potassium chloride in aqueous solution to produce silver chloride.

$$AgNO_{3(aq)} + KCl_{(aq)} \rightarrow AgCl_{(s)} + KNO_{3(aq)}$$

The reaction of 250 mL of $AgNO_{3(aq)}$ with excess aqueous potassium chloride produces 15.0 g of precipitate.

1. If all the silver ions in the reactants are removed following reaction, the limiting species in the reaction is

   A. $KNO_{3(aq)}$ **B.** $KCl_{(aq)}$

   C. $AgNO_{3(aq)}$ **D.** $AgCl_{(s)}$

2. The intramolecular bonding in CH_2FCF_3 is called

   A. ionic bonding $MgCl_2$

   B. hydrogen bonding

   C. van der Waal's bonding   (London Dispersion)

   D. covalent bonding O_2

The Hindenburg airship made regular transatlantic flights in 1936 and 1937. The German-built Hindenburg, the largest aircraft ever flown, made its final flight in May 1937. During this fatal flight, the hydrogen gas-filled dirigible burst into flames, killing 35 people on board.

3. The bonding within H$_{2(g)}$ could be described as

A. mutual attraction of valence electrons
B. intermolecular bonding   ~Covalent~
C. hydrogen bonding   H and O, N, F
D. ionic bonding   NaCl

Use the following information to answer the next question.

Ethanethiol is a foul smelling compound that is used by utility companies. Pure natural gas is odourless, which makes gas leaks difficult to detect. Small amounts of ethanethiol are added to natural gas, butane, and propane so that the smell and any subsequent leaks are easily detected. The structure of ethanethiol is shown below.

$$CH_3 - \overset{\overset{\displaystyle H}{|}}{\underset{\underset{\displaystyle H}{|}}{C}} - SH$$

4. The bonding within ethanethiol involves

A. valence orbital repulsion
B. the simultaneous attraction of electrons by the atomic nuclei
C. equal and unequal sharing of electrons by the nuclei
D. hydrogen bonding by the hydrogen sulphur

Use the following information to answer the next question.

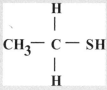

5. Chemical bonds such as those in anethole, the molecule responsible for the odour of licorice, are a result of

A. non-valence electron interactions
B. dipole-dipole interactions
C. complete electron transfer
D. simultaneous attraction of electrons by adjacent nuclei

Use the following information to answer the next two questions.

Compounds can be as structurally simple as $NaCl_{(s)}$, or more complex as chloroacetophenone, which has the following structure.

$$\underset{\substack{\| \\ C}}{\overset{O}{\|}}$$

(benzene ring)–C(=O)–CH_2Cl

Chloroacetophenone is the volatile liquid more commonly known as MACE or tear gas.

6. Both $NaCl_{(s)}$ and chloroacetophenone maintain their structural integrity because of

   A. electron-electron attraction

   B. nucleus-nucleus attraction

   C. simultaneous electron attraction between two nuclei

   D. electron transference and electron sharing, respectively

7. The main type of bonding in each of these compounds differs in that

   A. $NaCl_{(s)}$ is covalently bonded and MACE is molecularly bonded

   B. $NaCl_{(s)}$ is ionically bonded and MACE is hydrogen bonded

   C. $NaCl_{(s)}$ is covalently bonded and MACE is ionically bonded

   D. $NaCl_{(s)}$ is ionically bonded and MACE is covalently bonded

8. The type of bonding interactions that would occur in glass ($SiO_{2(s)}$) would most likely involve

   A. electron transfer

   B. equal sharing of electrons

   C. unequal sharing of electrons

   D. ionic bonding

Use the following information to answer the next question.

Historically, oxidation was the term used to refer to the reaction of an element with oxygen. Today, such reactions are called reduction-oxidation (redox) reactions. One such reaction might be

$$2Mg_{(s)} + O_{2(g)} \rightarrow 2MgO_{(s)}$$

9. The type of bonding in the product of this reaction is

   A. hydrogen bonding

   B. covalent bonding

   C. dipole-dipole bonding

   D. ionic bonding

Use the following information to answer the next question.

The rechargeable nickel-cadmium battery relies on a cadmium metal anode and a nickel (III) oxide hydroxide cathode. These batteries are more costly than the traditional dry cell and alkaline batteries, but they are easily recharged and are more economical in the long run.

10. The bonding in nickel (III) oxide hydroxide can be described as a result of

    A. complete transfer of electrons

    B. equal sharing of electrons

    C. unequal sharing of electrons

    D. partial bond formation resulting from dipole formation

11. Which of the following statements most accurately reflects a property of $NO_{(g)}$?

    A. It separates into ions in aqueous solution.

    B. It experiences dipole-dipole forces.

    C. It is isoelectronic with $N_{2(g)}$ molecules.

    D. It is isoelectronic with $O_{2(g)}$ molecules.

12. Hydrogen bonds are weaker than __*i*__ but are stronger than__*ii*__ .

The statement above is completed by the information in row

Row	*i*	*ii*
A.	Covalent bonds	Ionic bonds
B.	London forces	Covalent bonds
C.	Covalent bonds	Regular dipole—dipole forces
D.	Ionic bonds	Covalent bonds

13. Since most alkaloids are non-polar molecular compounds, they would be

    A. soluble in both water and hexane

    B. insoluble in both water and hexane

    C. soluble in water but insoluble in hexane

    D. insoluble in water but soluble in hexane

Solubility: "Like dissolves like" C_6H_{14}

14. The intermolecular bonding in $CH_2FCF_{3(l)}$ can be described as

    A. hydrogen bonding and dispersion forces

    B. dispersion forces and dipole-dipole attraction

    C. hydrogen bonding and dipole-dipole attraction

    D. covalent bonding and dispersion forces

Use the following information to answer the next question.

Glucose is consumed by the body in order to fuel the production of adenosine triphosphate (ATP), the energy "currency" of many biochemical reactions. Glucose breakdown can be represented as

$$C_6H_{12}O_6 + 6O_2 \rightarrow 6CO_2 + 6H_2O$$

15. The strongest bonds made and broken during glucose consumption are

    A. intermolecular bonds

    B. hydrogen bonds

    C. London dispersion forces

    D. intramolecular bonds

Use the following information to answer the next two questions.

It takes about 7 times as much energy to split one mole of water into hydrogen and oxygen as is required to vapourize one mole of water at its boiling point.

CHALLENGER QUESTION

16. Which bonds are broken when liquid water is split into hydrogen and oxygen gases?

    A. intermolecular bonds

    B. both intermolecular and intramolecular bonds

    C. intramolecular bonds

    D. neither intermolecular nor intramolecular bonds

17. The energy required to boil one mole of water compared to the energy required to split one mole of water indicates that

    A. intermolecular bonds are stronger than intramolecular bonds

    B. intramolecular bonds are stronger than intermolecular bonds

    C. hydrogen bonds are stronger than covalent bond

    D. dipole-dipole bonds are stronger than covalent bonds

Use the following information to answer the next question.

Researchers at the University of Alberta are using state of the art technology and innovative experiments to study van der Waals forces in certain substances. These experiments will expand our understanding of what happens in a substance at a microscopic level.

18. The subject of their research is **most likely**

    A. interactions between molecules of H_2O

    B. interactions between atoms of Ne

    C. bonding of atoms in molecules of NaCl

    D. bonding of atoms in molecules of O_2

Use the following information to answer the next question.

Chemists at the University of Alberta use infrared (IR) spectroscopy to obtain molecular information about nucleic acids.
IR spectroscopy is used to gain insight into the structure of molecules by learning more about the types of bonds between their atoms.
Different peaks are shown on a graph, each of which pertains to a different bond type.
Hydrogen bonding, if present, causes a characteristic broadening in some of the peaks of the compound's infrared spectrum.

19. IR spectroscopy would show no evidence of hydrogen bonding for

    A. $H_2O_{(s)}$ B. $NH_{3(l)}$

    C. $HF_{(aq)}$ D. $CH_{4(g)}$

20. Water exists as a liquid at room temperature, whereas the isoelectronic, non-polar compound, methane, exists as a gas at room temperature. Which of the following statements is false?

A. Intermolecular forces can be important in affecting the nature of a substance.

B. Hydrogen bonding occurs in water.

C. Intermolecular bonds between water molecules help stabilize the liquid state.

D. Both water and methane experience hydrogen bonding.

Use the following information to answer the next question.

The air in the vicinity of areas of geothermal activity (e.g., Yellowstone National Park) have a characteristic "rotten egg" aroma. The smell is due to the toxic gas, hydrogen sulfide. Water (H_2O) is a liquid at standard atmospheric temperature and pressure and yet hydrogen sulfide, hydrogen selenide (H_2Se), and hydrogen telluride (H_2Te) are all gases under the same standard conditions.

21. What might account for the obviously different boiling points of these compounds?

A. The relatively small electronegativity difference between H and O

B. Hydrogen bonding

C. Ionic bonding

D. Metallic bonding

Use the following information to answer the next question.

At the high temperatures normally found in gasoline and diesel engines, nitrogen monoxide is produced by the reaction of nitrogen and oxygen.

$$N_{2(g)} + O_{2(g)} \rightarrow 2NO_{(g)}$$

The formation of nitrogen monoxide requires the energy supplied by the heat from the engine. Nitrogen monoxide is a major player in photochemical smog.

22. Nitrogen monoxide formation requires heat because

A. it is an exothermic process

B. it is an endothermic process

C. it is a spontaneous process

D. the energy required to break the bonds in $N_{2(g)}$ and $O_{2(g)}$ is less than the energy released in the bonds formed in $NO_{(g)}$

Use the following information to answer the next question.

Aluminium powder improves a propellant's efficiency by engaging in formation reactions with oxygen and chlorine products. In solid fuel rocket exhaust, aluminium metal combines with oxygen and chlorine to form the ionic compounds $Al_2O_{3(s)}$ and $AlCl_{3(s)}$.

23. The statement that **best** describes these redox reactions in rocket exhaust is the

A. non-metals are reduced and the metal is oxidized

B. non-metals are oxidized and the metal is reduced

C. non-metals and metal are both reduced

D. non-metals and metal are oxidized

Use the following information to answer the next question.

The basic formula illustrating the formation of iron oxide (rust) is as follows.

$$2Fe_{(s)} + nO_{2(g)} + nH_2O_{(l)} \rightarrow Fe_xO_y \times xH_2O_{(s)}$$

24. During rust formation, the chemical entity that gains electrons is

A. O_2

B. Fe

C. H_2O

D. $(OH)_2$

Use the following information to answer the next question.

Calcium carbonate, $(CaCO_3)$, known as calcite when crystalline, is the primary mineral found in limestone, marble, chalk, pearls, and the shells of marine animals.

25. Calcium carbonate would be considered

A. an organic compound

B. an inorganic compound

C. a molecular compound

D. covalently bonded

Use the following information to answer the next question.

1. Ionic bonding

2. Covalent bonding

3. Hydrogen bonding

4. London dispersion forces

Numerical Response

1. When the four bonding types above are listed in order from strongest to weakest the four digit number obtained is

___ ___ ___ ___ .

Use the following information to answer the next question.

1. intermolecular bonds

2. hydrogen bonds

3. London dispersion forces

4. dipole

5. protons

6. electrons

7. polar

8. non-polar

Numerical Response

2. The circulation of _____ within a molecule leads to the generation of a momentary _____ within that molecule that induces dipoles in its near neighbours. The types of bonds that result are called _____. These kinds of bonds are the only kind available to _____ molecules.

The four digit number corresponding to the words needed to fill the blanks in the passage is ___ ___ ___ ___.

Written Response

1. Provide a suitable explanation for the limited number of common shapes for molecules containing between two and five atoms. (For full credit an answer must provide a specific example of and the names for, all the common shapes).

(8 marks)

Use the following information to answer the next question.

Four different strips of metal were placed in six different solutions, and the results were observed and recorded in the chart below.

	Cu	**Fe**	**Zn**	**Mg**
AgNO$_3$	reaction	reaction	reaction	reaction
CuNO$_3$	no reaction	reaction	reaction	reaction
Fe(NO$_3$)$_3$	no reaction	no reaction	reaction	reaction
HCl	no reaction	reaction	reaction	reaction
Zn(NO$_3$)$_2$	no reaction	no reaction	no reaction	reaction
Mg(NO$_3$)$_2$	no reaction	no reaction	no reaction	no reaction

2. **a)** Place the metals in an activity series, in order from **most** reactive to **least** reactive

(1 mark)

b) Why should all the metal strips be cleaned with sandpaper prior to immersion in each solution?

(1 mark)

c) Write a balanced chemical equation for one of the reactions in this series of tests.

(2 marks)

d) In your own words, explain what the terms oxidation and reduction mean.

(2 marks)

e) Are the metal elements in this series of reactions oxidized or reduced? Explain.

(2 marks)

26. A metal wi h three valence electrons forms an oxide by forming a compound with oxygen, which has a valence of negative two. The ratio of metal atoms to oxygen atoms in the compound is 3:2 because each metallic atom loses

A. 1 electron to each oxygen atom

B. 6 electrons to each oxygen atom

C. 3 electrons to each oxygen molecule

D. 6 electrons to a pair of oxygen atoms

27. The formula, Al$_2$O$_3$, means

A. 2 aluminium atoms combine with 3 atoms of oxygen to form a molecule of aluminium oxide

B. 2 aluminium atoms combine with 3 atoms of oxygen to form an ion of aluminium oxide

C. 2 aluminium atoms combine with 3 atoms of oxygen to form a mole of aluminium oxide

D. No matter what amount of Al$_2$O$_3$ is formed, the ratio of aluminium atoms to oxygen atoms will be 3:2

28. Given the manner in which ionic compounds form, the formula for ammonium phosphate would be

A. NH$_4$PO$_{4(s)}$

B. (NH$_4$)$_3$PO$_{4(s)}$

C. NH$_{4\,3}$(PO$_4$)$_{4(s)}$

D. NH$_4$(I)PO$_4$(III)$_{(s)}$

29. The formula for zinc oxide is

A. ZnO$_2$ **B.** ZnO$_2$

C. Zn$_2$O$_3$ **D.** ZnO

30. The tendency of an atom to attract pairs of electrons when combined in a compound is called electronegativity. When the elements Cl, Mg, C, and S are arranged in order from lowest electronegativity to highest electronegativity, they are

  A. Mg < C < S < Cl

  B. Mg < S < C < Cl

  C. Mg < Cl < C < S

  D. C < Mg < Cl < S

31. The elements in the periodic table with the highest Electronegativity are the

  A. halogens

  B. alkali metals

  C. transition elements

  D. alkaline earth metals

32. For an assignment, Aden named three molecular compounds from the chemical formulas that were given to her.

Compound.	Formula (Given)	Name (Answer)
1	NF_3	nitrogen trifluoride
2	N_2O	dinitrogen dioxide
3	CCl_4	carbon tetrachloride

Which of the compounds did Aden name correctly?

  A. 1 and 2   **B.** 1 and 3

  C. 2 and 3   **D.** 1, 2, and 3

33. One molecule of phosphorous pentachloride contains 1 phosphorous atom.
The number of chlorine atoms contained in one molecule of phosphorous pentachloride is

  A. 2   **B.** 3

  C. 4   **D.** 5

34. The molecule Al_2O_3 contains

  A. 6 atoms   **B.** 5 atoms

  C. 3 atoms   **D.** 1 atom

35. The bonding in molecular nitrogen can be described as

  A. ionic bonding

  B. covalent bonding

  C. hydrogen bonding

  D. dipole-dipole bonding

36. The intramolecular bonding in CH_2FCF_3 is called

  A. ionic bonding

  B. hydrogen bonding

  C. van der Waal's bonding

  D. covalent bonding

37.

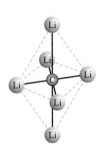

The hypervalent molecule was observed for the first time in the gas phase in 1992. This observation was significant because of the unusual bonding within the molecule.

According to Lewis bonding theory, how many electrons does carbon appear to have surrounding it?

  A. 6   **B.** 8

  C. 10   **D.** 12

Use the following information to answer the next question.

Hydrogen cyanide, a highly poisonous compound, undergoes additional reactions with organic compounds such as the aldehydes to form a compound known as cyanohydrin.

38. The shape of hydrogen cyanide (HCN) is

    A. linear

    B. pyramidal

    C. tetrahedral

    D. trigonal planar

39. The shape of a CO_2 molecule is

    A. linear

    B. pyramidal

    C. tetrahedral

    D. trigonal planar

40. Which of the following diagrams shows the correct Lewis structure of methanol?

    A.

$$\begin{array}{c} H \\ H:C:O:H \\ H \end{array}$$

    B.

$$\begin{array}{c} H \\ H:C:O:H \\ H \end{array}$$

    C.

$$\begin{array}{c} H \\ H \cdot C \cdot O \cdot H \\ H \end{array}$$

    D.

$$\begin{array}{c} H \\ H:C:O:H \\ H \end{array}$$

NOTES

FORMS OF MATTER: GASES

TABLE OF CORRELATIONS		
General Outcome	**Specific Outcome**	**Related Questions**
	Students are expected to:	
1. Students will explain molecular behaviour, using models of the gaseous state of matter.	1.1 describe and compare the behaviour of real and ideal gases in terms of kinetic molecular theory	1, 7, 8
	1.2 convert between the Celsius and Kelvin temperature scales	NR2, 5
	1.3 explain the law of combining volumes	4
	1.4 illustrate how Boyle's and Charles's laws, individually and combined, are related to the ideal gas law ($PV = nRT$) • express pressure in a variety of ways, including units of kilopascals, atmospheres and millimetres of mercury • perform calculations, based on the gas laws, under STP, SATP and other defined conditions	2, 3, NR1, 6, NR3, NR4, 9

20-B1.1k   Describe and compare the behaviour of real and ideal gases in terms of kinetic molecular theory

An ideal gas is a gas that obeys all the gas laws perfectly:

- Pressure and volume vary inversely with each other
- Volume varies directly as *absolute temperature* (measured in Kelvins)
- Volume varies directly as number of moles of gas

An ideal gas will never condense no matter how low the temperature or how high the pressure. According to (kinetic molecular theory), the following differences exist:

Real Gas	Ideal Gas
molecules have a distinct size and are "soft"	molecules are point masses (have no size) and are "hard"
forces of attraction between molecules cause them to condense into a liquid if the temperature gets low enough	molecules do not have forces of attraction among them so there is no cause for them to condense into liquid
molecules move about randomly, but because of the attraction between them, they do not travel in straight lines — they are influenced by each other	molecules of gas move about randomly; only collisions with container walls and other molecules cause them to change direction
collisions between molecules are inelastic — kinetic energy is not conserved	collisions between molecules are elastic — kinetic energy is conserved

Related Questions: 1, 7, 8

20-B1.2k   convert between the Celsius and Kelvin temperature scales

According to Charles' Law, volume of gas varies directly with temperature. If this is true, at 0 degrees, a sample of gas in a closed flexible walled container should occupy a volume of zero. What does 0 degrees mean?

0°C? 0°F? The arbitrary position of the zero on these 2 scales illustrates the problem.
If we were dealing with an ideal gas that never condensed, the volume would be zero at absolute zero, the lowest possible temperature, the temperature where all molecular motion stops. Absolute zero is –273.15°C.
This temperature is zero Kelvins (0 K) on the absolute or Kelvin temperature scale.
–273.15°C = 0 K.

Example:
Celsius(°C)   Kelvin(K)

$$-273.15 \xrightleftharpoons[\text{subtract } 273.15]{\text{add } 273.15} 0$$

Related Questions: NR2, 5

20-B1.3k   explain the law of combining volumes

The law of combining volumes loosely states that in reactions of gases, volumes of gaseous reactants and products, measured at the same temperature and pressure, will always be related by simple whole number ratios.

This law is explained by Avogadro's theory (also known as Avogadro's hypothesis and Avogadro's Law), which states that equal volumes of gases at the same temperature and pressure contain equal numbers of particles (atoms or molecules).

Today we believe that molecules are made up of a fixed number of atoms.

Example:
In a water molecule there are 2 hydrogen atoms for every one oxygen atom.
If water is decomposed by electrolysis, there will be 2 times as many hydrogen, H_2, molecules as oxygen, O_2, molecules, and the volume of hydrogen will be double that of oxygen.

Related Questions: 4

20-B1.4k *illustrate how Boyle's and Charles's laws, individually and combined, are related to the ideal gas law (PV = nRT)*

- express pressure using variety of units, including kilopascals, atmospheres and millimetres of mercury
- perform calculations, based on the gas laws, under STP (standard temperature and pressure), SATP (standard ambient temperature and pressure) and other defined conditions

According to Boyle's Law, for a closed system, a system where matter can not enter or leave, at constant temperature, $PV = k$, a constant. $PV = k$ (Boyle's Law) and $PV = nRT$ (ideal gas law) show that k from Boyle's Law = nRT. In a closed system, n is constant. At constant temperature, T is constant. The universal gas law constant, $R = 8.314$ j/K • mol is always constant. Therefore, nRT is a constant.

According to Charles' Law, $\left(\dfrac{V}{T} = k \right)$

If $PV = nRT$ is rearranged into this form, $\dfrac{V}{T} = \dfrac{nR}{P}$. Therefore, $k = \dfrac{nR}{P}$.

For a closed system at constant pressure, n is constant and R is always constant.

Therefore, $\dfrac{nR}{P}$ is a constant.

Pressure is force per unit area, it can be expressed in kilopascals, kPa.

$$1 \text{ kPa} = 1\,000 \text{ N/m}^2$$

Standard air pressure is 101.325 kPa.

Pressure can also be measured in units of atmospheres, atm.
1 atm is standard air pressure.

Another unit of pressure is millimeters of mercury, *mm Hg*. If you fill a test-tube with water, and turn it upside down under water, when you lift it up, water will stay in the test-tube. This is because air pressure pushes down on the water, keeping it in the test-tube. If the liquid is mercury, standard air pressure will support a column of mercury 760 mm tall. Standard air pressure is 760 mm Hg.

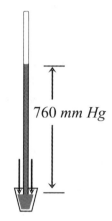

760 mm Hg

Sample calculations:

What is the volume of 0.750 mol of nitrogen gas at SATP?

The identity of the gas is unimportant. At SATP {100.0 kPa and 298.15 K (25°C)}, the molar volume of any gas is 24.8 L/mol. Number of moles, n = volume, v, divided by molar volume, V, $n = \dfrac{v}{V}$.

$$n = \frac{v}{V}$$
$$v = nV$$
$$= 0.750 \text{ mol} \times 24.8 \text{ L/mol}$$
$$= 18.6 \text{ L}$$

What pressure is exerted by 25.5 g of $N_{2(g)}$ in a 25.0 L container at 20.0°C?

First find moles of nitrogen:

$$n = \frac{m}{M}$$

$$= \frac{25.5 \text{ g}}{28.02 \text{ g/mol}}$$

$$= 0.910 \text{ mol}$$

Change 20.0°C to Kelvins (+273.15) = 293.2 K. Use the ideal gas law to calculate pressure.

$$PV = nRT$$

$$P = \frac{nRT}{V}$$

$$= \frac{0.910 \text{ mol} \times 8.31 \text{ }^{kPa\times L}/_{mol\times K} \times 293.2 \text{ K}}{25.0 \text{ L}}$$

$$= 88.7 \text{ kPa}$$

For a closed system question where one variable is changed, it is possible to use either

Boyle's Law: $PV = k$

Charles' Law: $\frac{V}{T} = k$, but it is easier to use the

combined gas law $\frac{PV}{T} = k$.

This will cover all situations and may reduce down to Boyle's or Charles' Law depending on what, if anything, is constant.

Examples:

1. If a syringe is filled with air to a volume of 20 cm³ at an air pressure of 93.5 kPa, what will be the new pressure in the syringe, if the end is sealed off and it is squeezed down to a new volume of 12 cm³ (assume constant temperature)?

$$\frac{PV}{T} = k \rightarrow \frac{P_1V_1}{T_1} = \frac{P_2V_2}{T_2}$$

$$93.5 \text{ kPa} \times 20 \text{ cm}^3 = P_2 \times 12 \text{ cm}^3$$

$$P_2 = \frac{93.5 \text{ kPa} \times 20 \text{ cm}^3}{12 \text{ cm}^3}$$

$$= 1.6 \times 10^2 \text{ kPa} \text{ or } 0.16 \text{ MPa}$$

2. If a sample of gas at 120 kPa occupies a volume of 40.0 L at 20.0°C, how many moles of gas are present?

$$PV = nRT$$

$$n = \frac{PV}{RT}$$

$$= \frac{120 \text{ kPa} \times 40.0 \text{ L}}{8.314 \text{ kPa} \times \text{L/mol} \times 293 \text{ K}}$$

$$= 1.97 \text{ mol}$$

3. If the gas in the previous example was chlorine, what would be its mass?

Hint: Don't forget that chlorine is Cl_2.

$$m = 1.97 \text{ mol} \times 70.90 \text{ g/mol} = 140 \text{ g}$$

Related Questions: 2, 3, NR1, 6, NR3, NR4, 9

1. If gas in a rigid steel container is heated from 0°C to 300°C, the **least** change will occur in

   A. the force with which the molecules impact the cylinder walls

   B. the average kinetic energy of the molecules

   C. the gas density

   D. the average speed of the gas molecules

Use the following information to answer the next question.

Researchers at the University of Alberta use a "helium liquefier" to change helium gas into liquid helium. Liquid helium is used to cool substances to very low temperatures in order to study the properties of superconductivity. (The boiling point of helium is approximately 4 K.)

2. How many litres of helium gas at 20°C would be required make one litre of helium gas at 5 K? (Use the Ideal Gas Law. Assume equal pressure.)

   A. 4 L   B. 58.6 L

   C. 100 L   D. 1 465 L

3. Before a long journey, the air in an automobile's tires were measured to have a pressure of 35 psi and a temperature of 10°C. The air temperature of the tire at the end of the journey was measured to be 56°C. Assuming that there was no change in tire volume, what was the final air pressure?

   A. 30 psi   B. 35 psi

   C. 38 psi   D. 41 psi

CHALLENGER QUESTION

Numerical Response

1. If a 5.00 g sample of ethyl mercaptan (MW = 62.14 g/mol) was allowed to fill a 3.50 L sealed container, then the theoretical pressure exerted at 25°C, assuming the container did not expand, would be _____ kPa.
(Record your answer to three digits.)

Use the following information to answer the next question.

A superconductor is a substance that conducts electricity without resistance.
Most known superconductors work only at very low temperatures. Researchers at the University of Alberta are investigating the properties of superconductors to discover compounds that can show superconductivity at higher temperatures. Currently, we know of compounds that will show superconductivity at temperatures of about 125 K. To bring a substance to superconducting temperature, scientists will often evaporate a liquid on it. Below is a list of substances and their respective boiling points.

Substance	Boiling Point
iodine	184°C
water	100°C
chlorine	−36.4°C
nitrogen	−196°C

4. Which of the following substances (in liquid form) would a researcher use to change the temperature of a substance to 125 K from room temperature?

   A. Iodine   B. Water

   C. Chlorine   D. Nitrogen

Use the following information to answer the next question.

Venus is roughly the same size as Earth but is approximately 26% closer to the Sun. This is one reason for Venus's  incredibly high surface temperature relative to Earth's. Another reason for this difference in temperature is that Venus's atmosphere is 95% carbon dioxide, producing a tremendous greenhouse effect that inhibits the escape of heat radiation. In contrast, Earth's atmosphere is only 0.035% carbon dioxide because most of the carbon dioxide has been trapped in rocks such as limestone and dolomite by biological processes throughout Earth's evolution.

Numerical Response

2. If Venus's surface is 750 K, the equivalent temperature in degrees Celsius would be _____ °C.
(Record your answer to three digits.)

Use the following information to answer the next question.

In 1960, it was discovered that interstellar dust clouds contained carbon chains at temperatures below 50 K.  The chain molecules C_3 and C_5 were found in these frozen clouds.

5. When expressed in degrees Celsius, the temperature of these interstellar dust clouds is

A. below –223°C

B. between –203°C and –223°C

C. above –223°C

D. between –323°C and –323°C

Use the following information to answer the next question.

Researchers have been able to convert carbon into diamond at 2 000°C and at 1.00×10^5 atm.

6. The IUPAC equivalent of this temperature and pressure is

A. 1 727 K and 987 kPa

B. 1 727 K and 1.01×10^7 kPa

C. 2 273 K and 987 kPa

D. 2 273 K and 1.01×10^7 kPa

Use the following information to answer the next question.

The advent of the steam engine was one of the major breakthroughs of the Industrial Revolution.  In a typical steam engine, water vapor, formed in the boiler, expands into the cylinder where it forces the piston up (thereby doing work). The steam is then condensed and collected in order to repeat the cycle.

Numerical Response

3. If a 3.4 L cylinder filled with steam has a temperature of 100°C and a pressure of 500 kPa, the number of moles of water in the cylinder is _____ mol.
(Record your answer to two digits.)

After World War I, Fritz Haber perfected the industrial production of large quantities of ammonia from the catalyzed reaction of nitrogen and hydrogen, as shown below.

$$N_{2(g)} + 3H_{2(g)} \rightarrow 2NH_{3(g)}$$

This is done at high temperatures and pressure.

Numerical Response

4. The volume occupied by a mole of ammonia in reaction conditions of 400°C and 250 atm is _____ L.
(Record your answer to two digits.)

Neon signs emit an unmistakable glow, making them a popular choice for many night time-based small businesses. Neon is an extremely inert (unreactive) gas but it is not an ideal gas.

7. In which of the following ways does neon and all other real gases differ from an ideal gas?

A. Real gas molecules are not in constant motion and ideal gas molecules are.

B. Real gas molecules do not exert pressure on the walls of a container but ideal gas molecules do.

C. Real gas molecules are attracted to each other but ideal gas molecules are not.

D. Real gas molecules have no volume and ideal gas molecules have volume.

Carbon monoxide is a toxic by-product of incomplete fuel combustion. Its toxicity derives from the fact that it can bind to hemoglobin almost 230 times more effectively than oxygen can. For this reason, it is a dangerous gas.

8. Carbon monoxide is a real gas rather than an ideal gas because

A. it is comprised of more than one element

B. it has a finite volume

C. the kinetic energy of carbon monoxide molecules does not increase with temperature

D. carbon monoxide molecules cannot form intermolecular bonds

Low density polyethylene (LDPE) is the plastic used for packaging most consumer goods. In the absence of catalysts, the synthesis of LDPE requires pressures as high as 3.00×10^5 atm and temperatures of 500°C.

9. The approximate pressure (in kPa) and temperature (in Kelvin) required for this process is

A. 3.01×10^3 and 227 K

B. 3.01×10^3 and 773 K

C. 3.01×10^7 and 227 K

D. 3.01×10^7 and 773 K

MATTER AS SOLUTIONS, ACIDS AND BASES

TABLE OF CORRELATIONS		
General Outcome	**Specific Outcome**	**Related Questions**
	Students are expected to:	
1. Investigate solutions, describing their physical and chemical properties.	1.1 recall the categories of pure substances and mixtures and explain the nature of homogeneous mixtures	68
	1.2 provide examples from living and non-living systems that illustrate how dissolving substances in water is often a prerequisite for chemical change	69
	1.3 explain dissolving as an endothermic or exothermic process with respect to the breaking and forming of bonds	70
	1.4 differentiate between electrolytes and non-electrolytes	34, 35, 36
	1.5 express concentration in various ways; i.e. moles per litre of solution, percent by mass and parts per million	40, 41, 42, 43, 44
	1.6 calculate, from empirical data, the concentration of solutions in moles per litre of solution and determine mass or volume from such concentrations	NR1, NR2
	1.7 calculate the concentrations and/or volumes of diluted solutions and the quantities of a solution and water to use when diluting	56, 57
	1.8 use data and ionization/dissociation equations to calculate the concentration of ions in a solution	58, 59
	1.9 define solubility and identify related factors; i.e., temperature, pressure and miscibility	25, 26, 27, 28, 31, 32, WR1
	1.10 explain a saturated solution in terms of equilibrium, i.e., equal rates of dissolving and crystallizing	29, 30, 48, 49, 50, 51
	1.11 describe the procedures and calculations required for preparing and diluting solutions	45, 46, 47

TABLE OF CORRELATIONS		
General Outcome	**Specific Outcome**	**Related Questions**
	Students are expected to:	
2. Describe acidic and basic solutions qualitatively and quantitatively	2.1 recall International Union of Pure and Applied Chemistry (IUPAC) nomenclature of acids and bases	71, 72
	2.2 recall the empirical definitions of acidic, basic and neutral solutions determined by using indicators, pH and electrical conductivity	4, 5, 9, 10, 11, 12, 13, 14, 20, 21, 52, 53
	2.3 calculate $H_3O^+_{(aq)}$ and $OH^-_{(aq)}$ concentrations and the pH and pOH of acidic and basic solutions based on logarithmic expressions; i.e., $pH = -\log [H_3O^+]$ and $pOH = -\log [OH^-]$	8, 15, 55
	2.4 use appropriate SI units to communicate the concentration of solutions and express pH and concentration answers to the correct number of significant digits; i.e., use the number of decimal places in the pH to determine the number of significant digits of the concentration	54
	2.5 compare magnitude changes in pH and pOH with changes in concentration for acids and bases	60, 61
	2.6 explain how the use of indicators, pH paper or pH meters can be used to measure $H_3O^+_{(aq}$	19, 23, 62, 63
	2.7 define Arrhenius (modified) acids as substances that produce $H_3O^+_{(aq)}$ in aqueous solutions and recognize that the definition is limited	1, 2, 6, 7, 22, 24, 50
	2.8 define Arrhenius (modified) bases as substances that produce $OH^-_{(aq)}$ in aqueous solutions and recognize that the definition is limited	
	2.9 define neutralization as a reaction between hydronium and hydroxide ions	3, 64, 65
	2.10 differentiate, qualitatively, between strong and weak acids and between strong and weak bases on the basis of ionization and dissociation; i.e., pH, reaction rate and electrical conductivity	16, 17, 18, 33, 37, 38, 39
	2.11 identify monoprotic and polyprotic acids and bases and compare their ionization/dissociation	66, 67

20-C1.1k   *recall the categories of pure substances and mixtures and explain the nature of homogeneous mixtures*

Pure substances are *substances* that cannot be separated by physical processes.
Elements and *compounds* are pure substances.

Any mixture of pure substances that is the same throughout is a *solution* or *homogeneous mixture*. This would include solutions of solids dissolved in liquids, liquids dissolved in liquids, gases dissolved in liquids, gases dissolved in gases, and even solids dissolved in solids.

Heterogeneous mixtures are not the same throughout. Often you can see different components of the mixture within a heterogeneous mixture.

Related Questions: 68

20-C1.2k   *provide examples from living and no-nliving systems that illustrate how dissolving substances in water is often a prerequisite for chemical change*

Many ionic compounds in solution react readily with each other in double replacement reactions to form precipitates. If the same compounds are simply placed side by side in the solid state in a beaker, nothing happens. Even if you stir them together nothing happens. In some cases, if you grind a pair of ionic substances together with a mortar and pestle, you may see evidence of a reaction, but it does not happen readily as it does in solution. In solution, the solute particles have been separated into individual molecules or ions depending on the type of solute.
The increased surface area between reacting particles allows the reaction to occur.

In the human digestive system, digestion begins in the mouth, where enzymes in the saliva begin the break-down of carbohydrates into simpler sugars. Water in the saliva carries these enzymes to the food and allows them to react with the food.

Related Questions: 69

20-C1.3k   *explain dissolving as an endothermic or exothermic process with respect to the breaking and forming of bonds*

Breaking bonds is always endothermic; forming bonds is always exothermic.
When an ionic solute dissolves in water, ionic bonds between ions in the ionic crystal lattice break. This is endothermic.
Intermolecular bonds between water molecules also break. This is also endothermic.
New bonds form between the ions and water molecules. This is exothermic.
If the total energy released is greater than the energy absorbed, the dissolving is exothermic.
If the total energy absorbed is greater than the energy released, the dissolving is endothermic.

When a molecular solute dissolves, the process is similar except that the there is no separation of ions. Molecules are separated from other molecules as intermolecular bonds are broken. This is endothermic. Energy is released as new intermolecular bonds form between water and the solute molecules.

Related Questions: 70

20-C1.4k   *differentiate between electrolytes and non-electrolytes*

Electrolytes are substances that conduct electricity when dissolved in water.
Non-electrolytes do not conduct electricity when dissolved in water. Ionic compounds are electrolytes. Most molecular compounds are non-electrolytes.

Related Questions: 34, 35, 36

20-C1.5k   express concentration in various ways; i.e. moles per litre of solution, percent by mass and parts per million

Molarity or **molar concentration** is the number of moles of solute per litre of solution.

Molarity can then be calculated as $C = \dfrac{n}{v}$,

where C = molarity, n = number of moles of solute, and v = number of litres of solution.

Molarity or molar concentration is the most common way of expressing solution concentration in the study of chemistry, but solution concentrations are so commonly used in other situations, that other units are often used to express them.

Note: All of these units, including molarity, are with respect to volume of solution, not volume of solvent. This will affect how solutions are prepared.

It will be necessary to memorize some of these conversions so that you can make calculations based on them.

Parts per million (ppm)   The number of milligrams (mg) of solute per litre (L) of solution, or the number of grams (g) of solute per 1 000 litres (1 000 L) of solution.

Used for very small concentrations, for example, the concentrations of pollutants in a river.

Percent mass to volume (% W/V)
The number of grams of solute per 100 mL of solution.
Consumer hydrogen peroxide is 3% W/V.

Percent by mass
The number of grams of solute per 100 g of solution.

Percent volume to volume (% V/V)
The number of milliliters of solute per 100 mL of solution. The concentration of propan-2-ol (isopropyl alcohol) in rubbing alcohol is 70% V/V.

Related Questions: 40, 41, 42, 43, 44

20-C1.6k   calculate, from empirical data, the concentration of solutions in moles per litre of solution and determine mass or volume from such concentrations

Examples:

1.   What is the molarity or molar concentration of a solution containing 1.50 mol of solute in 500 mL of solution?

$C = \dfrac{n}{v}$, where C is molar concentration (mol/L),

n is the number of moles of solute and v is the volume of solution.

The solution is the same whether you consider using a formula or doing unit analysis.

$$C = \frac{n}{v} = \frac{1.50 \text{ mol}}{0.500 \text{ L}} = 3.00 \text{ mol/L}$$

2.   What is the mass of solid necessary to prepare 500 mL of 0.100 mol/L $Na_2CO_{3(aq)}$?

$$C = \frac{n}{v} \rightarrow n = C \times v$$
$$= 0.100 \text{ mol/L} \times 0.500 \text{ L}$$
$$= 0.050\,0 \text{ mol}$$
$$n = \frac{m}{M} \rightarrow m = n \times M$$
$$= 0.050\,0 \text{ mol} \times 105.99 \text{ g/mol}$$
$$= 5.30 \text{ g}$$

3.   If a student has 4.50 g of $KOH_{(s)}$, what volume of 0.250 mol/L $KOH_{(aq)}$ can he prepare?

$$n = \frac{m}{M}$$
$$= \frac{4.50 \text{ g}}{56.11 \text{ g/mol}} = 0.080\,2 \text{ mol}$$
$$C = \frac{n}{v}$$
$$v = \frac{n}{C}$$
$$= \frac{0.080\,2 \text{ mol}}{0.250 \text{ mol/L}} = 0.321 \text{ L}   \text{ or } 321 \text{ mL}$$

Related Questions: NR1, WR2

20-C1.7k *calculate the concentrations and/or volumes of diluted solutions and the quantities of a solution and water to use when diluting*

When an aqueous solution is diluted, the number of moles of solute does not change.

Water is added to make the concentration smaller. If the n_i stands for initial number of moles of solute and n_f for final number of moles of solute, then

$$n_i = n_f \text{ and since } c = \frac{n}{v} \rightarrow n = c \times v$$

$$c_i v_i = c_f v_f$$

Examples:

1. If concentrated $HCl_{(aq)}$ has a concentration of 11.6 mol/L, what volume of concentrated $HCl_{(aq)}$ will be required to prepare 500 mL of 0.100 mol/L diluted $HCl_{(aq)}$?

$$c_i v_i = c_f v_f$$

$$v_i = \frac{c_f v_f}{c_i}$$

$$= \frac{0.100 \text{ mol/L} \times 500 \text{ mL}}{11.6 \text{ mol/L}}$$

$$= 4.31 \text{ mL}$$

2. If 200 mL of water are added to 500 mL of 0.250 mol/L $CuSO_{4(aq)}$ solution, what is the new concentration?

Vf is 500 mL + 200 mL = 700 mL

$$c_i v_i = c_f v_f$$

$$c_f = \frac{c_i v_i}{v_f}$$

$$= \frac{0.250 \text{ mol/L} \times 500 \text{ mL}}{700 \text{ mL}}$$

$$= 0.179 \text{ mol/L}$$

Related Questions: 56, 57

20-C1.8k *use data and ionization/dissociation equations to calculate the concentration of ions in a solution*

When ionic compounds dissolve in water, they dissociate or separate into individual aqueous ions.

Examples:

$$NaCl_{(s)} \rightarrow Na^+_{(aq)} + Cl^-_{(aq)}$$
$$Al_2(SO_4)_{3(s)} \rightarrow 2Al^{3+}_{(aq)} + 3SO_4^{2-}_{(aq)}$$

Note: The solute is indicated as solid on the left side and the ions are aqueous on the right side of the dissociation equation. This is because the equation shows what happens to the solid solute as it dissolves.

In a similar fashion, acids will have ionized into aqueous ions in solution. Strong acids will ionize completely, weak acids only partially.

Examples:

$$HCl_{(aq)} \rightarrow H^+_{(aq)} + Cl^-_{(aq)}$$
$$HNO_{3(aq)} \rightarrow H^+_{(aq)} NO_3^-_{(aq)}$$

Dissociation and ionization equations can be used to calculate the concentration of individual ions in solution.

Examples:

What is the concentration of $Na^+_{(aq)}$ and $PO_4^{3-}_{(aq)}$ in a solution of 0.500 mol/L $Na_3PO_{4(aq)}$?

"[ ]" means "concentration" of whatever is inside the brackets. You must use this style of brackets.

$$\left[Na^+_{(aq)} \right] = \frac{3}{1} \times 0.500 \text{ mol/L} = 1.500 \text{ mol/L}$$

$$\left[PO_4^{3-}_{(aq)} \right] = \frac{1}{1} \times 0.500 \text{ mol/L} = 0.500 \text{ mol/L}$$

The fraction is the mole ratio, $\dfrac{looking\ for}{given}$,

from the dissociation or ionization equation.

Related Questions: 58, 59

20-C1.9k   *define solubility and identify related factors; i.e., temperature, pressure and miscibility*

Solubility is the amount or mass of a solute that dissolves in a given volume of solvent.
It is often recorded in units of g/100 mL.
A large solubility means the substance dissolves well.

Solubility of <u>solids in liquids</u> increases with *temperature*. Solubility of <u>liquids in liquids</u> is unaffected by *temperature*. Solubility of <u>gases in liquids</u> decreases with *temperature*.

Solubility of <u>solids in liquids</u> is unaffected by changes in *pressure*. Solubility of <u>gases in liquids</u> increases as the *pressure* of the particular gas above the solution increases.

Substances that mix completely with each other in all proportions are said to be *miscible*. Miscibility depends on the nature of the solute and solvent. In general *like dissolves like*. Polar (Unit A) solutes dissolve well in polar solvents; non-polar solutes dissolve well in non-polar solvents.

Related Questions: 25, 26, 27, 28, 31, 32, WR1

20-C1.10k   *explain a saturated solution in terms of equilibrium, i.e., equal rates of dissolving and crystallizing*

A saturated solution is a solution that has its maximum concentration at a given temperature. This does not mean a solution in which no more solute will dissolve. The reason is that dissolving does not stop. Crystallizing and dissolving are both occuring, and when the solution is saturated, the rate of dissolving and crystallizing are equal. This is one type of *dynamic equilibrium*.

Related Questions: 29, 30, 48, 49, 50, 51

20-C1.11k   *describe the procedures and calculations required for preparing and diluting solutions*

Example 1
What are the correct steps for preparing 100.0 mL of a 0.100 mol/L solution of NH_4Cl?

1. Calculate the mass of NH_4Cl required: (this will be shown using unit analysis and formula methods)

<u>Unit Analysis</u>
$0.100 \text{ mol/L} \times 0.1000 \text{ L} \times 53.50 \text{ g/mol} = 0.535 \text{ g}$
<u>Formula</u>
$$n = c \times v$$
$$= 0.100 \text{ mol/L} \times 0.100\,0 \text{ L}$$
$$= 0.010\,0 \text{ mol}$$
$$m = n \times M$$
$$= 0.010\,0 \text{ mol} \times 53.50 \text{ g/mol}$$
$$= 0.535 \text{ g}$$

2. Using a balance, measure 0.535 g of NH_4Cl into a 100 mL beaker.

3. Add approximately 40 mL of water to the NH_4Cl in the beaker and stir to dissolve. If the solute will not completely dissolve you may go as high as 60 mL of water, but try not to exceed this limit. Do **not** remove your stirring rod from the beaker.

4. Pour the NH_4Cl solution through a funnel into a 100.0 mL volumetric flask. Wash the beaker, stirring rod, and funnel into the volumetric flask, using distilled water rinse bottle.

5. Add additional distilled water to make the water's meniscus sit on the 100.0 mL mark on the volumetric flask.

6. Stopper flask and invert to mix.

Example 2

What are the correct steps for diluting a commercially available 0.500 mol/L $Fe(NO_3)_{3(aq)}$ solution to prepare 100 mL of 0.150 mol/L necessary for an experiment?

1. Calculate the volume of concentrated solution necessary for the dilution. Students generally prefer to use the formula $c_i \times v_i = c_f \times v_f$ for this calculation, where ci and vi are the initial concentration and volume and cf and vf are the final concentration and volume.

$$c_i \times v_i = c_f \times v_f$$
$$0.500 \text{ mol/L} \times v_i = 0.150 \text{ mol/L} \times 100 \text{ mL}$$
$$v_i = \frac{0.150 \text{ mol/L} \times 100 \text{ mL}}{0.500 \text{ mol/L}}$$
$$= 30.0 \text{ mL}$$

2. Use a graduated pipet to obtain the 30.0 mL of concentrated solution by pouring approximately 50 mL into a 100 mL beaker. Rinse the pipet with a small volume of solution and discard this solution.
    Fill the pipet using a rubber bulb to beyond the 30 mL mark and dispense 30 mL of this solution into a clean 100.0 mL volumetric flask.

3. Add distilled water to the line on the volumetric flask.

4. Stopper flask and invert to mix.
    Note: When diluting a concentrated acid you need to put slightly less than the required volume of water into the flask before adding the concentrated acid. Once the acid is partially diluted the remaining water can be added.
    Also it is a good idea, particularly with sulfuric acid, not to invert and mix until the solution is cooled down. (You will also notice that the solution volume will decrease as the temperature drops. Volumetric flasks are calibrated at 20°C.)

Related Questions: 45, 46, 47

20-C2.1k   recall International Union of Pure and Applied Chemistry (IUPAC) nomenclature of acids and bases

To name acids, begin by naming the substance *as if it was* ionic. This is NOT the acid name. Recent IUPAC updates have allowed acids to be named simply by putting the word *aqueous* in front of this name. The more traditional acid name is determined using the following rules:

as if it was ionic name	traditional acid name
hydrogen _____ ide	hydro_____ ic acid
hydrogen _____ ate	_____ ic acid
hydrogen _____ ite	_____ ous acid

Examples:

formula	as if it was ionic name	IUPAC name	traditional name
$HClO_4$	hydrogen perchlorate	aqueous hydrogen perchlorate	perchloric acid
$HClO_3$	hydrogen chlorate	aqueous hydrogen chlorate	chloric acid
$HClO_2$	hydrogen chlorite	aqueous hydrogen chlorite	chlorous acid
$HClO$	hydrogen hypochlorite	aqueous hydrogen hypochlorite	hypochlorous acid
HCl	hydrogen chloride	aqueous hydrogen chloride	hydrochloric acid

Related Questions: 71, 72

20-C2.2k *recall the empirical definitions of acidic, basic and neutral solutions determined by using indicators, pH and electrical conductivity*

Empirical definitions are based on observations.

Acids, by observation, turn litmus paper red (or leave it red), are electrolytes (some are weak electrolytes), react with *active metals* e.g. Zn and Mg to produce hydrogen gas, taste sour (do not try it with lab acids), and neutralize bases.

Bases, by observation, turn litmus paper blue (or leave it blue), are electrolytes (<u>some</u> are weak electrolytes), taste bitter (do not try it with lab bases), feel slippery, and neutralize acids.

Neutral solutions have no effect on litmus paper, may be electrolytes or non-electrolytes, and have no characteristic taste or feel.

Related Questions: 4, 5, 9, 10, 11, 12, 13, 14, 20, 21, 52, 53

20-C2.3k *calculate $H_3O^+_{(aq)}$ and $OH^-_{(aq)}$ concentrations and the pH and pOH of acidic and basic solutions based on logarithmic expressions; i.e., $pH = -log\ [H_3O^+]$ and $pOH = -log\ [OH^-]$*

Related Questions: 8, 15, 55

20-C2.4k *use appropriate SI units to communicate the concentration of solutions and express pH and concentration answers to the correct number of significant digits; i.e., use the number of decimal places in the pH to determine the number of significant digits of the concentration*

By definition:

$$pH = -\log\left[H^+_{(aq)}\right] \text{ and}$$

$$\left[H^+_{(aq)}\right] = 10^{-pH}$$

$$pOH = -\log\left[OH^-_{(aq)}\right] \text{ and}$$

$$\left[OH^-_{(aq)}\right] = 10^{-pOH}$$

$$pH + pOH = 14.000 \text{ at } 25°C$$

$$\left[H^+\right] \times \left[OH^-\right] = 1.00 \times 10^{-14} \left(mol/L\right)^2$$

where $[H^+_{(aq)}]$ and $[OH^-_{(aq)}]$ are in units of mol/L.

$[H^+]$ *can be replaced by* $[H_3O^+]$ *in all of these formulas*

Examples:

1. What is the pH of 1.6 mol/L $HCl_{(aq)}$?

$$pH = -\log\left[H^+_{(aq)}\right] \text{ but}$$

$$\left[H^+_{(aq)}\right] = \left[HCl_{(aq)}\right]$$

$$pH = -\log\left(1.6\ mol/L\right) = \underline{-0.20}$$

A 1.6 mol/L $HCl_{(aq)}$ solution has a pH of –0.20. (The number of decimal places in a pH equals the number of significant digits in the $[H^+_{(aq)}]$. The same rule applies to pOH.)

2. What is the pH of 2.0 mol/L $NaOH_{(aq)}$?

$$pOH = -\log\left[OH^-_{(aq)}\right] \text{ but}$$

$$\left[OH^-_{(aq)}\right] = \left[NaOH_{(aq)}\right]$$

$$pOH = -\log(2.0\ mol/L) = -0.30$$
$$pH = 14.00 - pOH$$
$$= 14.00 - (-0.30) = 14.30$$

A 2.0 mol/L $NaOH_{(aq)}$ solution has a pH of 14.30.

3. What is the $[H_3O^+]$ of
    0.015 mol/L $NaOH_{(aq)}$?

    $[OH^-] = [NaOH] = 0.015$ mol/L

    $$\left[H_3O^+\right] = \frac{1.00 \times 10^{-14}}{0.015 \text{ mol/L}} = 6.7 \times 10^{-13} \text{ mol/L}$$

4. What is the $[H_3O^+]$ in a solution of
    pH = 2.57?

    What is the $[OH^-]$ in the same solution?

    Because the pH has 2 decimal places, the
    concentrations will have 2 significant digits.

    $$\left[H_3O^+\right] \text{ or } \left[H^+\right] = 10^{-pH} = 10^{-2.57}$$

    $$= 2.7 \times 10^{-3} \text{ mol/L}$$

    $$\left[OH^-\right] = \frac{1.00 \times 10^{-14}}{2.7 \times 10^{-3}}$$

    $$= 3.7 \times 10^{-12} \text{ mol/L}$$

    It is also possible to solve for $[OH^-]$ by using
    the following root

    $$pOH = 14.000 - pH = 1.000 - 2.57 = 11.43$$

    $$\left[OH^-\right] = 10^{-pOH} = 10^{-11.43} = 3.7 \times 10^{-12} \text{ mol/L}$$

Related Questions: 54

*20-C2.5k   compare magnitude changes in pH
          and pOH with changes in
          concentration for acids and bases*

pH and pOH are numbers on log scales.

As pH <u>increases</u>, $\left[H_3O^+\right]$ $\left(\left[H^+\right]\right)$ <u>decreases</u>.

An <u>increase</u> of 1 pH unit is a <u>decrease</u> in
$\left[H_3O^+\right]$ $\left(\left[H^+\right]\right)$ by a factor of 10.

An <u>increase</u> of 2 pH units is a <u>decrease</u> in
$\left[H_3O^+\right]$ $\left(\left[H^+\right]\right)$ by a factor of 100, and an
<u>increase</u> of 3 pH units is a <u>decrease</u> in
$\left[H_3O^+\right]$ $\left(\left[H^+\right]\right)$ by a factor of 1 000!

As pOH <u>increases</u> $\left[OH^-\right]$ <u>decreases</u>.

The pattern is exactly the same as for pH.

Related Questions: 60, 61

*20-C2.6k   explain how the use of indicators,
          pH paper or pH meters can be used
          to measure $H_3O^+_{(aq)}$*

Acid/base indicators change colour around a
transition pH. Different indicators have
transition pH values. Bromothymol blue
changes from yellow to blue as the pH of a
solution goes from below 6.0 to above 7.6.
If bromothymol blue is yellow in a solution, you
know that pH is less than or equal to 6.0.
If it is blue, you know that the pH is greater than
or equal to 7.6.
Using several indicators allows you to narrow
the pH down to a small range.

Example:

What is the pH of a solution if separate samples
turn methyl orange yellow, thymolphthalein
blue, and indigo carmine blue? You will need to
consult the indicator chart in the data charts in
this booklet.

Methyl orange conclusion: pH $\geq$ 4.4

Thymolphthalein conclusion: pH $\geq$ 10.6

Indigo carmine conclusion: pH $\leq$ 11.4

pH is between 10.6 and 11.4

pH paper is filter paper soaked in a solution of
multiple indicators and then allowed to dry.
The result is that it will have different shades
depending on how the test solution affects all of
the indicators in the paper.

A pH meter determines pH electrochemically.
The pH probe contains an internal solution that,
together with the outside solution and the
necessary attachments produces a voltage that is
affected by the solution pH.

Related Questions: 19, 23, 62, 63

20-C2.7k *define Arrhenius (modified) acids as substances that produce $H_3O^+_{(aq)}$ in aqueous solutions and recognize that the definition is limited*

20-C2.8k *define Arrhenius (modified) bases as substances that produce $OH^-_{(aq)}$ in aqueous solutions and recognize that the definition is limited*

Modified Arrhenius acids react with water to produce $H_3O^+_{(aq)}$, and a familiar balancing species. Modified Arrhenius bases react with water to produce $OH^-_{(aq)}$ and a familiar balancing species.

Examples:

$HNO_{3(aq)}$: write equations producing $H_3O^+_{(aq)}$ and $OH^-_{(aq)}$ to see which produces a familiar balancing species.

$$HNO_{3(aq)} + H_2O_{(l)} \rightarrow H_3O^+_{(aq)} + NO^{3-}_{(aq)}$$

$NO_3^-{}_{(aq)}$ is familiar – predict acid

$$HNO_{3(aq)} + H_2O_{(l)} \rightarrow OH^-_{(aq)} + H_2NO_3^+{}_{(aq)}$$

$H_2NO_3^+{}_{(aq)}$ is not familiar – predict acid

$NH^3_{(aq)}$:

$$NH_{3(aq)} + H_2O_{(l)} \rightarrow H_3O^+_{(aq)} + NH_{2(aq)}$$

$NH_2^-{}_{(aq)}$ is not familiar – predict base

$$NH_{3(aq)} + H_2O_{(l)} \rightarrow OH^-_{(aq)} + NH_4^+{}_{(aq)}$$

$NH_4^+{}_{(aq)}$ is familiar – predict base

$CO_{2(aq)}$:

$$CO_{2(aq)} + 2H_2O_{(l)} \rightarrow H_3O^+_{(aq)} + HCO_3^-{}_{(aq)}$$

$HCO_3^-{}_{(aq)}$ is familiar – predict acid

$$CO_{2(aq)} + H_2O_{(l)} \rightarrow OH^-_{(aq)} + HCO_2^+{}_{(aq)}$$

$HCO_2^+{}_{(aq)}$ is not familiar – predict acid

$HSO_4^-{}_{(aq)}$:

$$HSO_4^-{}_{(aq)} + H_2O_{(l)} \rightarrow H_3O^+_{(aq)} + SO_4^{2-}{}_{(aq)}$$

$SO_4^{2-}{}_{(aq)}$ is familiar – predict acid

$$HSO_4^-{}_{(aq)} + H_2O_{(l)} \rightarrow OH^-_{(aq)} + H_2SO_{4(aq)}$$

$H_2SO_{4(aq)}$ is familiar – predict base

The last example shows the limitation of the theory. Equations can be written to explain either the acid or base behaviour of different substances, but in some cases, like the last example the theory cannot be used to predict whether the substance is an acid or a base.

Related Questions: 1, 2, 6, 7, 22, 24, 50

20-C2.9k *define neutralization as a reaction between hydronium and hydroxide ions*

Since acids produce hydronium ions $H_3O^+_{(aq)}$ and bases produce hydroxide ions, $OH^-_{(aq)}$ in solution, an acid base neutralization can be shown as the net-ionic equation:

$$H_3O^+_{(aq)} + OH^-_{(aq)} \rightarrow 2H_2O_{(l)}$$

Related Questions: 3, 64, 65

20-C2.10k *differentiate, qualitatively, between strong and weak acids and between strong and weak bases on the basis of ionization and dissociation; i.e., pH, reaction rate and electrical conductivity*

Strong acids ionize completely (quantitatively) in water to $H_3O^+_{(aq)}$ and a balancing anion. Weak acids ionize only partially (sometimes only very slightly) to $H_3O^+_{(aq)}$ and a balancing anion.

Strong bases dissociate completely (quantitatively) in water to $OH^-_{(aq)}$ and a balancing cation. Weak bases react only partially (sometimes only very slightly) to $OH^-_{(aq)}$ and a balancing species.

Because of the greater ion concentration, strong acids have a lower pH, react more quickly, and have a greater conductivity than weak acids of the same concentration.

A similar statement can be made for bases.

Related Questions: 16, 17, 18, 33, 37, 38, 39

20-C2.11k identify monoprotic and polyprotic acids and bases and compare their ionization/dissociation

Monoprotic acids like $HCl_{(aq)}$ have 1 hydrogen atom that can ionize and react with water to produce $H_3O^+_{(aq)}$. Polyprotic acids like $H_2SO_{4(aq)}$ and $H_3PO_{4(aq)}$ have more than 1 hydrogen atom that can ion ionize and react with water to produce $H_3O^+_{(aq)}$.

Monoprotic bases like $NO_2^-_{(aq)}$ react with water to produce 1 mole of $OH^-_{(aq)}$ for every 1 mole of base. Polyprotic bases like $CO_3^{2-}_{(aq)}$ react with water to produce more than mole of $OH^-_{(aq)}$ for every 1 mole of base:

$$CO_3^{2-}_{(aq)} + 2H_2O_{(l)} \rightarrow 2\,OH^-_{(aq)} + H_2CO_{3(aq)}$$

Related Questions: 66, 67

1. Which of the following equations represents the reaction where CH_3COOH acts as an acid does with water?

   A. $CH_3COOH_{(aq)} + H_2O_{(l)}$
   $$\rightleftharpoons H_3O^+_{(aq)} + CH_3COO^-_{(aq)}$$

   B. $CH_3COO^-_{(aq)} + H_3O^+_{(aq)}$
   $$\rightleftharpoons CH_3COOH^+_{(aq)} + H_2O_{(l)}$$

   C. $H^+_{(aq)} + OH^-_{(aq)} \rightleftharpoons H_2O_{(l)}$

   D.
   $CH_3COOH_{(aq)} + H^+_{(aq)} + OH^-_{(aq)}$
   $$\rightleftharpoons H_2O_{(l)} + H^+_{(aq)} + CH_3COO^-_{(aq)}$$

2. Which of the following equations describes the dissociation of hydrogen chloride in water?

   A.
   $$H^+_{(aq)} + Cl^-_{(aq)} + H^+_{(aq)} + OH^-_{(aq)}$$
   $$\rightleftharpoons HCl_{(aq)} + H_2O_{(l)}$$

   B. $HCl_{(aq)} + H_2O_{(l)}$
   $$\rightleftharpoons H_3O^+_{(aq)} + Cl^-_{(aq)}$$

   C. $Cl^-_{(aq)} + H_2O_{(l)}$
   $$\rightleftharpoons HCl_{(aq)} + OH^-_{(aq)}$$

   D. $H^+_{(aq)} + Cl^-_{(aq)} \rightleftharpoons HCl_{(aq)}$

3. Which of the following balanced equations represents the reaction of NH_3 and H_2O?

   A. $NH_2^- + H_3O^+ \rightleftharpoons NH_3 + H_2O$

   B. $H_2O + NH_3 \rightleftharpoons NH_4^+ + OH^-$

   C. $H^+ + OH^- \rightleftharpoons H_2O$

   D. $2NH_3 \rightleftharpoons N_2 + 3H_2$

4. Solution X turns phenolphthalein (an indicator) solution pink when a few drops are added to it. What does solution X represent ?

   A. An alkali   **B.** An acid

   C. An oxide   **D.** A salt

5. A solution turns yellow when methyl orange is added to it. What is the nature of the solution ?

   A. Acidic

   B. Alkaline

   C. Strongly acidic

   D. Neutral

6. Which of the following rows correctly pair the ions which are obtained after ionization of water?

	I	II
A.	OH^-	O_2^-
B.	H_3O^+	OH^-
C.	H_3O^+	H^+
D.	H^+	O_2^-

7. Which of the following equations correctly represents the ionization of water?

   A. $2H_2O_{(l)} \rightleftharpoons H_3O^+_{(aq)} + OH^-_{(aq)}$

   B. $2H_2O_{(l)} \rightleftharpoons H_3O_{(aq)} + H^+_{(aq)} + O^-_{(aq)}$

   C. $H_2O_{(aq)} \rightleftharpoons 2H^+_{(aq)} + O^-_{2(aq)}$

   D. $2H_2O_{(aq)} \rightleftharpoons H_3O^+_{(l)} + OH^-_{(l)}$

Use the following information to answer the next question.

The K_w at 25°C is 10^{-14}

8. Which of the following equations is used to calculate [OH^-]?

   A. $\left[OH^- \right] = \dfrac{1.00 \times 10^{-14}}{\left[H_3O^+ \right]}$

   B. $\left[OH^- \right] = 1.00 \times 10^{-14} \times \left[H_3O^+ \right]$

   C. $\left[OH^- \right] = 1.00 \times 10^{-14} + \left[H^+ \right]$

   D. $\left[OH^- \right] = \sqrt{\dfrac{1.00 \times 10^{-14}}{H^+}}$

9. Which of the following statements is **TRUE** for a basic solution at 25°C?

   A. $\left[OH^- \right] > \left[H_3O^+ \right]$

   B. $\left[H^+ \right] > \left[OH^- \right]$

   C. $\left[H^+ \right] = \left[OH^- \right]$

   D. $\left[OH^- \right] = \left[H_3O^+ \right]$

10. Which of the following statements is true for an acidic solution at 30°C?

    A. $\left[H_3O^+ \right] > \left[OH^- \right]$

    B. $\left[OH^- \right] > \left[H_3O^+ \right]$

    C. $\left[H^+ \right] < \left[OH^- \right]$

    D. $\left[OH^- \right] = \left[H_3O^+ \right]$

11. Which of the following expressions is **NOT** true for a neutral solution at room temperature?

    A. $\left[H_3O^+ \right] = \left[OH^- \right]$

    B. pOH = 7.0

    C. $\left[H_3O^+ \right] = \left[OH^- \right] = 1.00 \times 10^{-7}$ mol/L

    D. pH > 7.0

12. Which alternative is **TRUE** for a basic aqueous solution ?

    A. $\left[H_3O^+ \right] = 1.00 \times 10^{-7}$ mol/L

    B. $\left[H_3O^+ \right] = \left[OH^- \right]$

    C. $\left[H_3O^+ \right] > \left[OH^- \right]$

    D. $\left[H_3O^+ \right] < \left[OH^- \right]$

13. Which is true for a basic solution at 30°C?

  A. $\left[OH^-\right] = \left[H_3O^+\right]$

  B. $\left[OH^-\right] > \left[H_3O^+\right]$

  C. $pH < 7.0$

  D. $pOH > 7.0$

14. Which of the solutions is **NOT** correctly matched with their respective ions?

Solution	Ions
A) Acidic	$[H_3O^+] > [OH^-]$
B) Neutral	$[H_3O^+] = [OH^-]$
C) Strongly Basic	$[OH^-] > [H_3O^+]$
D) Strongly Acidic	$[OH^-] \leq [H_3O^+]$

15. What is the value of $[OH^-_{(aq)}]$ if $[H_3O^+_{(aq)}]$ is 1.75×10^{-4} mol/L?

  A. 5.01×10^{-10} mol/L

  B. 5.71×10^{-11} mol/L

  C. 6.01×10^{-10} mol/L

  D. 6.71×10^{-11} mol/L

16. Which of the following solutions would typically show the least electrical conductivity?

  A. 0.8 M weak acid

  B. 1.0 M weak base

  C. 0.5 M strong base

  D. 0.1 M strong acid

17. Which of the following alternatives defines a strong acid correctly?

  A. An acid that ionizes 100% to produce H^+ ion and the conjugate base.

  B. Any metal hydroxide salt that completely dissociates into its ions in water.

  C. Any acid that ionizes only slightly in aqueous solution.

  D. A metal hydroxide salt that reacts with water produce hydroxide ions to only a slight extent in aqueous solution.

18. What is the main difference between a strong acid and a strong base?

  A. Their degree of ionization

  B. Their concentration in solution

  C. Their nature of ions

  D. Their degree of electrical conduction

19. Which row best represents an acidic solution?

	Litmus colour	Reaction with Mg
A.	blue	reaction
B.	blue	no reaction
C.	red	reaction
D.	red	no reaction

20. Which alternative represents the typical 'pH' value of dishwashing solutions?

  A. 2.0   B. 6.0

  C. 10.0   D. 14.0
  NaOH

21. Which of the following properties is found in an acid solution?

  A. Has a pH less than 7.0

  B. Has a pH greater than 7.0

  C. Is slippery

  D. Turns red litmus blue

Use the following information to answer the next question.

All acids contain hydrogen but all hydrogen containing compounds are not acids.

22. Which hydrogen containing compound is an acid?

   A. NH_3

   B. CH_4

   C. PH_3

   D. H_2SO_4

Use the following information to answer the next question.

A few drops of phenolphthalein are added separately to two beakers containing an acid and an alkali.

23. Which of the following rows indicates the colour change in the two solutions?

	Colour in acid solution	Colour in alkaline solution
A.	colourless	pink
B.	pink	colourless
C.	red	blue
D.	blue	red

24. An Arrhenius acid is:

   A. substance that dissociates in water to produce hydroxide ions

   B. substance that produces hydrogen ions in water

   C. proton donor

   D. proton acceptor

25. Which of the following compounds has the greatest solubility in water?

   A. $MgSO_4$ B. $CaSO_4$

   C. $BaSO_4$ D. $PbSO_4$

26. Which of the following pairs of compounds have high solubility in water?

   A. $AgNO_3$, $Pb(NO_3)_2$

   B. $AgCl$, $PbCl_2$

   C. $BaSO_4$, $CaSO_4$

   D. $CaCO_3$, $FeCO_3$

27. Which precipitate is formed when diluted HCl is added to $AgNO_3$ solution?

   A. $AgCl$ B. HNO_3

   C. Ag_2CO_3 D. $NaCl$

28. Which precipitate is formed when $Pb(NO_3)_2$ and NaCl solutions are mixed together?

   A. $NaNO_3$ B. $PbCl_2$

   C. Na_2CO_3 D. $PbSO_4$

29. Which of the following cations can not precipitate SO_4^{2-} (aq)?

   A. Pb^{2+} B. Cu^+

   C. Ca^{2+} D. Na^+

Use the following information to answer the next question.

An experiment is conducted to identify an unknown cation that is present in each of the four beakers.

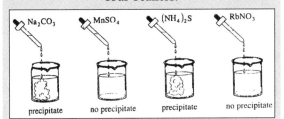

30. Which of the following cations may be the unknown cation?

   A. Pb^{2+} B. Sr^{2+}

   C. Fe^{3+} D. Ag^+

31. The oven cleaner Easy-Off ® is a concentrated aqueous solution of sodium hydroxide. With reference to Easy Off ® the term solute refers to

    A. a saturated solution of sodium hydroxide

    B. the sodium

    C. the sodium hydroxide component of the cleaner

    D. the water component of the cleaner

Use the following information to answer the next question.

Cocaine is addictive, illegal, and among other things, can lead to paranoid psychosis and heart failure. Cocaine exists in two forms:
1) an ammonium salt or ionic compound (a hydrochloride), and
2) in a free base form (a non polar molecule).

CHALLENGER QUESTION

32. Which form of cocaine would be more soluble in a non-polar solvent?

    A. Neither form is soluble

    B. Both forms are highly soluble

    C. The hydrochloride form

    D. The free base form

Use the following information to answer the next question.

Acetic acid comprises 5% of white vinegar by weight. Pure acetic acid is called glacial acetic acid. It is used by photographers to prepare a "stop bath" for photographic film during print development.

33. If a stop bath solution composed solely of acetic acid and water was tested for its electrical conductivity, the solution would be expected to

    A. conduct an electrical current well

    B. conduct an electrical current no better than water

    C. conduct an electrical current weakly

    D. conduct an electrical current less effectively than water

Use the following diagram to answer the next question.

Glucose has the following molecular structure

$$HO\text{—}C\text{—}H \quad CH_2OH$$

(molecular structure diagram of glucose)

CHALLENGER QUESTION

34. Glucose can be described as

    A. an electrolyte that is water soluble

    B. an electrolyte that is insoluble in water

    C. a non-electrolyte that is water soluble

    D. a non-electrolyte that is insoluble in water

35. Phosphoric acid is a component of many soft drinks. In an aqueous solution, phosphoric acid is a

    A. strong electrolyte and a strong conductor of electricity

    B. strong electrolyte and a weak conductor of electricity

    C. weak electrolyte and a strong conductor of electricity

    D. weak electrolyte and a weak conductor of electricity

36. NaOCl$_{(aq)}$ is __*i*__ at conducting electricity in water because NaOCl$_{(aq)}$ is __*ii*__.
The statement above is completed by the information in row.

Row	*i*	*ii*
A.	poor	non-electrolyte
B.	poor	weak electrolyte
C.	good	non-electrolyte
D.	good	strong electrolyte

Use the following information to answer the next question.

Nitric acid, which is used in the manufacture of fertilizers and explosives, is a good conductor of electricity.

37. Nitric acid has excellent electrical conductivity as a result of its

A. partial dissociation in aqueous solution

B. complete dissociation in aqueous solution

C. maintenance of its molecular structure in solution

D. inability to dissociate into ions

38. If an electrical current were applied to a liquid CO$_2$ sample, in all likelihood, the current would

A. be readily conducted

B. not be conducted

C. conduct well if the concentration of CO$_2$ was high

D. conduct well if the concentration of CO$_2$ was low

39. Of the following solutes, the one that will **not** conduct electricity well in aqueous solution is

A. NaCl   B. HNO$_3$

C. KOH   D. C$_{12}$H$_{22}$O$_{11}$

Use the following information to answer the next question.

Although for health reasons it is gradually being phased out, high concentrations of aqueous formaldehyde (HCHO$_{(aq)}$), or formalin, are used to preserve biological specimens.

Numerical Response

1. The mass of formaldehyde in 3.00 L of 11.6 mol/L formalin is _____ kg.
(Record your answer to three digits.)

Use the following information to answer the next question.

In 125 mL of reasonably strong English Breakfast tea, there is approximately 110 mg of caffeine.

40. The concentration of caffeine in this tea, expressed as a percentage of weight for this volume, is

A. 0.088 0%   B. 0.138%

C. 1.14%   D. 1.25%

41. By mass, the percentage composition of potassium permanganate is

A. 40.50% O, 34.76% Mn, and 24.74% K

B. 49.93% Mn, 35.53% K, and 14.54% O

C. 50.23% O, 30.69% K, and 19.08% Mn

D. 49.24% K, 30.61% Mn, and 20.15% O

CHALLENGER QUESTION

42. If 3.00 kg of liquid CO_2 dissolves 43.2 g of grease in the presence of 200 g of surfactant, the percent, by mass, of grease in this mixture is

A. 0.133%   **B.** 1.33%

C. 2.12%   **D.** 6.17%

Use the following information to answer the next question.

Hydrogen peroxide (H_2O_2), a strong oxidizing agent, was once used as rocket fuel, but today it is commercially sold as a disinfectant. Hydrogen peroxide decomposes over time to form water and oxygen.

CHALLENGER QUESTION

43. A 1 L bottle of liquid labelled "30% hydrogen peroxide by weight" was analyzed after three years, and its concentration was determined to be 6.0 mol/L. Assuming the density of the entire solution is 1.10 g/mL, the percent, by mass, of hydrogen peroxide in the bottle is

A. 0.016%   **B.** 0.019%

C. 16%   **D.** 19%

Use the following information to answer the next question.

Despite the key role it plays in the transport of oxygen in blood, the abundance of iron in the body is only 0.004% by weight.

44. Based on this information, the mass of iron in a person with a body mass of 68 kg is

A. 0.3 kg

B. 3 g

C. 0.06 g

D. 0.000 6 g

Use the following information to answer the next question.

Sodium fluoride is an important cavity-fighting ingredient in toothpaste. The fluoride ion acts by replacing a hydroxide ion in tooth minerals.

CHALLENGER QUESTION

Numerical Response

2. If a 75 mL tube of toothpaste is 0.243% sodium fluoride by weight, the concentration of fluoride in the toothpaste (assuming the density of the toothpaste is 4.5 g/mL) would be_____ mol/L. (Record your answer to two digits.)

45. The **best** way to prepare 100 mL of 0.040 0 mol/L $HCl_{(aq)}$ from a standard 0.200 mol/L $HCl_{(aq)}$ solution is to

A. use a burettte and transfer 20.0 mL of 0.200 mol/L $HCl_{(aq)}$ to a 100 mL Erlenmeyer flask and then top up the solution volume to the 100 mL line with distilled water. Finally, put a stop in the flask and invert it several times to mix the contents thoroughly

B. use a volumetric pipette and transfer 20.0 mL of 0.200 mol/L $HCl_{(aq)}$ to a 100 mL volumetric flask and then top up the solution volume to the calibration mark with distilled water. Finally, put a stop in the flask and invert it several times to mix the contents thoroughly

C. measure 20 mL of 0.200 mL/L $HCl_{(aq)}$ in a 100 mL volumetric cylinder and then top up the solution volume to 100 mL with distilled water

D. dissolve 20 mL of 0.200 mol/L $HCl_{(aq)}$ in exactly 80 mL of distilled water in a beaker and then swirl the mixture to thoroughly mix the solution

46. Which of the following techniques is the **best** way of preparing 100 mL of a 0.050 0 mol/L sodium carbonate $Na_2CO_{3(aq)}$ standard solution?

   A. Carefully pipet 10 mL of a 0.050 0 mol/L sodium carbonate stock solution into a 100 mL volumetric flask and then add water to the 100 mL mark.

   B. Carefully pour 0.500 mol/L sodium carbonate stock solution into a 100 mL graduated cylinder to the 10 mL mark then add water to the 100 mL mark.

   C. Dissolve 0.530 g of solid sodium carbonate in a 200 mL beaker, add water to the 100 mL mark, then carefully transfer the solution to a 100 mL volumetric flask.

   D. In a 50 mL beaker, dissolve 0.530 g of solid calcium carbonate in deionized water, carefully transfer the solution to a 100 mL volumetric flask, then add water to the 100 mL mark.

47. Which of the following is the **best** way to prepare 250 mL of 1.0 mol/L aqueous silver nitrate solution?

   A. Obtain 42.5 g of solid silver nitrate in a 100 mL beaker, dissolve it in about 80 mL of water, transfer the solution to a 250 mL volumetric flask with rinsing, and fill to the 250 mL mark with more water.

   B. Obtain 42.5 g of solid silver nitrate in a 300 mL Erlenmeyer flask, dissolve in a minimal volume of water and add more water to the 250 mL mark.

   C. Obtain 42.5 g of solid silver nitrate in a beaker, dissolve in a minimal volume of water, pipet into a 250 mL volumetric flask and fill to the mark with water.

   D. Pour water into a 250 mL volumetric flask to just below the 250 mL mark, add 42.5 g of solid silver nitrate, and swirl.

Use the following information to answer the next question.

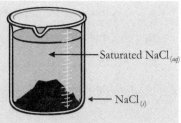

A sample of radioactively labelled $NaCl_{(s)}$ is added to the system shown. If radioactive salt is present, either as a solid or in a solution, it will make a nearby Geiger Counter click intensely.

Saturated $NaCl_{(aq)}$

$NaCl_{(s)}$

CHALLENGER QUESTION

48. After adding the radioactive $NaCl_{(s)}$, it can be observed that

   A. only the $NaCl_{(s)}$ will register as radioactive

   B. only the $NaCl_{(aq)}$ will register as radioactive

   C. both the $NaCl_{(s)}$ and the $NaCl_{(aq)}$ will register as radioactive

   D. neither the $NaCl_{(s)}$ nor the $NaCl_{(aq)}$ will register as radioactive

Use the following information to answer the next question.

Researchers at the University of Alberta have discovered accumulation of uric crystals in the fossils of the Tyrannosaurus Rex species of dinosaur. The scientists found that the fossils of these dinosaurs had erosions on the bone similar to bone erosion in humans with gout.
Gout is a metabolic disorder in humans caused by high levels of uric acid in blood.
In high concentrations, uric acid precipitates out of the blood and accumulates in the kidneys, joints, and toes, resulting in painful inflammation of these areas.

49. In patients with gout, the rate of dissolving uric acid is

  A. less than the rate of precipitation

  B. equal to the rate of precipitation

  C. greater than the rate of precipitation

  D. independent of the rate of precipitation

Use the following information to answer the next question.

The Dow process for the production of magnesium exploits the high magnesium ion concentrations in seawater. By this process, magnesium is precipitated from seawater by the addition of calcium hydroxide. The magnesium hydroxide formed is then treated with hydrochloric acid to give aqueous magnesium chloride by the following reaction.

$$Mg(OH)_{2(s)} + 2HCl_{(aq)}$$
$$\rightarrow MgCl_{2(aq)} + 2H_2O_{(l)}$$

Subsequent evaporation and electrolysis of magnesium chloride gives the desired magnesium metal.

50. Based on Arrhenius's definition, the formation of magnesium chloride as shown above is a neutralization reaction because

  A. the acid, $Mg(OH)_{2(s)}$, is reacting with the base, $HCl_{(aq)}$

  B. the acid, $HCl_{(aq)}$, is reacting with the base, $Mg(OH)_{2(aq)}$

  C. the acid is neutralized to form the base, $Mg(OH)_{(aq)}$

  D. $HCl_{(aq)}$ donates hydrogen ions

Use the following information to answer the next question.

1.	acidic	5.	> 7
2.	basic	6.	< 7
3.	neutral	7.	> 1.0×10^{-7} mol/L
4.	molecular	8.	> 1.0×10^{-7} mol/L

Numerical Response

3. The four numbers, corresponding to the pieces of information above, that will fill the blanks I, II, III and IV respectively in the table below are

___ ___ ___ ___

pH	$[H^+_{(aq)}]$(mol/L)	Solution is
I	II	acidic
>7	III	basic
7	$=1.0 \times 10^{-7}$	IV

51. A saturated solution at equilibrium with an undissolved solute could be **best** described as a system in which

  A. change in the reaction favours crystallization

  B. dissolution and crystallization are equal

  C. competing processes are occurring that can not balance each other

  D. change in the reaction favours dissolution

*Use the following information to answer
the next question.*

In 1909, Danish biochemist Peer Laurizt Sorensen, proposed a practical means of gauging the acidity of a solution. Sorensen called the pH (he wrote it as P_H) the "hydrogen ion exponent".

52. According to Sorensen, the pH of a solution is defined as

    A. $pH = -\log\left[H^+_{(aq)}\right]$

    B. $pH = -\log\left(-\left[H^+_{(aq)}\right]\right)$

    C. $\left[H^+_{(aq)}\right] = -\log pH$

    D. $pH = 10 - \left[H^+_{(aq)}\right]$

53. Gastric juice has a pH of about 2, while pure water has a pH of 7. Given this information, we can say that

    A. gastric juice is 5 times more acidic than pure water

    B. gastric juice is 10^5 times more acidic than pure water

    C. pure water is 5 times more acidic than gastric juice

    D. pure water is 10^5 times more acidic than gastric juice

---

CHALLENGER QUESTION

54. A particular solution has a pH of 2. By what factor is the concentration of $H^+_{(aq)}$ in that solution greater than $H^+_{(aq)}$ in a solution with a pH of 12?

    A. 6   **B.** 10

    C. 10^{10} **D.** 2^6

---

*Use the following information to answer
the next question.*

55. If a tablet of the weak acid Acetylsalicylic Acid (ASA) is dissolved in a glass of water and then gives a solution pH of 3, then the corresponding hydrogen ion concentration is

    A. 10^{-3} mol/L

    B. 10^{-4} mol/L

    C. 3 mol/L

    D. 4 mol/L

Written Response

1. Describe the factors that affect the solubility of gases, liquids, and solids in liquid solutions.

(8 marks)

Use the following table to answer the next question.

The concentrations of several minerals in natural spring water from the French Alps are as shown below:

Minerals	Concentration (ppm)
Calcium ($Ca^{2+}_{(aq)}$)	78
Magnesium ($Mg^{2+}_{(aq)}$)	24
Sodium ($Na^{+}_{(aq)}$)	5
Potassium ($K^{+}_{(aq)}$)	1

2. a) What is the molar concentration of calcium ions? (2 marks)

b) What mass of magnesium would be present in a 250 mL glass of this spring water? (2 marks)

c) Express the sodium concentration as a percentage weight per volume. (2 marks)

d) Calcium and magnesium ions are commonly associated with the hardness of water. Suggest a chemical reagent that will remove these ions thereby softening the water. (2 marks)

56. If the laboratory technician at your school wants to make 4.0 L of a 0.125 mol/L solution, what initial volume of a 1.50 mol/L solution is required?

A. 0.333 L

B. 4.50 L

C. 24.0 L

D. 48.0 L

57. What mass of pure solid sodium chloride is required to make 200 mL of a 2.3% W/V solution?

A. 0.004 6 mg

B. 4.6 mg

C. 4.6 g

D. 4.6 kg

58. If the concentration of a lead (II) nitrate solution is 0.16 mol/L, what is the concentration of nitrate ions?

A. 0.04 mol/L

B. 0.16 mol/L

C. 0.32 mol/L

D. 0.64 mol/L

59. An aqueous solution of lead (IV) nitrate contains 0.32 mol/L of nitrate ions. What is the concentration of the lead (IV) nitrate solution?

A. 0.08 mol/L

B. 0.16 mol/L

C. 0.32 mol/L

D. 0.64 mol/L

60. If the pH of a solution rises from 10 to 11, the H^{+} concentration

A. increased by 10%

B. decreased by 10%

C. increased by a factor of 10

D. decreased by a factor of 10

61. If the pH of an acid solution increases, the

   A. the number of H^+ and OH^- ions increases

   B. the number of H^+ and OH^- ions decreases

   C. the number of H^+ ions increases

   D. the number of OH^- ions increases

62. If phenolphthalein is colourless, chlorophenol red is red, and bromocresol green when added to samples of a solution, the solution pH could be

   A. 3.5

   B. 5.5

   C. 7.5

   D. 11.5

63. If a sample of a solution is tested with 3 different pH indicators, it is found to have a pH of 5.7.

The indicator colours that would match this evidence are

	Bromothymol blue	bromocresol green	litmus
A.	blue	blue	blue
B.	blue	green	blue
C.	yellow	yellow	red
D.	yellow	blue	red

64. The reaction of the hydrogen ions from an acid and the hydroxide ions from a base, to produce salt and water, is known as

   A. desalination

   B. neutralization

   C. precipitation

   D. dissociation

65. Neutralization reactions involve

   A. hydronium ions and hydrogen ions

   B. hydroxide ions and water

   C. hydrogen ions and water

   D. hydronium ions and hydroxide ions

66. A substance that can act as a polyprotic base is

   A. $KOH_{(aq)}$

   B. $Ba(OH)_{2(aq)}$

   C. $KHSO_{4(aq)}$

   D. $K_2CO_{3(aq)}$

67. An example of a polyprotic acid is

   A. $HCl_{(aq)}$

   B. $H_2SO_{3(aq)}$

   C. $KHSO_{4(aq)}$

   D. $H_2O_{(aq)}$

68. When sugar dissolves in water, the type of mixture formed is best classified as

   A. heterogeneous

   B. homogenous

   C. non-uniform

   D. uniform

69. Which of the following substances will undergo a chemical change if it is dissolved in water?

 A. common salt

 B. baking soda

 C. honey

 D sugar

Use the following information to answer the next question.

Household bleach can be a dangerous substance. A significant hazard may result from the mixing of bleach with ammonia cleansers. The initial product of this reaction is the toxic and volatile gas chloramine ($NH_2Cl_{(g)}$). It is formed as follows.

$$NH_{3(aq)} + ClO^-_{(aq)}$$
$$\rightarrow NH_2Cl_{(g)} + OH^-_{(aq)}$$

70. If this reaction is exothermic, then the best definition of this process is that the energy

 A. needed to break bonds in the reactants is greater than the energy released from bond formation in the products

 B. needed to break bonds in the reactants is equal to the energy released from bond formation in the products

 C. needed to break bonds in the reactants is less than the energy released from bond formation in the products

 D. is being created in the form of heat

Use the following information to answer the next question.

An iron ion can have a charge of 3+.
An oxygen ion has a charge of 2–.
Iron and oxygen readily combine to form a compound commonly known as rust.
$$Fe^{3+} O^{2-}$$

71. Which of the following rows identifies the correct formula and IUPAC name for rust?

 A.

Chemical formula	IUPAC Name
Fe_3O_2	Iron (III) oxide

 B.

Chemical formula	IUPAC Name
Fe_3O_2	Iron (II) oxide

 C.

Chemical formula	IUPAC Name
Fe_2O_3	Iron (III) oxide

 D.

Chemical formula	IUPAC Name
Fe_2O_3	Iron (II) oxide

Use the following information to answer the next question.

A calcium ion has a charge of 2+. It readily combines with oxygen to form an ionic compound. An oxygen ion has a charge of 2–.

$$Ca^{2+} \ O^{2-}$$

72. Which of the following rows gives the formula and IUPAC name for the compound formed by calcium and oxygen?

A.

Chemical formula	IUPAC Name
CaO	Calcium oxide

B.

Chemical formula	IUPAC Name
CaO	Calcide

C.

Chemical formula	IUPAC Name
Ca_2O_2	Calcium oxide

D.

Chemical formula	IUPAC Name
Ca_2O_2	Calcide

NOTES

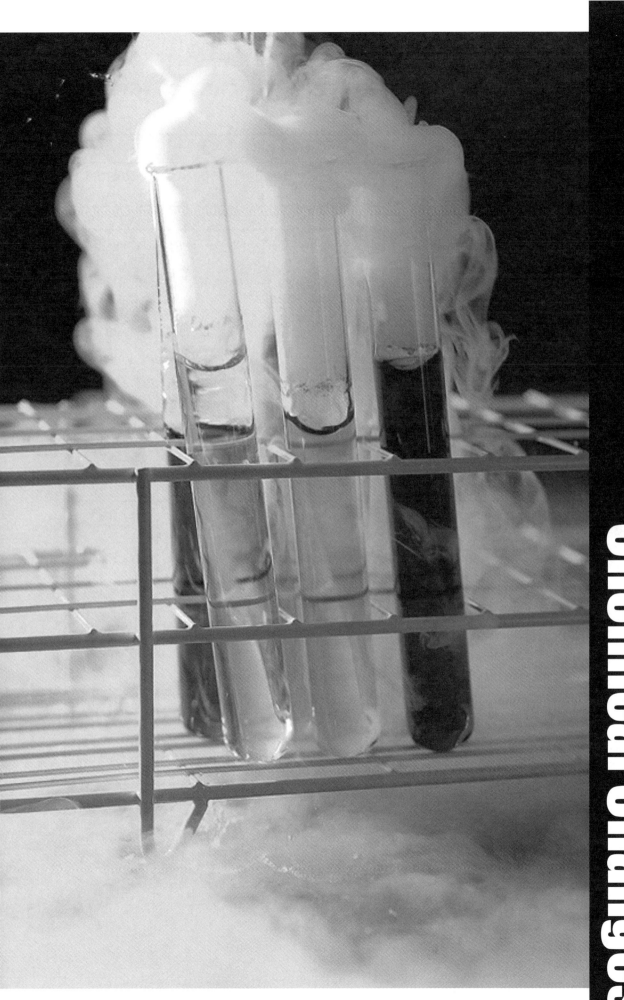

Quantitative Relatoinships in Chemical Changes

QUANTITATIVE RELATIONSHIPS IN CHEMICAL CHANGES

TABLE OF CORRELATIONS		
General Outcome	**Specific Outcome**	**Related Questions**
Students will:		
1. explain how balanced chemical equations indicate the quantitative relationships between reactants and products involved in chemical changes.	1.1 predict the products(s) of a chemical reaction based upon the reaction type	1, 10, 19, 38, 39
	1.2 recall the balancing of chemical equations in terms of atoms, molecules and moles	3, 12
	1.3 contrast quantitative and qualitative analysis	4, 9
	1.4 write balanced ionic and net ionic equations, including identification of spectator ions, for reactions taking place in aqueous solutions	2, 5, 6, 7, 11, 40, 41, 42, 43, 44
	1.5 calculate the quantities of reactants and/or products involved in chemical reactions, using gravimetric, solution or gas stoichiometry	NR1, 13, 14, 15, 16, 17, 18, 22, 23, 24, 25, 26, 27, 28, 29
2. use stoichiometry in quantitative analysis.	2.1 explain chemical principles (i.e. conservation of mass in a chemical change), using quantitative analysis	36, 37, 45, 46
	2.2 identify limiting and excess reagents in chemical reactions	31, 34, WR1
	2.3 define theoretical yields and actual yields	30, 32, 33, 35, 47, 48
	2.4 explain the discrepancy between theoretical and actual yields	49, 50
	2.5 draw and interpret titration curves, using data from titration experiments involving strong monoprotic acids and strong monoprotic bases	20, 21, 51, 52
	2.6 describe the function and choice of indicators in titrations	8, 53, 54
	2.7 identify equivalence points on strong monoprotic acid-strong monoprotic base titration curves and differentiate between the indicator end point and the equivalence point	55, 56

20-D1.1k   *recall the balancing of chemical equations in terms of atoms, molecules and moles*

Chemical reactions can be classified as follows:

Formation:

X + Y → XY

Example:

$$4Al_{(s)} + 3O_{2(g)} → 2Al_2O_{3(s)}$$

Decomposition:

XY → X + Y

Example:

$$2H_2O_{(g)} → 2H_{2(g)} + O_{2(g)}$$

Single Replacement:

AB + C → CB + A, where C is a metal

Example:

$$2AgNO_{3(aq)} + Cu_{(s)} → Cu(NO_3)_{2(aq)} + 2Ag_{(s)}$$

AB + C → AC + B, where C is a non-metal

Example:

$$2KI_{(aq)} + Cl_{2(g)} → 2KCl_{(aq)} + I_{2(aq)}$$

Double Replacement

AB + CD → AD + BC

Example:

$$2NaI_{(aq)} + Pb(NO_3)_{2(aq)}$$
$$→ PbI_{2(s)} + 2NaNO_{3(aq)}$$

Complete Combustion

$$C_xH_y + O_2 → CO_2 + H_2O$$

Example:

$$C_3H_{8(g)} + 5O_{2(g)} → 3CO_{2(g)} + 4H_2O_{(g)}$$

Other: Any reaction that does not fit the previous classifications – you will not be able to predict the products in "other" reactions. Knowing the reaction type enables you to predict the products.

Related Questions: 1, 10, 19, 38, 39

20-D1.2k   *recall the balancing of chemical equations in terms of atoms, molecules and moles*

When chemical reaction equations are balanced, there will be an equal number of atoms (number of moles of atoms) of each type on each side of the reaction equation.

Consider the equation:

$$C_3H_{8(g)} + 5O_{2(g)} → 3CO_{2(g)} + 4H_2O_{(g)}$$

On each side of the equation there are 3 carbon atoms (3 moles of carbon atoms), 8 hydrogen atoms (8 moles of hydrogen atoms), and 10 oxygen atoms (10 moles of oxygen atoms). On the left side there is 1 molecule of $C_3H_{8(g)}$ (1 mole of $C_3H_{8(g)}$ molecules) and 5 molecules of $O_{2(g)}$ (5 moles of $O_{2(g)}$ molecules). On the right side there are $3CO_{2(g)}$ molecules (3 moles of $CO_{2(g)}$ molecules) and 4 molecules of $H_2O_{(g)}$ (4 moles of $H_2O_{(g)}$ molecules).

Related Questions: 3, 12

20-D1.3k   *contrast quantitative and qualitative analysis*

Qualitative analysis determines whether or not a certain substance is present in a sample to be tested. Quantitative analysis determines how much (mass, concentration, etc) of that substance is present.

Related Questions: 4, 9

20-D1.4k   *write balanced ionic and net ionic equations, including identification of spectator ions, for reactions taking place in aqueous solutions*

Electrolytes in solution will exist in dissociated (ionic) or ionized (strong acid) form. In either case there will be "free" ions in solution. Taking a formula equation and changing into ionic and net ionic equations begins by identifying electrolytes and determining whether or not they are dissolved. If they are then they are written as "free" ions.

Example:
Formula equation

$$2AgNO_{3(aq)} + Cu_{(s)} \rightarrow Cu(NO_3)_{2(aq)} + 2Ag_{(s)}$$

(dissolved electrolyte)   (dissolved electrolyte)

Ionic equation

$$2Ag^+_{(aq)} + 2NO_3^-_{(aq)} + Cu_{(s)}$$

(spectator ion)

$$\rightarrow Cu^{2+}_{(aq)} + 2NO_3^-_{(aq)} + 2Ag_{(s)}$$

(spectator ion)

Spectator ions are cancelled out to produce a net ionic equation.

Net ionic equation

$$2Ag^+_{(aq)} + Cu_{(s)} \rightarrow Cu^{2+}_{(aq)} + 2Ag_{(s)}$$

Example:
Formula equation

$$2NaI_{(aq)} + Pb(NO_3)_{2(aq)}$$
$$\rightarrow PbI_{2(s)} + 2NaNO_{3(aq)}$$

Ionic equation

$$2Na^+_{(aq)} + 2I^-_{(aq)} + Pb^{2+}_{(aq)} + 2NO_3^-_{(aq)}$$

(spectator ion)   (spectator ion)

$$\rightarrow PbI_{2(s)} + 2Na^+_{(aq)} + 2NO_3^-_{(aq)}$$

(undissolved electrolyte)   (spectator ions)

Net ionic equation:

$$Pb^{2+}_{(aq)} + 2I^-_{(aq)} \rightarrow PbI_{2(s)}$$

Related Questions: 2, 5, 6, 7, 11, 40, 41, 42, 43, 44

20-D1.5k   *calculate the quantities of reactants and/or products involved in chemical reactions, using gravimetric, solution or gas stoichiometry*

Gravimetric stoichiometry example:

In a precipitation reaction, $KOH_{(aq)}$ reacts with excess $Sn(NO_3)_{2(aq)}$ to produce a precipitate. If the mass of precipitate is 2.57 g, what mass of $KOH_{(s)}$ was present in the original solution?

Begin by writing the reaction equation, and all pertinent information underneath the substances in the reaction equation.

Note: from the *solubility chart* that the precipitate will be $Sn(OH)_{2(s)}$.

$$2KOH_{(aq)} + Sn(NO_3)_{2(aq)}$$
$$\rightarrow Sn(OH)_{2(s)} + 2KNO_{3(aq)}$$

Moles:	n_2	n_1
Mass:	?	2.57 g
Molar Mass:	56.11 g/mol	152.71 g/mol

This shows the pathway to do the question. First find the number of moles, n_1, for the substance whose mass is given.

Use the mole ratio: $\dfrac{looking\ for}{given}$ to find the

moles of the required substance, n_2, then convert n_2 into mass which is the final answer.

$$n_1 = 2.57\ g \times \frac{1\ mol}{152.71\ g} = 0.016\ 8\ mol$$

$$n_2 = 0.016\ 8\ mol \times \frac{2}{1} = 0.033\ 7\ mol$$

$$m = 0.033\ 7\ mol \times \frac{56.11\ mol}{g} = \underline{1.89\ g}$$

Special notes: The coefficients 2 and 1 are not included in the molar masses because they are already part of the mole ratio. You must show all of your work on these questions completely.

Solution stoichiometry example:

25.0 mL of 0.100 mol/L sulfuric acid reacts with 10.0 mL of potassium hydroxide solution. What is the concentration of the potassium hydroxide solution?

As before, it is necessary to write a reaction equation, find moles of the substance for which you have both concentration and volume, n_1. Use the mole ratio to find moles of the required substance, n_2, and convert this either to concentration or volume as required in the question.

$$H_2SO_{4(aq)} + 2KOH_{(aq)}$$
$$\rightarrow K_2SO_{4(aq)} + 2HOH_{(l)}$$

Moles:	n_1	n_2
Concentration:	0.100 mol/L	?
Volume:	25.0 mL	10.0 mL

$$n_1 = 0.100\,mol/L \times 0.025\,0\,L = 0.002\,50\,mol$$

$$n_2 = 0.002\,50\,mol \times \frac{2}{1} = 0.005\,00\,mol$$

$$\left[KOH_{(aq)}\right] = \frac{0.005\,00\,mol}{0.010\,0\,L} = \underline{0.500\,mol/L}$$

Note: It is possible to work directly with *mL* and get *mmol* instead of *mol* for n_1 and n_2, but do not use this unless you are very comfortable with the units.

Gravimetric and solution stoichiometry questions are always very similar, but gas stoichiometry questions will vary in approach. Always find the number of moles, first then multiply by the mole ratio, and finally convert the final number of moles into the required quantity.

Gas stoichiometry example:

In a combustion reaction, 150 g of methanol, $CH_3OH_{(l)}$, is completely burned. What volume of $CO_{2(g)}$ at 95.0 kPa and 20.0°C will be produced?

$$2CH_3OH_{(l)} + 3O_{2(g)} \rightarrow 2CO_{2(g)} + 4H_2O_{(l)}$$

n_1	n_2
150 g	95.0 kPA
32.05 g/mol	20.0°C

Labels have been dropped this time, but the information is still listed underneath each substance as shown above.

$$n_1 = 150\,g \times \frac{1}{32.05}\,mol/g = 4.68\,mol$$

$$n_2 = 4.68\,mol \times \frac{2}{2} = 4.68\,mol$$

$$v = \frac{nRT}{P}$$

$$= \frac{4.68\,mol \times 8.314\,{}^{kPa \times L}\!/_{mol \times K} \times 293\,K}{95.0\,kPa}$$

$$= \underline{120\,L}$$

Related Questions: NR1, 13, 14, 15, 16, 17, 18, 20, 22, 23, 24, 25, 26, 27, 28, 29

20-D2.1k   explain chemical principles (i.e. conservation of mass in a chemical change), using quantitative analysis

In a chemical reaction, mass is conserved. This means that the mass of products = mass of reactants. In the reaction $2AgNO_{3(aq)} + Cu_{(s)} \rightarrow Cu(NO_3)_{2(aq)} + 2Ag_{(s)}$, the mass of $AgNO_{3(aq)}$ and $Cu_{(s)}$ equals the mass of $Cu(NO_3)_{2(aq)}$ and $Ag_{(s)}$. This can be explained by the fact that there are an equal number of moles of each element before and after the reaction. If this reaction was performed with excess $Cu_{(s)}$, and the concentration of $AgNO_{3(aq)}$ was known, when the reaction goes to completion, all of the $AgNO_3$ will be used, some of the $Cu_{(s)}$ will be used, and $Cu(NO_3)_{2(aq)}$ and $Ag_{(s)}$ will be produced. The mass of $AgNO_3$ will be known from the solution concentration and volume.

The $Ag_{(s)}$ can be carefully removed from the piece of $Cu_{(s)}$ washed, dried, and its mass determined. The $Cu_{(s)}$ mass, after the silver is removed, can be determined and compared to the original mass. Finally the $Cu^{2+}_{(aq)}$ could be removed from the solution by precipitation with excess $NaOH_{(aq)}$. The mass of $Cu(OH)_{2(s)}$ precipitate could be used to calculate the mass of $Cu(NO_3)_2$ in the solution using gravimetric stoichiometry. Within experimental error, this should verify the law of conservation of mass.

Related Questions: 45, 46

20-D2.2k   identify limiting and excess reagents in chemical reactions

A limiting reagent is completely consumed in a chemical reaction. The excess reagent is present in greater quantity (number of moles times mole ratio) than is necessary to consume the limiting reagent. The limiting reagent is the one that is being analyzed in a quantitative analysis where limiting and excess reagents are present.

Related Questions: 31, 34, WR1

20-D2.3k   define theoretical yields and actual yields

The theoretical yield of a chemical reaction is the quantity of product formed if all the limiting reagent is consumed. It is calculated by stoichiometry. The actual yield is the actual quantity of product collected. In most cases, the actual yield will be less than the theoretical yield.

Related Questions: 30, 32, 33, 35, 47, 48

20-D2.4k   explain the discrepancy between theoretical and actual yields

Actual yields will be less than theoretical yields for the following reasons:

- the purity of the reacting chemicals
- uncertainty in measurements
- losses due to various experimental factors

e.g. mass of precipitates will be less because some of the precipitate substance actually dissolves, washing the precipitate with water

to clean it causes a little bit more to dissolve.

E.g. small amounts of solid will stick to spatulas and stirring rods.

- the reaction may be thought to be complete, but is not because it is a slow reaction
- some reactions never go to completion; they reach a state of dynamic equilibrium before doing so

Related Questions: 49, 50

20-D2.5k   draw and interpret titration curves, using data from titration experiments involving strong monoprotic acids and strong monoprotic bases

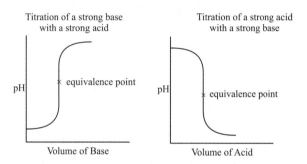

As a strong acid is added to a strong base, (or a strong base to a strong acid) the pH does not change dramatically because there is always a significant amount of the initial acid or base present. When moles of acid = moles of base the titration is at its equivalence point. Just before the equivalence point, the pH begins to change rapidly as the original base (or acid) is used up. The pH levels out again after the equivalence point as it approaches the pH of the solution being added.

Related Questions: 20, 21, 51, 52

I

20-D2.6k describe the function and choice of indicators in titrations

Indicators are chosen so that the equivalence point is in the middle of the transition range for the indicator. For example, bromothymol blue changes colour from yellow to blue in pH range 6.0 to 7.6. (See indicator chart) Below pH 6.0, it is yellow; above pH 7.6, it is blue. Between 6.0 and 7.6, it is various shades of green. For a monoprotic strong acid – strong base titration it is an ideal indicator since the equivalence point is in the middle of the transition range. When titrating, a lab worker would attempt to get a green bromothymol blue end point.

Related Questions: 8, 53, 54

20-D2.7k identify equivalence points on strong monoprotic acid-strong monoprotic base titration curves and differentiate between the indicator end point and the equivalence point

The *equivalence point* is indicated on each of the titration curves in section 20-D2.5k. It is the point at which equivalent numbers of moles of acid and base are present. The *end point* refers to a physical change that is observed at the *equivalence point*. For an acid/base indicator, it is the colour of the indicator at the equivalence point. A strong acid/strong base titration would have a green bromothymol blue end point (see indicator chart). Its equivalence point occurs at pH = 7.0, and bromothymol blue is green at this point.

Related Questions: 55, 56

1. The reaction of $Ba(OH)_{2(aq)}$ and $H_2SO_{4(aq)}$ produces a precipitate with the chemical formula being

   A. $Ba(OH)_{2(s)}$ B. $BaSO_{4(s)}$

   C. $H_2SO_{4(s)}$ D. $H_2O_{(s)}$

Use the following information to answer the next two questions.

Hydrochloric acid, $HCl_{(aq)}$, is produced in the stomach to aid in the breakdown of food. Excess stomach acid, however, can irritate the lower esophagus causing heartburn. Milk of Magnesia, a suspension of $Mg(OH)_{2(s)}$ in water, can usually provide effective relief from heartburn pain.

2. A balanced equation for the reaction of Milk of Magnesia with excess stomach acid is

   A. $HCl_{(aq)} + Mg(OH)_{2(s)}$
   $\rightarrow HOH_{(l)} + MgCl_{(aq)}$

   B. $HCl_{(aq)} + Mg(OH)_{2(s)}$
   $\rightarrow H_2O_{(l)} + MgCl_{(aq)}$

   C. $2HCl_{(aq)} + Mg(OH)_{2(s)}$
   $\rightarrow 2HOH_{(l)} + MgCl_{2(aq)}$

   D. $2HCl_{(aq)} + 2Mg(OH)_{(s)}$
   $\rightarrow HOH_{(l)} + 2MgCl_{(aq)}$

3. How many moles of stomach acid are neutralized for every mole of magnesium hydroxide in Milk of Magnesia?

   A. 3

   B. 1

   C. 2

   D. 4

Use the following information to answer the next question.

The Enzyme Multiplied Immunoassay Technique (EMIT) can be used to detect the presence of a particular substance in urine, serum, or plasma. The EMIT is used in laboratories to screen for the presence of illicit drugs such as marijuana, barbiturates, amphetamines, and opiates.

4. EMIT is an example of a

   A. titration analysis

   B. gravimetric analysis

   C. quantitative analysis

   D. qualitative analysis

Use the following information to answer the next question.

Carbon dioxide levels on board the space shuttle must be controlled in order to prevent the accumulation of exhaled $CO_{2(s)}$. Canisters of LiOH are commonly used for this purpose. The unbalanced reaction that occurs is
$LiOH_{(s)} + CO_{2(g)} \rightarrow Li_2CO_{3(s)} + H_2O_{(l)}$

5. The mole ratio of lithium hydroxide to carbon dioxide in the balanced chemical equation is

   A. 1:1

   B. 1:2

   C. 1:3

   D. 2:1

Use the following information to answer the next two questions.

Sodium hydroxide has been used to make "lye soap" for centuries. The soap forms when fatty acids are heated with $NaOH_{(s)}$. Soaps made with $NaOH_{(s)}$ usually feel hard to the touch. NaOH is also used in the chemical and pulp and paper industries.

6. The concentration of $NaOH_{(aq)}$ in a soap sample was established by titrating it with $HCl_{(aq)}$. The dissolved ions present in this titration were

   A. $H^+_{(aq)}, OH^-_{(aq)}$ and $Cl^-_{(aq)}$

   B. $Na^+_{(aq)}, Cl^-_{(aq)}$ and $H_2O_{(l)}$

   C. $H_2O_{(l)}, H^+_{(aq)}$ and $OH^-_{(aq)}$

   D. $Na^+_{(aq)}, OH^-_{(aq)}, H^+_{(aq)}$ and $Cl^-_{(aq)}$

Use the additional information to answer the next question.

Sodium bicarbonate ($NaHCO_{3(s)}$) can also be used to neutralize excess stomach acid.

$NaHCO_{3(s)} + HCl_{(aq)}$
$\rightarrow NaCl_{(aq)} + CO_{2(g)} + H_2O_{(l)}$

7. In the reaction of sodium bicarbonate with excess stomach acid, the spectator ions are

   A. CO_3^{2-} and H^+

   B. Na^+ and Cl^-

   C. HCO^{3-} and Na^+

   D. Cl^- and H^+

Use the following information to answer the next question.

If a vivid blue colour develops when a few drops of 1.0 mol/L aqueous copper (II) sulphate solution are added to a 1.0 mL aqueous solution of an unknown compound, then the unknown compound is **probably** an amine or an amino acid.

8. The statement that best describes the above information is

   A. a diagnostic test for amino acids and amines

   B. a quantitative analysis

   C. a colour change, and thus, a negative result

   D. a vivid blue solution that results when amines or amino acids are combined with copper (II) sulphate

Use the following information to answer the next question.

In 1995, chemists Sherry Rowland and Mario Molina shared the Nobel Prize in Chemistry for the discovery of the ozone damaging effects of chlorofluorocarbon compounds (CFCs).

9. Presently, the detection of CFCs in the atmosphere would

   A. be a quantitative observation

   B. be a qualitative observation

   C. not be a result of a diagnostic test

   D. be accomplished using spectator ions

Use the following information to answer the next question.

The mantle of a camping lantern is covered in thorium hydroxide and ceramic nitrate. They burn when the mantle is ignited and provide a catalytic surface for the pressurized fuel-air combustion. The equation for this "pre-burn" reaction involving thorium hydroxide is:

$$Th(OH)_{4(s)} \rightarrow ThO_{2(s)} + 2H_2O_{(g)}$$

10. This reaction is best classified as

  A. formation

  B. single replacement

  C. decomposition

  D. double replacement

Use the following information to answer the next two questions.

Alchemy is the precursor of modern chemistry and metallurgy. Many alchemists tried to change baser metals into gold.
Gold was believed to be the perfect metal and a key to immortality. Several "aurifaction" recipes were created. One such process, which resulted in golden crystals of tin (IV) sulfide, is shown:

#1. $KAl(SO_4)_2 \rightarrow K_2SO_4 + Al_2O_3 + SO_3$

#2. $SO_3 + 2Sn \rightarrow SnS_2 + SnO_2$

(This reaction sequence was described by the Chinese alchemist Ko Hung.)

11. When equation #1 is balanced, the mole ratio of potassium aluminum sulfate, $KAl(SO_4)_2$, to aluminum oxide, Al_2O_3, is

  A. 1:1

  B. 2:3

  C. 1:2

  D. 2:1

12. The anions in reaction 2 are

  A. S^{2-} and Sn^{2+}

  B. O^{2-} and Sn^{4+}

  C. S^- and O^-

  D. S^{2-} and O^{2-}

Use the following information to answer the next question.

Carbon dioxide fire extinguishers work because carbon dioxide is non-flammable and is denser than air. Consequently, carbon dioxide displaces air around a fire, thereby smothering it. Carbon dioxide in a pressurized tank is a liquid. However, as soon as it is released, it vaporizes.

CHALLENGER QUESTION

Numerical Response

1. If the pressure inside a 5.00 L $CO_{2(g)}$ tank is 5 times the room pressure, the volume of $CO_{2(g)}$ released when the valve is left open will be _____ L.
(Record your answer to three digits.)

Use the following information to answer the next question.

Scientists often analyze different sources of water to determine their chloride concentration. The majority of chloride present in natural bodies of water derives from dissolved rocks and minerals, although human activity can elevate these levels. High concentrations of chloride can be damaging to pipes, bridges, and agricultural crops. Chloride analysis can be done by titration with 0.004 0 mol/L $AgNO_{3(aq)}$.

CHALLENGER QUESTION

13. If three 100 mL samples of water required an average volume of 26.8 mL of $AgNO_{3(aq)}$ titrant for complete reaction, then the concentration of chloride ions in the water samples would have been

    A. 1.1 mmol/L

    B. 0.11 mol/L

    C. 11 mmol/L

    D. 15 mmol/L

Use the following information to answer the next question.

Decay occurs quite quickly in places like forest floors where the oxygen supply is abundant. In oxygen poor environments, such as stagnant swamps, decay is promoted by anaerobic bacteria. These bacteria obtain their oxygen by splitting off methane and carbon dioxide from carbohydrates.

$$C_6H_{12}O_{6(s)} \rightarrow 3CO_{2(g)} + 3CH_{4(g)}$$

The net effect is often a build-up of carbon-rich residue. These environments can eventually become sources of fossil fuels such as coal or even natural gas.

14. If 100 kg of glucose is broken down, the mass of methane gas produced would be

    A. 26.7 mg

    B. 73.3 kg

    C. 73.3 mg

    D. 26.7 kg

Use the following information to answer the next question.

The 1999 Acura Integra RS Coupe has one of the most advanced air bags in any production car available on the market today.

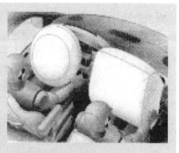

The Supplemental Restraint System (SRS) uses gold-plated, corrosion resistant electrical connectors to improve conductivity. This allows the air bag to inflate at a faster rate than air bags with other types of connectors. Upon impact, a pendulum-type device swings to close an electrical switch that initiates the simple decomposition reaction of sodium azide, which produces the gas that inflates the bag.

$$2NaN_{3(s)} \rightarrow 2Na_{(s)} + 3N_{2(g)}$$

15. If the volume of an inflated air bag is 35.0 L at SATP, the mass of sodium azide required to fully inflate the airbag upon reaction is

    A. 61.2 g   B. 122 g

    C. 91.8 g   D. 138 g

Use the following information to answer the next two questions.

The chemical 3-methylimino-2-butanone has the intense aroma of corn chips and can be prepared from small quantities of 2, 3-butanedione, methylamine hydrochloride and a suitable base. 3-Methylimino-2-butanone has been patented as a flavouring agent for foodstuffs.

$$H_3C-\overset{\overset{O}{\|}}{C}-\overset{\overset{O}{\|}}{C}-CH_3 \xrightarrow[\substack{\text{Strong} \\ \text{Base}}]{CH_3NH_2.HCl} H_3C-\overset{\overset{O}{\|}}{C}-\overset{\overset{N^{\diagdown CH_3}}{\|}}{C}-CH_3$$

CHALLENGER QUESTION

16. The mass yield of 3-methylimino-2-butanone obtained from the reaction of 0.35 g of 2,3-butanedione with excess methylamine hydrochloride is

    A. 0.56 g   B. 0.36 g

    C. 0.40 g   D. 4.0 g

17. If 0.28 g of 3-methylimino-2-butanone was obtained, the percent yield of the experiment was

    A. 65%   B. 70%

    C. 56%   D. 78%

Use the following information to answer the next question.

Calcium carbonate $CaCO_{3(s)}$ is found in marble and limestone buildings and structures. Acid rain poses a problem as it reacts with $CaCO_{3(s)}$ to cause the deterioration of these structures. An example of this reaction may be

$$CaCO_{3(s)} + 2HCl_{(aq)}$$
$$\rightarrow CaCl_{2(aq)} + H_2O_{(l)} + CO_{2(g)}$$

18. The volume of rain, with an $H^+_{(aq)}$ concentration of 1.00×10^{-4} mol/L, that would be required to dissolve 3.50 g of $CaCO_{3(s)}$ is

    A. 69.9 L   B. 6.99 L

    C. 6.99 kL   D. 699 L

Use the following information to answer the next question.

Galvanized nails are used extensively because they do not rust. An experiment is designed to determine the mass of the zinc coating on hot-dipped galvanized nails by the following reaction.

$$Zn_{(s)} + 2HCl_{(aq)} \rightarrow ZnCl_{2(aq)} + H_{2(g)}$$

19. This reaction could be classified as a

    A. double replacement

    B. decomposition

    C. formation

    D. single replace, electron transfer reaction

Use the following information to answer the next question.

In 1986, more than 154 billion kilograms of sulfuric acid were produced in North America alone, making it the most produced chemical. The uses of sulfuric acid range from fertilizers and explosives to application in pharmaceuticals and dyes. A titration was performed to completely neutralize 45 mL of $H_2SO_{4(aq)}$ using 1.22 mol/L $Ba(OH)_{2(aq)}$. The initial burette reading was 1.2 mL and the final reading was 24.6 mL.

20. The molar concentration of the 45 mL sample of sulfuric acid was

    A. 0.63 mol/L   B. 0.029 mol/L

    C. 0.055 mol/L   D. 2.3 mol/L

Use the following information to answer the next question.

Pure acetic acid is called glacial acetic acid. It is used by photographers to prepare a "stop bath" for photographic film and print development. A 30.0 mL stop bath sample was titrated with 1.75 molar KOH to ensure it contained enough acetic acid. The volume of $KOH_{(aq)}$ used for each trial was 8.4 mL, 9.1 mL, 8.6 mL, and 8.5 mL

21. The acetic acid concentration of the stop bath was

   A. 0.015 mol/L   **B.** 0.50 mol/L

   C. 0.053 mol/L   **D.** 0.30 mol/L

CHALLENGER QUESTION

22. What is the concentration of the $H_2SO_{4(aq)}$ in a rainwater sample if 200 mL of rainwater require 43.2 mL of 0.001 05 mol/L $KOH_{(aq)}$ for complete neutralization?

   A. 1.13×10^{-4} mol/L

   B. 2.27×10^{-5} mol/L

   C. 2.27×10^{-4} mol/L

   D. 5.25×10^{-3} mol/L

Use the following information to answer the next question.

Sodium bicarbonate, $NaHCO_{3(s)}$ can be used to neutralize excess stomach acid as follows

$$NaHCO_{3(s)} + HCl_{(aq)}$$
$$\rightarrow NaCl_{(aq)} + CO_{2(g)} + H_2O_{(l)}$$

23. The mass of sodium bicarbonate needed to completely neutralize 75 mL of 0.110 mol/L $HCl_{(aq)}$ is

   A. 0.69 g   **B.** 0.57 g

   C. 0.17 g   **D.** 0.12 g

Use the following information to answer the next two questions.

An environmental chemist analyzes the effluent (waste material) released from an industrial process. The effluent contains benzoic acid ($HC_7H_5O_2$), the concentration of which must be monitored to ensure that it does not exceed environmentally safe levels.

A 100 mL effluent sample is titrated with 0.015 5 mol NaOH. The initial and final burette readings of an analysis are 28.7 mL and 40.2 mL, respectively.

Numerical Response

2. The average volume of $NaOH_{(aq)}$ added to the effluent is _____ mL.
(Record your answer to three digits.)

CHALLENGER QUESTION

24. The concentration of the benzoic acid in the effluent is

   A. 1.09×10^{-2} mol/L

   B. 9.10×10^{-3} mol/L

   C. 1.78×10^{-3} mol/L

   D. 0.135 mol/L

Use the following information to answer the next question.

Many tonnes of hydrochloric acid are produced every year. $HCl_{(aq)}$ is used in the manufacture of pharmaceuticals, alkyl chlorides, rubber, and for cleaning metals before galvanizing them. $HCl_{(aq)}$ is also used for simple titration in chemistry labs.

25. If a 15 mL sample of $KOH_{(aq)}$ is completely neutralized by 8.5 mL of 0.190 mol/L $HCl_{(aq)}$. The molar concentration of the $KOH_{(aq)}$ is

   A. 0.11 mol/L   **B.** 0.008 0 mol/L

   C. 0.008 1 mol/L   **D.** 0.13 mol/L

CHALLENGER QUESTION

26. When 15 mL of a 0.55 mol/L solution of $Na_2SO_{4(aq)}$ is mixed with 20 mL of a 0.50 mol/L solution of $Pb(NO_3)_{2(aq)}$, the predicted mass of the precipitate is

A. 8.3 g   B. 0.70 g

C. 3.0 g   D. 2.5 g

Use the following information to answer the next question.

In the canning industry, the determination of contaminant metal ion concentrations is necessary to ensure that food products meet safety standards. Tin (II) ion concentrations are measured after canning to see whether or not tin cans increase the tin (II) ion concentration to hazardous levels after storage.
Potassium phosphate can be used to precipitate any tin (II) ions that may enter the contents during this time, according to the following reaction

$$2K_3PO_{4(aq)} + 3Sn^{2+}_{(aq)} \rightarrow Sn_3(PO_4)_{2(s)} + 6K^+_{(aq)}$$

CHALLENGER QUESTION

27. The juice from a 2.00 L can was analyzed using 100 mL of aqueous potassium phosphate. It was found that 0.689 mg of tin (II) phosphate precipitated. The tin ion concentration in the juice was

A. 3.79×10^{-5} mol/L

B. 1.26×10^{-6} mol/L

C. 1.89×10^{-6} mol/L

D. 4.84×10^{-7} mol/L

Use the following information to answer the next question.

Barium sulphate ($BaSO_{4(s)}$) is opaque to x-rays and almost completely insoluble in water. When a slurry consisting of $BaSO_{4(s)}$ and water is ingested, it coats the soft tissue of the digestive system. Upon exposure to x-rays, this permits real-time imaging of the oesophagus, stomach, and intestines.

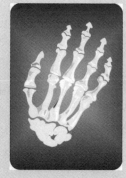

28. The volume of 0.700 mol/L $BaCl_{2(aq)}$ that will react with excess $K_2SO_{4(aq)}$ to produce 10.0 g of barium sulphate is

A. 48.0 mL

B. 68.6 mL

C. 42.8 mL

D. 61.2 mL

29. If 100 mL of 0.450 mol/L washing soda ($Na_2CO_{3(aq)}$) was just sufficient to remove all the $Mg^{2+}_{(aq)}$ in 5.00 L of hard water, then what is the mass of magnesium compound that could precipitate?

A. 6.49 g   B. 190 g

C. 4.89 g   D. 3.79 g

Use the following information to answer the next question.

The addition of small amounts of coloured metal impurities to glass is useful in colouring glass. Calcium sulfate is sometimes used to give glass a milky white colour. Calcium sulfate can be produced according to the following net ionic reaction.

$$Ca^{2+}_{(aq)} + SO_4^{2-}_{(aq)} \rightarrow CaSO_{4(s)}$$

CHALLENGER QUESTION

30. If the reaction produces 85% of the predicted yield, what volume of 2.33 mol/L $CaCl_{2(aq)}$ is needed to react with excess $Na_2SO_{4(aq)}$ to produce 300 g of $CaSO_{4(s)}$?

   A. 0.95 L   **B.** 1.1 L

   C. 2.6 L   **D.** 2.3 L

Use the following information to answer the next question.

Silver salts played a role in the early development of photography. It was reported in 1727 by Johann Heinrich Schulze that $AgCl_{(s)}$ darkens when exposed to light. Toward the end of the eighteenth century, Thomas Wedgewood produced a picture using paper soaked in silver nitrate. Silver nitrate can react with potassium chloride in aqueous solution to produce silver chloride, as shown:

$$AgNO_{3(aq)} + KCl_{(aq)} \rightarrow AgCl_{(s)} + KNO_{3(aq)}$$

The reaction of 250 mL of $AgNO_{3(aq)}$ with excess aqueous potassium chloride produces 15.0 g of precipitate.

Numerical Response

3. The concentration of the $AgNO_{3(aq)}$ solution is _____ $\times 10^{-1}$ mol/L.
(Record your answer to three digits.)

Use the following information to answer the next three questions.

300 mL of 0.100 mol/L $BaCl_{2(aq)}$ and 200 mL of 0.110 mol/L $Na_2CO_{3(aq)}$ are mixed.

31. The limiting reagent in the above reaction is

   A. $BaCl_{2(aq)}$ **B.** $Na_2CO_{3(aq)}$

   C. $BaCO_{3(s)}$ **D.** $NaCl_{(aq)}$

CHALLENGER QUESTION

32. The mass of precipitate predicted for the reactants is

   A. 1.29 g   **B.** 2.57 g

   C. 3.18 g   **D.** 4.34 g

CHALLENGER QUESTION

33. What mass of precipitate actually forms if the experimental yield is 78% of the predicted yield?

   A. 1.0 g   **B.** 2.0 g

   C. 2.5 g   **D.** 3.4 g

Use the following information to answer the next two questions.

Gasoline antifreeze (methylhydrate) is added to automobile gas tanks in winter to allow for cleaner combustion of water-contaminated gasoline. The IUPAC name for methylhydrate is methanol. The chief reaction by which methanol is manufactured is

$$CO_{(g)} + 2H_{2(g)} \rightarrow CH_3OH_{(l)}$$

34. If 70.0 kg of $CO_{(g)}$ are used in combination with 9.00 kg of $H_{2(g)}$ the limiting reagent(s) is/are

   A. $CO_{(g)}$ and $H_{2(g)}$ **B.** $CH_3OH_{(l)}$

   C. $CO_{(g)}$ **D.** $H_{2(g)}$

35. If the actual mass of methanol produced is 59.2 kg, then the percentage yield for this reaction is

 A. 82.9% **B.** 84.6%

 C. 73.9% **D.** 65.8%

Use the following information to answer the next question.

The fertilizer commonly used to "green up" lawns and increase crop yields is made by combining ammonia (NH_3) with concentrated sulfuric acid (H_2SO_4).

36. According to the law of conservation of mass, if 1.11 kg of ammonia is reacted with 3.20 kg of sulfuric acid, the fertilizer produced, $(NH_4)_2SO_4$, would have a mass of

 A. 1.11 kg

 B. 3.20 kg

 C. 4.31 kg

 D. 2.09 kg

Use the following information to answer the next question.

Titanium dioxide is used as a white pigment in paints, rubbers, plastics, and paper.
Titanium dioxide is formed in the following reaction.

$$TiCl_{4(g)} + O_{2(g)} \rightarrow TiO_{2(s)} + 2Cl_{2(g)}$$

37. If the masses of the products and reactants were accurately measured (with an equal number of moles of reactants present), then

 A. the masses of the products would outweigh the masses of the reactants

 B. the masses of the reactants would outweigh the masses of the products

 C. the mass of chlorine would be exactly twice the mass of titanium dioxide

 D. the combined mass of the products would equal the combined mass of the reactants.

Numerical Response

4. What is the mass of silver chloride precipitate predicted if excess silver nitrate is added to a 100 mL water sample containing 0.001 0 mol/L of $Cl^-_{(aq)}$?

_____ mg.
(Record your answer to three digits.)

Written Response

1. Describe the stoichiometric method.
   (Your response should include a simple
   reaction equation and an explanation of
   excess and limiting reagents.)

   (8 marks)

2. A man is found dead in a limestone cave
   primarily comprised of $CaCO_{3(s)}$.
   The man bears no bruise, wound, or mark on
   his body. You are asked to solve the
   mystery of how the man died.
   Upon searching the scene, you discover a
   deep hole in the limestone floor that
   contains traces of acetic acid.
   Some bubbling is still occurring.

   a) Write a balanced equation for the
      reaction of acetic acid with limestone

      (1 mark)

   b) What might be causing the bubbling to
      occur?
      (Hint: consider carbonated water.)

      (1 mark)

   c) If the room has an 11.0 kL capacity, and
      1 mole of gas occupies 24.8 L, how
      many litres of a 1.25 mol/L acetic acid
      would be needed to cause the room to
      completely fill with gas?

      (5 marks)

   d) How might the man have died?

      (1 mark)

38. Which net ionic equation best describes the
    reaction between $HCl_{(aq)}$ and $NaOH_{(aq)}$?

    A. $H^+_{(aq)} + OH^-_{(aq)} \rightarrow H_2O_{(l)}$

    B. $HCl_{(aq)} + NaOH_{(aq)}$
       $\rightarrow NaCl_{(aq)} + H_2O_{(l)}$

    C. $H^+_{(aq)} + Cl^-_{(aq)} + Na^+_{(aq)} + OH^-_{(aq)}$
       $\rightarrow Na^+_{(aq)} + Cl^-_{(aq)} + H_2O_{(l)}$

    D. $Na^+_{(aq)} + Cl^-_{(aq)} \rightarrow NaCl_{(aq)}$

39. Which of the following equations is a net
    ionic equation representing the precipitation
    of $CaCO_3$ when equal volumes of $Ca(NO_3)_2$
    and Na_2CO_3 are mixed?

    A. $Ca^{2+}_{(aq)} + CO^2_{3(aq)} \rightleftharpoons CaCO_{3(s)}$

    B. $Na^{2+}_{(aq)} + NO^-_{3(aq)} \rightleftharpoons NaNO_{3(s)}$

    C. $Ca(NO_3)_{2(aq)} + Na_2CO_{3(aq)}$
       $\rightleftharpoons 2NaNO_{3(s)} + CaCO_{3(s)}$

    D. $2NaNO_{3(aq)} + CaCO_{3(aq)}$
       $\rightleftharpoons Ca(NO_3)_{2(aq)} + Na_2CO_{3(aq)}$

40. Which of the following equations represents the formula equation for the precipitation reaction between $Pb(NO_3)_2$ and $NaCl$?

A. $Pb^{2+}_{(aq)} + 2Cl^-_{(aq)} \rightarrow PbCl_{2(s)}$

B. $Na^+_{(aq)} + NO_3^-_{(aq)} \rightarrow NaNO_{3(aq)}$

C.
$$Pb^{2+}_{(aq)} + 2NO_3^-_{(aq)} + 2Na^+_{(aq)} + 2Cl^-_{(aq)}$$
$$\rightarrow PbCl_{2(s)} + 2Na^+_{(aq)} + 2NO_{3(aq)}$$

D. $Pb(NO_3)_{2(aq)} + 2NaCl_{(aq)}$
$$\rightarrow PbCl_{2(s)} + 2NaNO_{3(aq)}$$

41. Which of the following equations represents a precipitation reaction?

A. $2H_3PO_{4(aq)} + 3Sr^{2+}_{(aq)} + 6OH^-_{(aq)}$
$$\rightarrow Sr_3(PO_4)_{2(s)} + 6H_2O_{(l)}$$

B. $H^+_{(aq)} + OH^-_{(aq)} \rightarrow H_2O_{(l)}$

C. $6H^+_{(aq)} + 6OH^-_{(aq)} \rightarrow 6H_2O_{(l)}$

D. $Sr^{2+}_{(aq)} + 2OH^-_{(aq)} \rightarrow Sr(OH)_{2(aq)}$

42. What is the net ionic equation for the precipitation reaction between $H_3PO_{4(aq)}$ and $Sr(OH)_{2(aq)}$?

A. $2H_3PO_{4(aq)} + 3Sr^{2+}_{(aq)} + 6OH^-_{(aq)}$
$$\rightarrow Sr_3(PO_4)_{2(s)} + 6H_2O_{(l)}$$

B. $H^+_{(aq)} + OH^-_{(aq)} \rightarrow H_2O_{(l)}$

C. $6H^+_{(aq)} + 6OH^-_{(aq)} \rightarrow 6H_2O_{(l)}$

D. $Sr^{2+}_{(aq)} + 2OH^-_{(aq)} \rightarrow Sr(OH)_{2(aq)}$

43. Which of the following equations represents the net ionic equation for the precipitation of $CaSO_4$ when $CaCl_2$ and Na_2SO_4 are mixed?

A.
$$CaCl_{2(aq)} + Na_2SO_{4(aq)}$$
$$\rightarrow 2NaCl_{(aq)} + CaSO_{4(s)}$$

B.
$$Ca^{2+}_{(aq)} + 2Cl^-_{(aq)} + 2Na^+_{(aq)} + SO_4^{2-}_{(aq)}$$
$$\rightarrow 2Na^+_{(aq)} + 2Cl^-_{(aq)} + CaSO_{4(s)}$$

C. $2Na^+_{(aq)} + SO_4^{2-}_{(aq)} \rightarrow Na_2SO_{4(aq)}$

D. $Ca^{2+}_{(aq)} + SO_4^{2-}_{(aq)} \rightarrow CaSO_{4(s)}$

44. What is the complete ionic equation for the reaction between $BaS_{(aq)}$ and $Sr(OH)_{2(aq)}$?

A. $Ba^{2+}_{(aq)} + 2OH^-_{(aq)} \rightarrow Ba(OH)_{2(s)}$

B.
$$Ba^{2+}_{(aq)} + S^{2-}_{(aq)} + Sr^{2+}_{(aq)} + 2OH^-_{(aq)}$$
$$\rightarrow Ba(OH)_{2(s)} + Sr^{2+}_{(aq)} + S^{2-}_{(aq)}$$

C. $BaS_{(aq)} + Sr(OH)_{2(aq)}$
$$\rightarrow SrS_{(aq)} + Ba(OH)_{2(aq)}$$

D. $Sr^{2+}_{(aq)} + S^{2-}_{(aq)} \rightarrow SrS_{(s)}$

45. 45.9 g of sodium metal reacts with 70.90 g of chlorine gas to form 116.80 g of solid sodium chloride. This evidence demonstrates the Law of

A. multiple proportions

B. definite composition

C. mass action

D. conservation of mass

46. To determine the amount, in moles, of a sample of butane gas, an experimenter measured mass, temperature, and pressure of the gas sample. A calculation of the molar mass would require

   A. mass and temperature measurements

   B. mass and pressure measurements

   C. temperature and pressure measurements

   D. a volume of measurement

47. The quantity of product that is predicted as a result of a stoichiometric calculation is known as the

   A. actual yield

   B. predicted yield

   C. percent yield

   D. theoretical yield

48. The actual yield of an experiment is the

   A. mass of product obtained from the reaction

   B. difference between the mass of the reactants and the mass of the products

   C. mass of the products that are expected from the reaction

   D. difference between the expected mass and the measured mass of the product

49. A precipitate formed when a student mixed two solutions together.
The student predicted a yield of 14.3 g. After washing and drying, it was found to have a mass of 11.7 g. What was the percent yield?

   A. 1.67

   B. 22.2%

   C. 81.8%

   D. 122%

50. Discrepancies between theoretical yield and actual yield can not be explained by

   A. the purity of the reactants

   B. very slight solubility of the product

   C. the size of the pores in the filter paper

   D. the combined mass of the reactants

51. If a 10.00 mL sample of 0.20 mol/L hydrochloric acid is titrated with a 0.20 mol/L solution of sodium hydroxide, the shape of the titration curve would be

A.

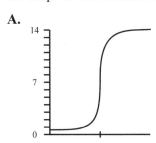

B.

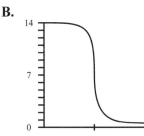

C.

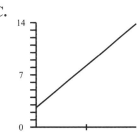

D.

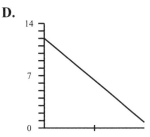

52. Using the data supplied, draw a curve for a sample of hydrochloric acid titrated with sodium hydroxide. Label the equivalence point and identify a suitable indicator.

vol NaOH added (mL)	pH
0	1.0
4	1.0
8	1.1
12	1.5
16	7.0
20	12.3
24	12.6
28	12.8
32	13.0

53. If a sample of HCl is titrated with NaOH to its endpoint, the best choice for an indicator would be

A. thymol blue

B. bromothymol blue

C. cresol red

D. alizarin yellow

54. A basic substance has 2 equivalence points when titrated with HCl. The second equivalence point occurs when the pH reaches 3.5. A suitable indicator for this endpoint would be

A. bromothymol blue

B. methyl orange

C. bromocresol green

D. thymol blue

55. A sample of NaOH is titrated with HCl. At the equivalence point,

A. an amount of HCl equivalent to the initial amount of NaOH has been added

B. there are more hydrogen ions than hydroxide ions in the solution

C. litmus paper would turn from blue to pink

D. sodium chloride would precipitate in the Erlenmeyer flask

Use the following information to answer the next question.

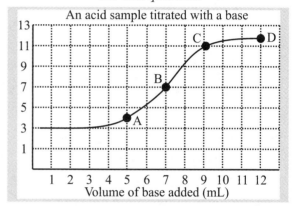

56. From the titration curve above, the pH at the equivalence point is at

A. 5

B. 7

C. 9

D. 12

ANSWERS AND SOLUTIONS – CHEMICAL BONDING

1. C	9. D	17. B	25. B	28. B	35. B
2. D	10. A	18 B	NR1. 2, 1, 3, 4	29. D	36. D
3. A	11. B	19. D	NR2. 6, 4, 3, 8	30. A	37. D
4. C	12. C	20. D	WR1. *	31. A	38. A
5. D	13 D	21. B	WR2. *	32. B	39. A
6. D	14. B	22. B	26. D	33. D	40. D
7. D	15. D	23. A	27. A	34. B	
8. C	16. B	24. A	*for written responses, see solutions		

1. **C**

The **limiting reagent** in a chemical reaction is the reactant that is completely consumed. Any reactant that is not completely consumed is an **excess reagent.**
If all the reactant silver ions from $AgNO_{3(aq)}$ are consumed, then the $AgNO_{3(aq)}$ is the limiting reagent (clearly, the $KCl_{(aq)}$ is the excess reagent).

2. **D**

Intramolecular bonding ("intra"means within) in molecules such as CH_2FCF_3 consists of shared pairs of electrons between atoms — otherwise known as covalent bonds.

Note: The complete transfer of a bonding pair of electrons to one of the bound atoms creates what is called an ionic bond. Reacting atoms with a large difference in electronegativity (metals versus non-metals) tend to favour the formation of ionic bonds. This involves the metal losing electrons (oxidized) and the non-metal gaining electrons (reduced).

3. **A**

Hydrogen is a molecular element composed of two hydrogen nuclei sharing a single pair of e^- in the bond that joins them.
Since the electronegativity of each H atom is identical, the bond pair of e^- is shared equally by each nucleus.

4. **C**

Ethanethiol is a very weakly polar molecular compound. Thus, the electrons in the covalent bonds of ethanethiol are probably equally shared between the C atoms but shared unequally between unlike atoms.

5. **D**

As in all molecules, the covalent bonds that hold the individual atoms to their nearest neighbours result from the simultaneous attraction of e^- between adjacent nuclei.

6. **D**

The important difference between an ionic bond and a covalent bond is the distribution of the bonding electrons of the nuclei involved. In a covalent bond, the bonding electrons are shared whereas in ionic bond formation, the bonding electrons are transferred completely to one of the nuclei (and ions are produced).
D adequately describes the bonding in $NaCl_{(s)}$ (ionic bonding) and chloroacetophenone/MACE (covalent bonding).

7. D

The structure of $NaCl_{(s)}$ comprises a lattice work of Na^+ and Cl^- ions packed close together such that each ion is surrounded by six oppositely charged neighbours. The mutual attraction between each ion and its oppositely charged neighbours constitutes **ionic bonding.**
The intramolecular bonding in molecular compounds such as chloroacetophenone/MACE involves the sharing of one or more pairs of valence electrons by bonded nuclei.
We call this **covalent bonding.**

8. C

The elements that make up sand (non-metals), favour covalent over ionic bond formation. The difference in their electronegativities is not large enough to allow the Si atoms to lose their valence electrons, but O atoms will have more of a share of the bonding electrons.
(O has the higher electronegativity.)

9. D

$MgO_{(s)}$ is formed from elements with a large difference in electronegativity.
It is an ionic compound. The ions Mg^{2+} and O^{2-} are strongly attracted to their nearest oppositely charged neighbours in the crystal lattice they form.
These strong attractions constitute ionic bonding.

10. A

Ionic compounds contain ions — entities formed from the complete transfer of electrons. In nickel (III) oxide, the electrons lost by the nickel in forming Ni^{3+} have been gained by the oxygen to form O^{2-}.

11. B

The electronegativity difference between N and O is too small to permit it to form ions, but it will make $NO_{(g)}$ a polar molecule. In addition, $NO_{(g)}$ is not an ideal gas — there are likely to be attractive forces between individual molecules if they are close enough. The **most likely** forces of attraction between $NO_{(g)}$ molecules arranged from strongest to weakest are dipole-dipole forces and dispersion forces.

12. C

Hydrogen bonds are the strongest of the available intermolecular bonds, but are about 10% the strength of typical covalent bonds. So, they are stronger than dipole-dipole forces but weaker than covalent bonds.

13. D

Water is a polar solvent, while hexane is a non-polar solvent. Most alkaloids, being non-polar, will tend to be soluble in hexane but have low solubility in water.
(Remember the saying: **like dissolves like**)

14. B

For any molecule, the type and extent of intermolecular bonding hinges on the nature of the molecules involved.
All molecules experience London Dispersion forces. Only polar molecules are affected by dipole-dipole forces. Only those molecules that contain O–H or N–H bonds, or HF itself, are capable of being affected by hydrogen bonding. CH_2FCF_3 is a polar molecule (see diagram).

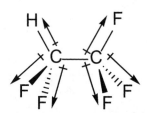

The dipoles do not all act in opposition. However, having no O–H or N–H bonds, CH_2FCF_3 will be affected by dispersion forces.

15. D

The bonds that hold the atoms together within a glucose molecule are called intramolecular bonds — in this case covalent bonds. If the atoms in $C_6H_{12}O_6$ and O_2 are to be "rearranged" to give CO_2 and H_2O, then it is intramolecular bonds that must be broken and reformed. Generally speaking, relative bond strengths (bond energies) follow the following pattern.

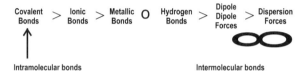

16. B

Changing liquid molecular substances like water into hydrogen and oxygen gases involves firstly breaking intermolecular bonds between molecules of H_2O in the liquid state before secondly breaking O–H intramolecular bonds within each molecule to generate oxygen and hydrogen as gases.

17. B

Since the energy required to split one mole of water far exceeds the energy required to vaporize the same quantity of water, stronger bonds must be broken in chemical reactions than in physical transformations. Splitting water involves breaking intramolecular bonds, while vaporizing water breaks intermolecular bonds. Clearly, intramolecular bonds are the stronger of the two.

18. B

Van der Waals' forces are types of relatively weak intermolecular attractions. Since both answers **C** and **D** are concerning intramolecular bonds, they are incorrect. The attractive force between water molecules is known as hydrogen bonding, so **A** is not correct. Neon is a noble gas and is monatomic. Since Ne atoms do not bond to each other to form molecules, interactions between atoms of neon would involve intermolecular or, more particularly, Van der Waals' forces. **B** is the correct answer.

19. D

Hydrogen bonds are those intermolecular attractions that form between molecules containing O–H and N–H bonds or in HF. Clearly $CH_{4(g)}$ does not have the necessary prerequisites for hydrogen bonding.

20. D

Consider the following table.

	# of e^-	Polarity	Types of bonding available
$H_2O_{(l)}$	10	polar	Dispersion forces, Dipole Dipole forces, and Hydrogen bonds
$CH_{4(g)}$	10	non-polar	Dispersion forces only

Water experiences intermolecular forces, primarily hydrogen bonding, as a result of its polar character. This is what generates its increased stability in the liquid state. Methane, CH_4, experiences no hydrogen bonding. Statement **D** is false and therefore the correct answer.

21. **B**

For molecular compounds, intermolecular forces exert great influence over their melting and boiling points.

Intermolecular interactions, collectively know as Van der Waals attractions, come in three varieties

(1) London Dispersion Forces,

(2) Dipole-Dipole interactions, and

(3) Hydrogen Bonds.

All molecular (and atomic) chemical entities experience dispersion forces. These short lived, weak dipole-dipole attractions result from the irregular circulation of electrons within atomic and/or molecular orbitals in neighbouring molecules. Dispersion forces are the only intermolecular attractions available to non-polar molecules and atoms.

Polar molecules are attracted to their near neighbours by dipole-dipole forces that, being comparable to dispersion forces, are weak. A molecule is polar if it has the right geometry and bonded atoms of different electro negativity to give it polar bonds. A molecule with non-polar bonds can never have an overall dipole. Hydrogen bonds are the strongest intermolecular forces, but only those molecules with very polar O–H, N–H bonds or in H–F itself are affected by them. The summary of attractive forces affecting H_2O, H_2S, H_2Se, and H_2Te in the following table make it clear that since water experiences all three types of intermolecular attractions, it will take more energy and a higher boiling point to vaporize water than is the case for the three gases.

Substance	# e$^-$	Polarity	London Dispersion Forces	Dipole Dipole Interactions	Hydrogen Bonds
$H_2O_{(l)}$	10	Polar	✓	✓	✓
$H_2S_{(g)}$	18	Weakly polar	✓	✓	✗
$H_2Se_{(g)}$	36	Non-polar	✓	✗	✗
$H_2Te_{(g)}$	54	Non-Polar	✓	✗	✗

22. **B**

Endothermic processes or reactions are those that require or absorb heat energy to proceed. Exothermic processes or reactions release heat energy as they progress.

23. **A**

When aluminum reacts to form $Al_2O_{3(s)}$ or $AlCl_{3(s)}$, the aluminum atoms become positive ions through loss of electrons (oxidation), while the non-metals O and Cl become negative ions by gaining electrons (reduction).

24. **A**

The $O_{2(g)}$ molecules in Step (1) and (2) become oxide ions in $Fe_2O_3 \times 3H_2O_{(s)}$. The only way neutral $O_{2(g)}$ molecules can become O^{2-} ions is by gaining electrons.

25. **B**

Calcium carbonate, as its name suggests, contains the ions calcium, (Ca^{2+}), and carbonate, (CO_3^{2-}). Clearly calcium carbonate is an inorganic/ionic compound.

NR 1. 2, 1, 3, 4

In order, from the strongest bond to the weakest bond are
Covalent bonds > Ionic bond > Metallic bonds > Hydrogen Bond > Dipole-Dipole bonds ≈ London Dispersion Forces.
The answer is: 2, 1, 3, 4.

NR 2. 6, 4, 3, 8

The circulation of electrons within a molecule leads to the generation of a momentary dipole within that molecule that induces dipole in its near neighbours. The types of bonds formed are called London Dispersion Forces. These kinds of bonds are the only kind available to non-polar molecules.
The answer is: 6, 4, 3, 8.

Written Response

1. Provide a suitable explanation for the limited number of common shapes for molecules containing between two and five atoms. (For full credit, an answer must provide a specific example of and the names for all the common shapes).

(8 marks)

Description	Example	
Linear		**(1 mark)**

$$Cl-Cl$$

| Trigonal planar | | **(1 mark)** |

| Pyramidal | | **(1 mark)** |

| Tetrahedral | | **(1 mark)** |

| Angular or 'V'-shaped | | **(1 mark)** |

$$H-O-H$$

The five common geometries of the molecules shown are determined entirely by the mutual repulsion of electron pairs (either as bonds or lone pairs) that force the bonds as for apart in space as possible.

(3 marks)

Four different strips of metal were placed in six different solutions, and the results were observed and recorded in the chart below.

	Cu	Fe	Zn	Mg
AgNO₃	reaction	reaction	reaction	reaction
CuNO₃	no reaction	reaction	reaction	reaction
Fe(NO₃)₃	no reaction	no reaction	reaction	reaction
HCl	no reaction	reaction	reaction	reaction
Zn(NO₃)₂	no reaction	no reaction	no reaction	reaction
Mg(NO₃)₂	no reaction	no reaction	no reaction	no reaction

2. Place the metals in an activity series, in order from most reactive to least reactive.
(1 mark)

Most Reactive – Mg, Zn, Fe, Cu – least reactive

a) *Why should all the metal strips be cleaned with sandpaper prior to immersion in each solution?*
(1 mark)

It is important that the pure metal is tested, rather than the oxide of the metal present on its surface. Each strip should be cleaned with sandpaper to ensure that only the metal itself is undergoing a possible reaction and not its oxide.

b) *Write a balanced chemical equation for one of the reactions in this series of tests.* **(2 marks)**

$$Cu_{(s)} + 2AgNO_{3(aq)} \rightarrow Cu(NO_3)_{2(aq)} + Ag_{(s)}$$

c) *In your own words, explain what the terms oxidation and reduction mean.*
(2 marks)

- Oxidation is the loss of electrons
- Reduction is the gaining of electrons

d) *Are the metal elements in this series of reactions oxidized or reduced? Explain.*
(2 marks)

Since the $Cu_{(s)}$ becomes Cu^{2+} in $Cu(NO_3)_{2(aq)}$, it has lost electrons and has clearly been oxidized. With the exception of $Ag_{(s)}$, all the metals here, by implication, have been oxidized.

26. D
$Al \rightarrow Al^{3+} + 3e^-$, so 2 Al atoms lose 6 electrons and $O^2 \rightarrow O + O$,
$O + 2e^- \rightarrow O^{2-}$, so 3 oxygen atoms gain 6 electrons.

27. A
Each pair of aluminium atoms lose 6 electrons to three oxygen atoms.

28. B
Ammonium (NH_4) is a polyatomic ion that has a charge of +1. Phosphate (PO_4) is a polyatomic ion that has a charge of –3. You require three ammonium ions (total charge +3) to balance one phosphate ion. To indicate that the 3 refers to both the nitrogen and the hydrogens of the ammonium, the ammonium must be in brackets. The Roman numerals in D are from Stock's system. They are used in the names of some transition metals, but never in a formula.

29. D

Zinc has an oxidation number of +2, and oxygen has an oxidation number of –2. When these two elements are combined to form a compound their charges cancel each other out, resulting in a net charge of zero. This is shown in the following equation: $Zn^{+2} + O^{-2} = ZnO$. Therefore the final formula for zinc oxide is ZnO.

30. A

When arranged in order of increasing electronegativity, the elements are $Mg < C < S < Cl$

31. A

Electronegativity is the relative attraction of an atom for a shared pair of electrons. It increases from left to right across the periodic table, such that the order in which electronegativity increases is: alkali metals, alkaline earth metals, transition metals, and halogens. Of the four groups, the halogens have the highest electronegativity.

32. B

The following steps show how to properly name a chemical formula:

Step 1: Write out the symbols of the ions in the compound. The element that appears first in the formula keeps its name. The second element ends with -ide.

Step 2: Look up the oxidation numbers of the ions involved in the formula and write them at the top right hand corner of each element.

Step 3: The combination of ions need to produce a net charge of zero. When there is more than one atom of an element in the formula, the name of the element usually contains a prefix that specifies the number of atoms present.

Number Prefix Examples:
1 mono
2 di
3 tri
4 tetra
5 penta
and so on...

Aden used the prefix examples correctly for NF_3 and CCl_4 but made a mistake in naming N_2O. The correct naming for N_2O nitrogen oxide and not dinitrogen dioxide. Therefore the correct answer is **B**.

33. D

Pentachlorine has the prefix "penta" therefore, the number of chlorine atoms is 5.

34. B

The number of atoms that each element has is indicated in the subscript number beside the element. If Al has two atoms and O has three atoms, you simply add them both up to get the final atom count of 5 atoms for Al_2O_3

35. B

Nitrogen (N_2) is a molecular species composed of two nitrogen atoms that bond together by sharing three pairs of electrons. This results in the formation of a triple bond. Since the bonding involves the sharing of electrons, it is a covalent bond.

36. D

Intramolecular bonding ("intra" means within) in molecules such as CH_2FCF_3 consists of shared pairs of electrons between atoms — otherwise known as covalent **bonds**.

Note: The complete **transfer** of a bonding pair of electrons to one of the bound atoms creates what is called an ionic bond. Reacting atoms with a large difference in electronegativity (metals versus non-metals) tend to favour the formation of ionic bonds. This involves the metal losing electrons (oxidized) and the non-metal gaining electrons (reduced).

37. D

If each atom in the molecule is bonded with a bonding pair of electrons, there ought to be $12e^-$, (6 pairs of bonding e^-) surrounding the carbon.

38. A

In a HCN molecule, the central carbon atom has zero lone pairs and two bonding pair sets. The only way both C and N can achieve stable octets is by sharing three pairs of electrons and forming a triple bond. This gives hydrogen cyanide a linear shape.

$$H - C \equiv N$$

39. A

The central carbon atom in CO_2 is seen to have two bonding pairs; the multiple bonding pair set counts as one bonding pair, and there are no lone pairs. The furthest apart these pairs can be is 180°, leading to a linear structure.

40. D

The number of valence electrons present in carbon, hydrogen, and oxygen are four, one, and six, respectively. Therefore, in order to complete their octet, carbon shares its four electrons, hydrogen shares one electron, oxygen shares two electrons, and two lone pairs still remain on oxygen. The Lewis structure of methanol is correctly shown in alternative **D**.

A. In the structure given in this alternative, the two lone pairs on the oxygen atom are not shown.

B. In the structure given in this alternative, oxygen has six electrons and one lone pair. In the correct Lewis structure of methanol, oxygen has eight electrons and two lone pairs.

C. In the structure given in this alternative, each bond is represented by a single dot, but in the correct Lewis structure, each bonded pair of electrons is represented by two dots.

The correct answer is **D**.

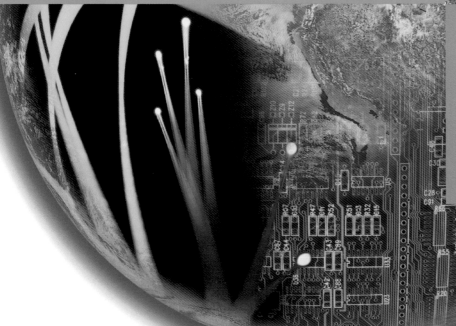

THE BEAR CHILDREN'S FUND

Think of it as 'Tough Love'

Since 1992, The Bear has been giving back to Edmonton's kids through The Bear Children's Fund. In the years since the Fund's inception, over $1,500,000 has been directed back into the greater Edmonton community and its charities. To make the Fund work requires the dedication of both management and staff, who have volunteered thousands of hours of their time to this worthwhile cause. As a rock station, The Bear may be loud, but it's proud too. Proud to be a part of a community as generous as Edmonton.

To apply for grants from the Bear Children's Fund please visit **www.thebearrocks.com**

Alberta Committee for Citizens with Disabilities | Alberta Rose Chapter | Alberta Special Olympics | Arbutus Volunteer Foundation Belmont Elementary School | Ben Calf Robe Native Elementary & Junior High Catholic School | Bent Arrow Traditional Healing Society | Boyle Street Co-op Playground | Boys & Girls Club of Edmonton | Canadian Progress Club | Century Services Inc. Stollery Children's Hospital Foundation | Children's Heart Society City Centre Education Project | CNIB | Cross Cancer Institute Early Head Start Program | Edmonton City Police D.A.R.E. Program | Edmonton Food Bank | Edmonton Garrison Base Fund Edmonton Jaycees | Edmonton School Lunch Program | Edmonton Spring Board & Platform Diving Club | Employabilities | EMS Social Club | Firefighter's Burn Unit | Fort Saskatchewan Boys & Girls Club | Friends of Rosecrest | Garden Valley Pony Club | Glenrose Rehabilitation Hospital | Griesbach School Council | Inner City Youth Development Association | Head First Foundation | Hug-A-Bear Express | Kid's Kottage | Kinsmen Club of St. Albert | Mansion Youth Drop-In Centre for Teens | McCauley Community After School Care Association | Morinville Panthers | New York City Police & Fire Widows' & Children's Benefit | Northern Alberta Brain Injury Society | Norwood Community Centre | Nottingham Playground Association | Parents Empowering Parents | P.A.R.T.Y. Program Project Literacy | Queen Mary Park School | Rainbow Society Ronald McDonald House | Royal Alexandra Hospital | Southwest Area Council of Community Leagues | St. Michael's School | St. Patrick's School (Edmonton) Parents Society | Terra Association | Uncles At Large | Various Trust Funds & Confidential Donations | Westview Regional Health Authority Youth Health Centre | Wetaskiwin Head Start Society | Yellowhead Youth Centre | Youth Emergency Shelter Society | Skills Woodcroft Respite Home | Royal Alexandra Hospital NICU Family Room (Bear Den) | Brightview Elementary School

ANSWERS AND SOLUTIONS – GASES

1. C	NR1. 57.0	NR2. 477	6. D	NR4. 0.221	8. B
2. B	4. D	5. A	NR3. 1.6	7. C	9. D
3. D					

1. C

If both the volume and the mass of the gas heated in a cylinder remain constant, then its density will also remain unchanged. Both of these criteria have been met since air can neither enter nor leave the cylinder and the cylinder is made of rigid steel and will not expand in volume.

2. B

By the Combined Gas Law

$$\frac{P_1 V_1}{T_1} = \frac{P_2 V_2}{T_2}$$

Since we are given that P_1 and P_2 are equal, we can reduce the equation to

$$\frac{V_1}{T_1} = \frac{V_2}{T_2} \text{ or } V_1 T_2 = V_2 T_1$$

Let V_1 be the initial volume and T_1 be the initial temperature. Let V_2 be the final volume and T_2 be the final temperature. Remember to convert T_2 from Celsius to Kelvin.

$$20°C = (20 + 273.15) \text{ K} = 293.15 \text{ K}$$

$$V_1 \times 5 \text{ K} = 1 \text{ L} \times 293.15 \text{ K}$$

$$V_1 = \frac{293.15}{5} \text{ L}$$

$$= 58.63 \text{ L}$$

To the nearest litre, the answer is 59 L.

3. D

Gay-Lussac's Law describes the relationship between the pressure and temperature of a fixed quantity of gas. This relationship can be described by the following equation.

$$\frac{P_1}{T_1} = \frac{P_2}{T_2}$$

P_1 and P_2 represent the initial and final pressures, respectively, of a fixed quantity of gas. T_1 and T_2 represent the initial and final temperature, respectively, of the same fixed quantity of gas.
Therefore,

$$\frac{35 \text{ psi}}{283 \text{ K}} = \frac{P_2}{329 \text{ K}}$$

$$P_2 = 329 \text{ K} \times \frac{35 \text{ psi}}{283 \text{ K}}$$

$$= 41 \text{ psi}$$

Note: When using any of the gas law equations, except for the Ideal Gas Equation, it is possible to use a wide variety of pressure and volume units with the condition that all units are consistent.

NR1.   57.0

The pressure of a known mass of gas at a fixed volume and temperature is calculated using the ideal gas law:

$$P = \frac{nRT}{V}$$

We must first determine the number of moles of ethyl mercaptan:

$$n = \frac{m}{M} = \frac{5.00 \text{ g}}{62.14 \text{ g/mol}} = 0.0805 \text{ g/mol}$$

Therefore,

$$P = \frac{(0.0805 \text{ mol})(8.314 \text{ kPa•L/mol•K})(298 \text{ K})}{(3.50 \text{ L})}$$

$$= \frac{199.44 \text{ kPa•L}}{3.50 \text{ L}}$$

$$= 57.0 \text{ kPa}$$

4.   D

To convert °C to K add 273.15.
To convert K back to °C subtract 273.15.
Thus,
$T(°C) = (125 - 273.15)°C = -147.85°C$.
Iodine, water and chlorine all boil at a temperature higher than –147.85°C. Only liquid nitrogen would boil at a low enough temperature.

NR2.   477

To convert °C to K add 273.15. So, to convert K back to °C you subtract 273.15.
Thus, $T(°C) = (750 - 273.15)°C = 477°C$
The surface temperature of Venus is 477°C.

5.   A

To convert °C to K add 273.15. So, to convert K back to °C, you subtract 273.15. Therefore,
$T = (50 - 273.15)°C = -223°C$.
Therefore, the temperature of the interstellar dust clouds is below –223°C.

6.   D

Remember, add 273.15 to convert °C to K.
$T(K) = (2\,000°C + 273.15) \text{ K} = 2\,273 \text{ K}$
The conversion of pressure is
1 atm = 101.325 kPa = 760 mm Hg.
This must be memorized.
Thus,

$$P_1(\text{kPa}) = 1.00 \times 10^5 \text{ atm} \times \frac{101.325 \text{ kPa}}{\text{atm}}$$

$$= 1.01 \times 10^7 \text{ kPa}$$

NR3.   0.55

At these pressures, the Ideal Gas Law may not apply but it is a responsible approximation.

$$n = \frac{PV}{RT} = \frac{500 \text{ kPa} \times 3.4 \text{ L}}{8.314 \dfrac{\text{kPa} \times \text{L}}{\text{mol} \times \text{K}} \times 373 \text{ K}} = 0.55 \text{ mol}$$

The cylinder contains some 0.55 mol of steam under the conditions given.

NR4.   0.221

At these pressures and temperatures, the Ideal Gas Law may not apply but it is a reasonable approximation.

$$V = \frac{nRT}{P} = \frac{1 \text{ mol} \times 0.082\,06 \dfrac{\text{L} \times \text{atm}}{\text{mol} \times \text{K}} \times 673 \text{ K}}{250 \text{ atm}}$$

$$= 0.221 \text{ L}$$

The estimated molar volume of ammonia under the conditions specified is 0.221 L.

7. **C**

    Except at low pressure and high
    temperature, real gases do not behave like
    ideal gases. The following table points out
    the differences between ideal and real gas
    molecules.

Ideal Gas Molecules	Real Gas Molecules
• Experience no intermolecular forces	• Can and do experience intermolecular forces
• Always fly in straight lines	• Curve when they pass by other molecules
• Collide elastically (no energy lost)	• Collide inelastically (energy lost as heat when molecules 'stick')
• Obey all the gas laws perfectly	• Obey the gas laws well at high temperature
• Have mass but zero volume	• Have mass and a finite volume
• Never condense—at any temperature	• Will always condense— low temperature

8. **B**

    The comparison table of real and ideal
    gases, shown above, shows that real gases
    have a finite molecular volume while ideal
    gas molecules have zero volume.

9. **D**

    Remember, add 273.15 to convert °C to K.
    $T(\text{K}) = (500°\text{C} + 273.15)\ \text{K} = 773\ \text{K}$
    The conversion of pressure is
    1 atm = 101.325 kPa = 760 mm Hg.
    This must be memorized.
    Thus,

    $$P_1 (\text{kPa}) = 3.00 \times 10^5\ \text{atm} \times \frac{101.325\ \text{kPa}}{\text{atm}}$$

    $$= 3.01 \times 10^7\ \text{kPa}$$

ANSWERS AND SOLUTIONS –
SOLUTIONS, ACIDS, BASES

1. A	14. D	27. A	NR1. 1.05	NR3. 678 3	61. D
2. B	15. B	28. B	40. A	51. B	62. C
3. B	16. A	29. D	41. A	52. A	63. D
4. A	17. A	30. C	42. B	53. B	64. B
5. B	18. C	31. C	43. D	54. C	65. D
6. B	19. C	32. D	44. B	55. A	66. D
7. A	20. C	33. C	NR2. 0.3	WR1. *	67. B
8. A	21. A	34. C	45. B	WR2. *	68. B
9. A	22. D	35. D	46. D	56. A	69. B
10. A	23. A	36. D	47. A	57. C	70. C
11. D	24. B	37. B	48. C	58. C	71. C
12. D	25. A	38. B	49. A	59. A	72. A
13. B	26. A	39. D	50. B	60. D	

*for written responses, see solutions

1. A

The question asks for a hydrolysis reaction of CH_3COOH. Hydrolysis is defined as the reaction of a chemical entity (ion or molecule) with water to produce H_3O^+ or OH^-.

2. B

Dissociation is the separation of an ionic compound into its individual ions in solution

$$HCl_{(aq)} + H_2O_{(l)}$$

$$\rightleftharpoons H^+_{(aq)} + Cl^-_{(aq)} + H_2O_{(l)}$$

$$\rightleftharpoons H_3O^+_{(aq)} + Cl^-_{(aq)}$$

3. B

The question asks for the hydrolysis reaction of NH^-_3. Hydrolysis is the reaction of a chemical entity (ion or molecule) with water to produce H_3O^+ or OH^-.

4. A

The colour of phenolphthalein in an alkaline solution is pink. Phenolphthalein solution remains colourless in an acid solution. Hence **B** is incorrect.
A salt is produced by the neutralization reaction i.e., the reaction of acids with bases and alkali. Hence at the point of neutralization, phenolphthalein is colourless. So **D** is incorrect.
An oxide itself cannot change the colour of any indicator. Oxides, when dissolved in water, produce either an acidic or basic solution.
This solution can change the colour of an indicator depending upon whether it is an acidic or a basic solution.

5. B

An alkaline solution turns yellow when methyl orange is added to it.

6. B

Ionization of water gives the ions H_3O^+ and OH^-. e.g. $2H_2O \rightleftharpoons H_3O + OH^-$

7. A

The ionization of water can be written as

$$2H_2O_{(l)} \rightleftharpoons H_3O^+_{(aq)} + OH^-_{(aq)} \text{ or,}$$

$$H_2O_{(l)} \rightleftharpoons H^+_{(aq)} + OH^-_{(aq)}$$

8. A

$$1.00 \times 10^{-14} = \left[H_3O^+\right]\left[OH^-\right]$$

So,

$$\left[OH^-\right] = \frac{1.00 \times 10^{-14}}{\left[H_3O^+\right]}$$

9. A

A base solution will always have

$$\left[OH^-\right] > \left[H_3O^+\right] \text{ or } \left[OH^-\right] > \left[H^+\right].$$

This is true at any temperature where water is liquid.

10. A

An acidic solution has $\left[H_3O^+\right] > \left[OH^-\right]$

at any temperature where water is liquid.

11. D

In a neutral solution at room temperature,

$$\left[H_3O^+\right] = \left[OH^-\right] = 1.00 \times 10^{-7} \text{ mol/L and}$$

their pH = 7. For acidic solution pH > 7.0.

12. D

For bases, $\left[OH^-\right] > \left[H_3O^+\right]$

i.e. $\left[H_3O^+\right] < \left[OH^-\right].$

For acids, $\left[H_3O^+\right] > \left[OH^-\right]$

For neutral solution,

$$\left[H_3O^+\right] = \left[OH^-\right] = 1.00 \times 10^{-7} \text{ mol/L}$$

13. B

A basic solution will have

$$\left[OH^-\right] > \left[H_3O^+\right], \text{ pH} > 7.0 \text{ and}$$
$$\text{pOH} < 7.0$$

14. D

For an acidic solution, $[H_3O^+] > [OH^-]$
So, for a strongly acidic solution
$[H_3O^+] > [OH^-]$, i.e. $[H_3O^+]$ will be much
higher than the $[OH^-]$.
For an acidic solution, $[H_3O^+]$ can never be
equal to $[OH^-]$.
Only neutral solutions have $[H_3O^+] = [OH^-]$

15. B

$$K_w \text{ at } 25°C = 1.00 \times 10^{-14}$$

$$K_w = \left[H_3O^+_{(aq)}\right]\left[OH^-_{(aq)}\right] \text{ or}$$

$$1.00 \times 10^{-14} = \left(1.75 \times 10^{-4}\right)\left[OH^-_{(aq)}\right] \text{ or}$$

$$\left[OH^-_{(aq)}\right] = \frac{1.00 \times 10^{-14}}{1.75 \times 10^{-4}}$$

$$\left[OH^-_{(aq)}\right] = 5.71 \times 10^{-11} \text{mol/L}$$

16. A

The solutions with the least ion concentration will have the least electrical conductivity. It must be either a weak acid or a weak base, since strong acids and strong bases dissociate completely, their solutions have a large ion concentration. Since the weak acid concentration in alternative **A** is lower than the weak base concentration in alternative **B**, it will have the least ion concentration and the least electrical conductivity.

17. A

Strong acids are completely ionized in
water i.e., $HCl \rightleftharpoons H + Cl^-$

18. C

Strong acids and strong bases ionize completely in water, but acids produce a large number of H^+ ions, and bases produce a large number of hydroxyl ions (OH^-).
So the nature of ions produced on dissociation differs in acids and bases.
So **C** is correct and **A** incorrect.
The concentration of an acid and a base may be the same or different depending upon the relative amounts of the solute and the solvent present in the solution.

19. C

Acids turn litmus paper red.
Active metals like 'Mg' react to some degree with all acids.

20. C

All soap solutions are basic and have a somewhat high pH. However, pH 14.0, (alternative **D**) is excessively high. Hence alternative **C** is correct and alternative **D** is incorrect.
Solutions with pH < 7 are acidic.
Alternatives **A** and **B** represent acidic solutions.
Hence they are incorrect.

21. A

All acids have a pH less than 7.0.
So alternative **A** is correct and alternative B is incorrect.
Alternative **C** and **D** are true for an alkaline solution. Hence these are incorrect.

22. D

A compound containing one or more hydrogen atoms in its molecule is termed as an acid only when its hydrogen atom(s) is/are replaced by a metal or a group of elements behaving like a metal producing salt.
For example, $Zn + H_2SO_4 = ZnSO_4 + H_2\uparrow$

23. A

Phenolphthalein turns colourless in acid solution and remains pink in alkaline solution.
So alternative **A** is correct and alternative B is incorrect.
Blue litmus turns red in acid solution and remains blue in alkaline solution.
Red litmus remains red in acid solution and turns blue in alkaline solution.
So alternatives **C** and **D** are incorrect.

24. B

Arrhenius acid is a substance which produces hydrogen ions in water.
A is the definition of an Arrhenius base.
C and **D** are the definition of a Bronsted – Lowry acid.

25. A

According to the solubility chart, $MgSO_4$ is the only compound having a solubility greater than 0.1 mol/L. 0.1 mol/L is the dividing line used in a solubility chart. Solubility > 0.1 mol/L is labeled as high solubility while a solubility ≤ 0.1 mol/L is labeled as low solubility.

26. A

The salts of nitrates have high solubility according to the solubility chart.
So **A** is correct. All chloride salts are soluble except Ag^+, Hg_2^{2+}, and Pb^{2+}.
So **B** is incorrect. $CaSO_4$ and $BaSO_4$ are insoluble. So **C** is incorrect.
All carbonates are insoluble except Group I-A and NH_4^+. So **D** is incorrect.

27. A

AgCl is sparingly soluble in water.
But the addition of HCl increases the concentration of Cl^- ion.
Under this condition, the amount of the products of the ions $[Ag^+][Cl^-]$ exceed the amount of the solubility products and hence a precipitate is left behind.

28. B

According to the question, either A or B is formed. $PbCl_2$ is insoluble.
According to the solubility chart, nitrates are soluble. So $NaNO_3$ cannot leave behind a precipitate and hence $PbCl_2$ leaves behind a precipitate.

29. D

According to the solubility chart, $Na^+_{(aq)}$ is soluble in all forms of salts, so it cannot precipitate $SO_4^{2-}{}_{(aq)}$.

30. C

According to the given data, the unknown cation forms a precipitate with carbonate (CO_3^{2-}) and sulfide (S^{2-}) but not with sulfate (SO_4^{2-}) and nitrate (NO^{3-}).
Again, according to the solubility chart, Pb^{2+}, Sr^{2+}, and Ag^+ form a precipitate with SO_4^{2-}.

31. C

A solution comprises two components —
the solvent and the solute. Usually, but not
always, the solvent is the major component
of the solution, while the solute is the
minor component
(in terms of molar amounts). Since Easy-
Off® is an aqueous solution of sodium
hydroxide, the sodium hydroxide is the
solute.

32. D

The least polar form of a molecule will
likely be more soluble in a non-polar
solvent. In this case, the free base form
of cocaine is the more non-polar molecule.

33. C

Since acetic acid is a weak acid
(it dissociates or ionizes partially at most
normal concentrations), it will be a weak
electrolyte. Weak electrolytes will conduct
electricity, but poorly.

34. C

Sugars are polar organic molecules that
tend to have high solubility in water, which
is a polar solvent (remember solutes
dissolve well in solvents of similar
polarity). However, molecular compounds,
such as sugars, do not dissociate into ions
in aqueous solution. This latter property
makes glucose in solution a non-electrolyte,
i.e., it will not conduct electricity.

35. D

Phosphoric acid is a weak acid in water
because it dissociates or ionizes only
partially.

$$H_3PO_{4(aq)} \leftrightarrow H^+_{(aq)} + H_2PO_4^-{}_{(aq)}$$

All weak molecular acids are weak
electrolytes. The low concentration of
dissolved ions makes them poor conductors
of electricity.

36. D

In solution, NaOCl would form
the following ions: Na^+ and OCl^-
Therefore, it would be effective
in conducting electricity.

37. B

Nitric acid, like all strong acids, dissociates
completely in aqueous solution.
Thus, with two moles of dissolved ions
per mole of acid, nitric acid is a good
conductor of electricity.

38. B

Since pure molecular liquids do not
dissociate to any degree, they are unlikely
to be electrolytes, i.e., they will not conduct
electricity.

39. D

Neutral molecular compounds tend
to be non-electrolytes. Sucrose is one such
compound.

NR1.   1.05

Solution concentration problems are done
as part of a stoichiometric calculation.

$$n_{HCHO} = 3.00\text{ L} \times \frac{11.6\text{ mol}}{L} = 35\text{ mol}$$

$$n_{HCHO} = 1.05 \times 10^3\text{ g} = 1.05\text{ kg}$$

There is 1.05 kg of formaldehyde/methanol
in 3.0 L of 11.6 mol/L formalin.

40. A

Percent weight for volume (%W/V) is a
solution concentration that measures the
mass of a solute, in grams, per 100 mL of
solution. Simply divide the solute's mass
(in grams) by the solution volume (in mL)
and multiply by 100%.

$$\% \text{ caffeine} = \frac{0.110\text{ g}}{125\text{ mL}} \times 100\% = 0.088\,0\%$$

41. A

The molar mass of potassium
permanganate, $KMnO_{4(s)}$, is 158.04 g/mol

$$\% \text{ Mn} = 54.94\text{ g}/158.04\text{ g} \times 100\% = 34.76\text{ Mn}$$

$$\% \text{ K} = 39.10\text{ g}/158.04\text{ g} \times 100\% = 24.74\% \text{ K}$$

$$\% \text{ O} = 4 \times 16.00\text{ g}/158.04\text{ g} \times 100\%$$
$$= 40.50\% \text{ O}$$

42. B

The percentage by mass (%W/W) of a solute in a solvent is the mass of the solute in grams per 100 g of solution. Therefore, the total mass of the solution is equal to the combined masses of its components.

$$\text{Total mass} = 3\,000\text{ g} + 43.2\text{ g} + 200\text{ g}$$
$$= 3\,243.2\text{ g}$$

$$\%\text{ grease} = \frac{43.2\text{ g}}{3\,243.2\text{ g}} = 0.013\,3 \times 100\%$$
$$= 1.33\%$$

The % grease by mass in this solution is 1.33%.

43. D

We must use stoichiometry to solve this problem. To determine the percent mass of H_2O_2 in the bottle, we need to first determine the mass of $H_2O_2 (mH_2O_2)$ in the bottle as well as the mass of the entire solution. From this, we get

$$\%\,H_2O_2\,(\text{by mass}) = \frac{mH_2O_2}{mSol}$$

We are given that the remaining H_2O_2 in the 1 L bottle has a concentration of 6.0 mol. Therefore,

$$mH_2O_2 = 6.0\text{ mol} \times \frac{34.02\text{ g}}{\text{mol}} = 0.204\text{ kg}$$

We are given that the density of the 1 L solution is 1.10 g/mL, therefore

$$mSol = \frac{1.10\text{ g}}{\text{mL}} \times 1\,000\text{ mL} = 1.10\text{ kg}$$

$$\text{The }\%\,H_2O_2\text{ by mass} = \frac{mH_2O_2}{mSol} = \frac{0.204\text{ kg}}{1.10\text{ kg}}$$

$$(0.19)100\% = 19\%$$

The % of H_2O_2 concentration by mass is 19%.

44. B

The amount of iron contained within a person (m_{Fe}) is 0.004% of their body mass. In the case of a 68 kg person,

$$m_{Fe} = \frac{0.004\%}{100\%} \times 68\text{ kg} = 3 \times 10^{-3}\text{ kg}$$

The mass of iron is 3 g.

NR2. 0.27

These types of concentration problems require a few stoichiometric steps to solve.

$$n_{NaF} = \frac{0.243\%}{100\%} \times 75\text{ mL} \times \frac{4.5\text{ g}}{\text{mL}} = 0.82\text{ g}$$

$$n_{NaF} = 0.82\text{ g} \times \frac{\text{mol}}{41.99\text{ g}} = 0.020\text{ mol of NaF}_{(s)}$$

$$[NaF] = \frac{0.020\text{ mol}}{0.075\text{ L}} = 0.27\text{ mol/L}$$

The concentration of sodium fluoride in toothpaste is 0.27 mol/L.

45. B

Using $C_1V_1 = C_2V_2$, we can calculate the initial volume of $HCl_{(aq)}$ required.

$$C_1 = \frac{C_2V_2}{V_1} = \frac{100\text{ mL} \times \dfrac{0.040\,0\text{ mol}}{\text{L}}}{0.200\text{ mol/L}} = 20.0\text{ mL}$$

20.0 mL of 0.400 mol/L are required to prepare the desired solution. Standard solutions are prepared in volumetric flasks of the appropriate volume, in this case, 100 mL. The instructions for preparing a standard solution are outlined in the solution chapter of most high school text books. To ensure a high level of precision, it is important to use quality glassware such as pipettes and volumetric flasks.

46. D

In order to prepare a standard solution of a solid solute, the important first step is calculating the mass of solute required.

$$n_{NaCO_3} = \frac{0.100\text{ L} \times 0.050\,0\text{ mol}}{\text{L}}$$
$$= 0.005\,00\text{ mol}$$

$$n_{NaCO_3} = 0.005\,0\text{ mol} \times \frac{105.99\text{ g}}{\text{mol}} = 0.530\text{ g}$$

0.530 g of $Na_2CO_{3(s)}$ are required to make 100 mL of a 0.050 0 mol/L aqueous solution. Whenever a standard solution is prepared, it is best to dissolve the solute (if it is solid and crystalline) in half the final solvent volume with the aid of a glass stirring rod.

47. A

The required mass of $AgNO_{3(s)}$ for a 250 mL, 1 mol/L solution is calculated as follows.

$$n_{AgNO_3} = 0.250\text{ L} \times \frac{1.00\text{ mol}}{\text{L}} = 0.250\text{ mol}$$

$$n_{AgNO_3} = 0.250\text{ mol} \times \frac{169.88\text{ g}}{\text{mol}} = 42.5\text{ g}$$

Whenever a standard solution is prepared, it is best to dissolve the solute (if it is solid and crystalline) in roughly half the final solvent volume with the aid of a glass stirring rod.

48. C

The dynamic solubility equilibrium
$$NaCl_{(s)} \leftrightarrow NaCl_{(aq)}$$

$$NaCl_{(s)} \leftrightarrow Na^+_{(aq)} + Cl^-_{(aq)}$$

that occurs in this situation explains just how the radioactive $NaCl_{(s)}$ will become distributed throughout both the solution and the undissolved solute.

49. A

The equilibrium
" Uric $Acid_{(s)} \rightleftharpoons$ Uric $Acid_{(aq)}$ "

operates in cases of gout such that the precipitant crystallizes more than it dissolves. Therefore, over long periods of time, this precipitant (uric acid) accumulates to levels which are eventually toxic.

50. B

The neutralization reactions of strong Arrhenius acids and bases produce water and a salt. The reaction of $Mg(OH)_{2(s)}$ and $HCl_{(aq)}$ is one such reaction.

NR3. 678 3

The pH of an acidic solution is less than 7. The $[H^+_{(aq)}]$ of an acidic solution exceeds that of pure water,
i.e. $[H^+_{(aq)}] > 10^{-7}$ mol/L.
A solution whose pH = 7 is a neutral solution. The four digit answer is

I	II	III	IV
6	7	8	3

51. B

During solution equilibria, the rates of forward and reverse process (dissolution and crystallization, respectively) are equal.

52. A

Sometimes it is necessary to memorize important formulas.
This is one such formula.
pH = $-\log[H^+_{(aq)}]$

53. B

$$\frac{\left[H^+_{(aq)}\right]_{gastric\ juice}}{\left[H^+_{(aq)}\right]_{pure\ water}} = \frac{10^{-2}\,(\text{mol/L})}{10^{-7}\,(\text{mol/L})} = 10^5$$

Therefore, gastric juice is 10^5 times more acidic than pure water.

54. C

To solve this question, we must first convert pH into mol/L. We are given that the $pH_{gastric\ juice} = 2$
Therefore,

$$pH = 2\left[H^+_{(aq)}\right] = 10^{-pH} = 10^{-2}\ mol/L$$

We are given that the $pH_{pure\ water} = 7$.
Therefore,

$$pH = 12[H^+_{(aq)}] = 10^{-pH} = 10^{-12}\ mol/L$$

Dividing the $[H^+_{(aq)}]$ of gastric juice by the $[H^+_{(aq)}]$ of pure water, we get

$$\frac{10^{-2}\ mol/L}{10^{-12}\ mol/L} = 10^{10}$$

Therefore, the $[H^+_{(aq)}]$ at pH 2 is 10^{10} times greater than the $[H^+_{(aq)}]$ at pH = 12

55. A

For a given pH, $[H^+_{(aq)}] = 10^{-pH}$
In this case, the pH of the ASA solution is 3.
Therefore, $[H^+_{(aq)}] = 10^{-3}\ mol/L$.

Written Response

1. *Describe the factors that affect the solubility of gases, liquids, and solids in liquid solutions.* **(8 marks)**

"Like dissolves like" polar solutes are more soluble in polar solvents — e.g., alcohol in water; non-polar solutes are more soluble on non-polar solvents — e.g., bike chain grease in white gasoline. **(2 marks)**

Gases dissolve exothermically — this means that they tend to be more soluble at low temperatures and high pressure — e.g., the $CO_{2(g)}$ in pop is more soluble when it is kept in the refrigerator with the lid on.

(2 marks)

Solids, which dissolve endothermically, tend to be more soluble at higher temperature — e.g., sugar is more soluble in hot coffee than it is in cold coffee.

(2 marks)

Liquids soluble in each other, in all possible ratios, are said to be miscible — e.g., methanol in water.

(2 marks)

Liquids that do not mix at all are said to be immiscible — e.g., oil and water.

(**4** of these **8** marks are normally awarded for well communicated answers.)

2. When solving solution concentration problems, students must be familiar with concentrations and their units.

- p.p.m. – mol/L
- % (W/V) – g/100 mL
- % (W/W) – g/100 g
- % (V/V) – mL/100 mL

Unit cancellation calculations are sufficient to do any solution calculations.

a) $\left[Ca^{2+}_{(aq)}\right] = 78\ ppm$

$$= \frac{78\ mg\ Ca^{2+}}{L}$$

$$\left[Ca^{2+}_{(aq)}\right] = \frac{78\ mg}{L} \times \frac{mol}{40.08\ g}$$

$$= 1.9\ mol/L$$

The calcium ion concentration is 1.9 mmol/L.

(2 marks)

b) $m_{Mg} = 250\ mL \times \dfrac{24\ mg}{1\ 000\ L} = 6.0\ mg$

Some 6.0 mg of $Mg^{2+}_{(aq)}$ are present in 250 mL of the spring water. **(2 marks)**

c) $\left[Na^{2+}_{(aq)}\right] = \dfrac{5 \times 10^{-3}\ g}{1\ 000\ mL} \times 100\%$

$$= 5 \times 10^{-4}\ \%(W/V)$$

The sodium ion concentration is $5 \times 10^{-4}\%(W/V)$.

(2 marks)

d) Adding $Na_2CO_{3(aq)}$, $NaOH_{(aq)}$, $NaOH_{(aq)}$, $Na_3PO_{4(aq)}$

$NaSO_{3(aq)}$ will precipitate the ions as follows.

$$Mg^{2+}_{(aq)} + CO_3^{2-}_{(aq)} \rightarrow MgCO_{3(l)}$$

$$Ca^{2+}_{(aq)} + CO_3^{2-}_{(aq)} \rightarrow CaCO_{3(s)}$$

These solids are removed by filtration.

(2 marks)

56. A

A concentration problem:

Inital = Final

$$n_i = n_f$$

$$v_i C_i = v_f C_f$$

$$(v_i)(1.50 \text{ mol/L}) = (4.0 \text{ L})(0.125 \text{ mol/L})$$

$$v_i = \frac{(4.0 \text{ L})(0.125 \text{ mol/L})}{(1.50 \text{ mol/L})}$$

$$v_i = \frac{0.5 \text{ mol}}{1.50 \text{ mol/L}}$$

$$= 0.3 \text{ L}$$

Using 3 significant digits, the answer is 0.333 L.

57. C

$$2.3\% \text{ W/V} = 2.3 \text{ g/100 mL}$$

$$m_{NaCl} = 2.3 \text{ g/100 mL} \times 200 \text{ mL}$$

$$= 4.6 \text{ g}$$

58. C

lead (II) nitrate

$$Pb(NO_3)_{2(aq)} \rightarrow Pb^{2+}{}_{(aq)} = 2NO_3{}^-{}_{(aq)}$$

1(0.16 mol/L):1(0.16 mol/L):2(0.16 mol/L)

59. A

lead (IV) nitrate

$$Pb^{4+}{}_{(aq)} + 4NO_3{}^-{}_{(aq)} \rightarrow Pb(NO_3)_{4(aq)}$$

$$(0.32 \text{ mol/L}) : \frac{1}{4}(0.32 \text{ mol/L})$$

60. D

pH = 10, [H⁺] = 10^{-10} mol/L and pH = 11,

[H⁺] = 10^{-11} mol/L since $\frac{10^{-10}}{10} = 10^{-11}$,

[H⁺] is decreased by a factor of 10

61. D

If pH increases, [H⁺] decreases, [OH⁻] increases.

62. C

phenolphthelein: colourless → pH < 8.2
chlorophenol red: red → pH > 6.8
bromocresol green: blue → pH > 5.4

Therefore, 6.8 < pH < 8.2
pH 7.5 is possible

63. D

Bromothymol blue is yellow below pH 6.0
Bromocresol green is blue above pH 5.4
Litmus is red below pH 6.0
Therefore, **D** is correct.

64. B

A neutralization reaction produces salt and water when an acid and a base are combined in solution. Acids dissociate in aqueous solution to create hydrogen or hydronium ions, while bases dissociate and create hydroxide ions. The hydrogen or hydronium ions combine with the hydroxide ions to form water, and the remaining ions in the solution combine to form a salt. This reaction of acids and bases result in a solution with a pH that is more neutral than either the original acid or base reactants.

65. D

Neutralization reactions involve the combination of positively charged hydrogen and hydronium ions with negatively charged hydroxide ions to produce water. As the quantity of water increases, and the quantity of ions decreases, the pH of the solution becomes increasingly neutral and approaches 7.

66. D

A polyprotic base can accept 2 or more protons(H⁺ ions)

first, $CO_3{}^{2-} + H^+ \rightarrow HCO_3{}^-$
then $HCO_3{}^- + H^+ \rightarrow H_2CO_3$

67. B

A polyprotic acid can accept 2 or more protons(H⁺ ions)

first, $H_2SO_3 \rightarrow HSO_3{}^- + H^+$
then $HSO_3{}^- \rightarrow SO_3{}^{2-} + H^+$

68. B

Sugar in water forms a homogenous mixture, or solution. It is virtually impossible to detect any differences in one part of the solution from another part of the solution. The mixture is uniform, or even throughout. In a heterogenous mixture, it is possible to see distinct phases, or different substances within the mixture.

This mixture could be described as non-uniform. Stirring a fine silty sand in water would produce a good example of a heterogenous mixture. Individual sand grains could still be distinguished as being separate from the water, and it may also be possible to note grain sizes that are slightly different sizes or colors.

69. B

Baking soda dissociates in water as does salt, however salt remains chemically unchanged as roaming sodium and chlorine ions. Baking soda is a base, and upon dissociation the carbonate ion further reacts with water to form hydrogen carbonate ions and hydroxide ions. The presence of hydroxide and corresponding absorption of hydrogen ions is characteristic of a bases ability to remove acid properties from a solution.

70. C

An exothermic reaction results in the net release of heat. It requires energy to break bonds in the reactants, and bond formation releases energy. If the energy of bond formation in the products exceeds that of bonds breaking in the reactants, then the result is a release of heat energy, or an exothermic reaction.

71. C

Fe_2O_3 is the correct chemical formula for the combination of these two ions in an ionic bond. The balance of charges is zero: two iron ions with a 3+ charge is a total of 6+ (positive) and three oxygen ions with a 2– charge is a total of 6 – (negative) charges.

The correct IUPAC name would have to indicate the charge on the positive ion by the use of an indicator in brackets.

Iron ions can commonly have two charges: a 2+ charge would indicate an Fe^{2+} ion, and an IUPAC name would include iron (II) in it. A 3+ charge would be written as iron (III). In this case the charge is 3+ and so the correct name for this compound would be iron (III) oxide.

72. A

CaO is the correct chemical formula for the combination of these two ions in an ionic bond. The balance of charges is zero: one calcium ion with a 2+ charge is balanced by a single oxygen ion with a 2– charge.

The correct IUPAC name would have to list the positive ion by its elemental name, followed by the negative ion with an ending of –ide. The correct name for this compound would be calcium oxide.

ANSWERS AND SOLUTIONS –
QUANTITATIVE RELATIONSHIPS IN CHEMICAL CHANGE

1. B	12. D	22. A	NR3. 4.19	WR2.*	47. D
2. C	NR1. 25.0	23. A	31. B	38. A	48. A
3. C	13. A	NR2. 11.5	32. D	39. A	49. C
4. D	14. D	24. C	33. D	40. D	50. D
5. D	15. A	25. A	34. D	41. A	51. A
6. D	16. D	26. D	35. A	42. A	52. *
7. B	17. B	27. C	36. C	43. D	53. B
8. A	18. D	28. D	37. D	44. B	54. B
9. B	19. D	29. D	NR4. 14.3	45. D	55. A
10. C	20. A	30. B	WR1.*	46. D	56. B
11. D	21. B		*see solutions for written response and question 52		

1. B

The complete neutralization of $H_2SO_{4(aq)}$ and $BaOH_{2(aq)}$ results in the release of $Ba^{2+}_{(aq)}$ and $SO^{2-}_{(aq)}$ ions that combine to produce a $BaSO_{4(s)}$ precipitate. After examining a solubility table, you will find that most sulphate compounds are highly soluble except for those containing Ca^{2+}, Sr^{2+}, Ba^{2+}, Ra^{2+}, Pb^{2+}, and Ag^+.

2. C

The reaction of $HCl_{(aq)}$ and $Mg(OH)_{2(s)}$ would be

$$HCl_{(aq)} + Mg(OH)_{2(s)}$$
$$\rightarrow HOH_{(l)} + MgCl_{2(aq)}$$

Balance the atom or ion that is present in the greatest number, in this case, either OH^- or Cl^- ions.

$$2HCl_{(aq)} + Mg(OH)_{2(s)}$$
$$\rightarrow HOH_{(l)} + MgCl_{2(aq)}$$

Then, balance the H^+ ions.

$$2HCl_{(aq)} + Mg(OH)_{2(s)}$$
$$\rightarrow 2HOH_{(l)} + MgCl_{2(aq)}$$

Note: You can also solve this question by elimination since **C** is the only equation of the four presented that is balanced.

3. C

This question asks what the mole ratio of $HCl_{(aq)}$ to $Mg(OH)_{2(s)}$ is in the neutralization reaction

$$2HCl_{(aq)} + Mg(OH)_{2(s)}$$
$$\leftrightarrow 2H_2O_{(l)} + MgCl_{(aq)}$$

2 and 1 are the coefficients of $HCl_{(aq)}$ and $Mg(OH)_{2(s)}$, respectively, in the balanced equation above.
Therefore,

$$\frac{n_{HCl}}{n_{Mg(OH)_2}} = \frac{2 \text{ mol}}{1 \text{ mol}} = \frac{2}{1} \text{ or } 2:1$$

2 moles of $HCl_{(aq)}$ are required to neutralize 1 mole of $Mg(OH)_{2(s)}$.

4. D

An analysis that detects the *presence* of a chemical but not its *concentration* is a qualitative analysis.

5. D

There are only two rules for balancing simple chemical equations by inspection
1) Balance the species in greatest amount.
2) Repeat rule (1) until all the atoms are balanced on each side of the equation arrow. If normal balancing rules are followed, you get

$$2LiOH_{(s)} + CO_{2(g)} \rightarrow Li_2CO_{3(s)} + H_2O_{(g)}$$

The mole ratio is

$$\frac{n_{LiOH}}{n_{Li_2CO}} = \frac{2\text{ mol}}{1\text{ mol}} = \frac{2}{1}\text{ or } 2:1$$

6. D

Both $NaOH_{(aq)}$ and $HCl_{(aq)}$ are strong electrolytes that are completely dissociated in aqueous solution.

$$HCl_{(aq)} \rightarrow H^+{}_{(aq)} + Cl^-{}_{(aq)}$$

$$NaOH_{(aq)} \rightarrow Na^+{}_{(aq)} + OH^-{}_{(aq)}$$

The dissolved ions in the reaction are $H^+{}_{(aq)}$, $Cl^-{}_{(aq)}$ $Na^+{}_{(aq)}$, $OH^-{}_{(aq)}$

7. B

Spectator ions in a chemical reaction are those entities that essentially take *no part* in a chemical reaction. Another way of saying this is that spectator ions are present in the reactants and appear *unchanged* in the products.
In the reaction given, $H^+{}_{(aq)}$ and $HCO_3{}^-{}_{(aq)}$ in the reactants become $CO_{2(g)}$ and $H_2O_{(l)}$ in the products — they are not spectator species.

8. A

Ideally, a diagnostic test is usually a short qualitative analytical procedure with results that indicate, with little or no chance of error, the presence or absence of a chemical constituent or property of a system.

9. B

Quantitative analyses seek to *measure* the mass, volume, concentration, etc. of a chemical entity while qualitative analyses (e.g., the starch test for iodine, lime water test for $CO_{2(g)}$ "squeaky pop" of burning hydrogen, etc.) only detect the *presence* of a chemical species. The mere detection of CFCs in the atmosphere is a qualitative analysis.

10. C

When a compound is broken down to other compounds (not to elements) a decomposition has taken place. A simple decomposition has occurred if the products are all elements.

11. D

There are only two rules for balancing simple chemical equations by inspection.
1) Balance the species in greatest amount
2) Repeat rule (1) until all the atoms are balanced on each side of the equation arrow.
When equation 1 is balanced you get
$$6KAl(SO_4)_2 \rightarrow 3K_2SO_4 + 3Al_2O_3 + 9SO_3$$

Therefore, the mole ratio of Al to Al_2O_3 is

$$\frac{n_{KAl(SO_4)_2}}{n_{Al_2O_3}} = \frac{6\text{ mol}}{3\text{ mol}} = \frac{2}{1}$$

12. D

Ions come in two forms: cations (which are positive) and anions (which are negative). In a correctly written ionic compound formula, the cation(s) usually appear first followed by the anion(s). The same convention applies when ionic compounds are named.
In the reaction
$$2SO_3 + 4Sn \rightarrow SnS_2 + 3SnO_2$$

the anions are S^{2-} in SnS_2 (tin IV sulfide) and O^{2-} in SnO_2 (tin IV oxide).

NR1. 25.0

Since temperatures are not stated, this question can be best answered using Boyle's Law.

$$P_1 = 5\,(P_{\text{room}}),\ V_1 = 5\text{ L},\ P_2 = P_{\text{room}},\ V_2 = ?$$

$$P_2 V_2 = P_1 V_1$$

$$V_2 = \frac{P_1 V_1}{P_2}$$

$$= \frac{5(P_{\text{room}}) \times 5.0\text{ L}}{P_{\text{room}}}$$

$$= 25\text{ L}$$

It has already been established that the gas in the cylinder occupies 25 L at the room pressure. However, 5 L of gas will remain in the cylinder as it "empties," since the pressures outside and inside the cylinder will be equal at this point. Thus, 20 L of gas will be released into the room.

13. A

It is possible to employ a stoichiometric method using any kind of chemical equation provided it is balanced.

$$AgNO_{3(aq)} + Cl^-{}_{(aq)} \rightarrow AgCl_{(s)} + NO_3^-{}_{(aq)}$$

26.8 mL   100 mL

0.004 0 mol/L $\left[Cl^-{}_{(aq)}\right] = ?$

$$n_{Cl^-} = \frac{1}{1} n_{AgNO_3} = \frac{1}{1} \times 0.11\text{ mmol/L}$$

$$= 0.11\text{ mmol/L}$$

$$\left[Cl^-{}_{(aq)}\right] = \frac{0.11\text{ mmol/L}}{100\text{ mL}}$$

$$= 0.0011\text{ mol/L}$$

$$\text{or } 1.1\text{ mmol/L}$$

The chloride ion concentration is 1.1 mmol/L.

Note: The equation $Ag^+{}_{(aq)} + Cl^-{}_{(aq)} \rightarrow AgCl_{(s)}$ could also have been used.

14. D

The stoichiometric method is needed to solve this problem.

$$C_6H_{12}O_{6(s)} \rightarrow CO_{2(g)} + 3CH_{4(g)}$$

100 kg   m = ?

180.18 g/mol   16.05 L/mol

$$n_{C_6H_{12}O_6} = 100\text{ kg} \times \frac{\text{mol}}{180.18\text{ g}} = 0.555\text{ kmol}$$

$$= \frac{3}{1} n_{C_6H_{12}O_6} = \frac{3}{1} \times 0.555\text{ kmol} \quad {}^{n_{CH_4}}$$

$$= 1.67\text{ kmol}$$

$$m_{CH_4} = 1.67\text{ kmol} \times \frac{16.05\text{ g}}{\text{mol}} = 26.7\text{ kg}$$

26.7 kg of methane gas are predicted from the anaerobic digestion of 100 kg of glucose.

15. A

$$2NaN_{3(s)} \rightarrow 2Na_{(s)} + 3N_{2(g)}$$

m = ?   35.0 L

65.02 g/mol   24.8 L/mol

$$n_{N_2} = 35.0\text{ L} \times \frac{\text{mol}}{24.8\text{ L}} = 1.41\text{ mol}$$

$$n_{NaN_3} = \frac{2}{3} n_{N_2} = \frac{2}{3} \times 1.41\text{ mol} = 0.941\text{ mol}$$

$$m_{NaN_3} = 0.941\text{ mol} \times \frac{65.02\text{ g}}{\text{mol}} = 61.2\text{ g}$$

The decomposition of 61.2 g of $NaN_{3(s)}$ will provide 35.0 L of gas at SATP.

16. D

or

$$C_4H_6O_2 \rightarrow C_5H_9NO$$

0.35 g   m = ?

86.10 g/mol   99.15 g/mol

$$n_{reactant} = 0.35\,g \times \frac{mol}{86.10\,g} = 0.0041\,mol$$

$$n_{product} = \frac{1}{1}n_{reactant} = \frac{1}{1} \times 0.0041\,mol = 0.004$$

$$m_{product} = 0.0041\,mol \times \frac{99.15\,g}{mol} = 4.0\,g$$

The predicted mass of the product of this reaction is 4.0 g.

17. B

$$\%\ yield = \frac{mass\ obtained}{mass\ predicted} \times 100\%$$

In this case, % yield

$$= \frac{0.28\,g}{0.40\,g} \times 100\% = 70\%$$

18. D

A straightforward stoichiometric calculation will work for this problem.

$$CaCO_{3(s)} + 2H^+_{(aq)} \rightarrow$$

$$Ca^{2+}_{(aq)} + H_2O_{(l)} + CO_{2(g)}$$

3.50 g   V = ?

100.09 g/mol 1.00×10^{-4} mol/L

It requires 699 L of acid rain with an $[H^+_{(aq)}]$ of 1.00×10^{-4} mol/L to dissolve 3.50 g of $CaCO_{(s)}$.

19. D

An electron transfer (redox) reaction has occurred when an element replaces a similar element in a compound during a chemical reaction.

20. A

A simple application of the stoichiometric method is all that's needed.

$$Ba(OH)_{2(aq)} + H_2SO_{4(aq)}$$

$$\rightarrow BaSO_{4(s)} + 2HOH_{(l)}$$

1.22 mol/L   45 mL

23.4 mL $[H_2SO_{4(aq)}] = ?$

$$V_{Ba(OH)_2} = 24.6\,mL - 1.2\,mL = 23.4\,mL$$

$$n_{Ba(OH)_2} = 23.4\,mL \times \frac{1.22\,mol}{L}$$

$$= 28.5\,mmol$$

$$n_{H_2SO_4} = \frac{1}{1}n_{Ba(OH)_2} = \frac{1}{1} \times 28.5\,mmol$$

$$= 28.5\,mmol$$

$$[H_2SO_{4(aq)}] = \frac{28.5\,mmol}{45\,mL} = 0.63\,mol/L$$

The sulfuric acid molar concentration is 0.63 mol/L.

21. B

A straightforward stoichiometric method approach is what is needed here.

$$CH_3COOH_{(aq)} + KOH_{(aq)}$$
$$\rightarrow KCH_3COO_{(aq)} + HOH_{(l)}$$

30.0 mL   8.5 mL

$$\left[CH_3COOH_{(aq)}\right] 1.75 \text{ mol/L}$$

$$V_{KOH} = \frac{8.4 \text{ mL} + 8.6 \text{ mL} + 8.5 \text{ mL}}{3}$$

$$= 8.5 \text{ mL}$$

$$n_{KOH} = 8.5 \text{ mL} \times \frac{1.75 \text{ mol}}{L} = 15 \text{ mol}$$

$$n_{CH_3COOH} = \frac{1}{1} n_{KOH}$$

$$= \frac{1}{1} \times 15 \text{ mmol}$$

$$= 15 \text{ mmol}$$

$$\left[CH_3COOH_{(aq)}\right] = \frac{15 \text{ mmol}}{30.0 \text{ mL}} = 0.50 \text{ mol/L}$$

The molar concentration of acetic acid in the stop bath is 0.50 mol/L.

22. A

The stoichiometric method is needed to solve this problem.

$$2KOH_{(aq)} + H_2SO_{4(aq)}$$
$$\rightarrow Na_2SO_{4(aq)} + 2HOH_{(l)}$$

43.2 mL   200 mL

0.001 05 mol/L $\left[H_2SO_{4(aq)}\right]$

The number of moles of $KOH_{(aq)}$ used was

$$n_{KOH} = 43.2 \text{ mL} \times \frac{0.001\,05 \text{ mol}}{L}$$

$$= 0.045\,4 \text{ mmol}$$

Since the molar ratio of $KOH_{(aq)}$:$H_2SO_{4(aq)}$ was 2:1, half the number of moles of $H_2SO_{4(aq)}$

$$n_{H_2SO_4} = \frac{1}{2} n_{KOH} = \frac{1}{2} \times 0.045\,4 \text{ mmol}$$

$$= 0.022\,7 \text{ mmol}$$

Therefore,

$$\left[H_2SO_{4(aq)}\right] = \frac{0.022\,7 \text{ mmol}}{200 \text{ mL}}$$

$$= 1.13 \times 10^{-4} \text{ mol/L}$$

The concentration of $H_2SO_{4(aq)}$ in the acid rain was 1.13×10^{-4} mol/L.

23. A

Use the stoichiometric method to calculate the mass of $NaHCO_{3(s)}$ required.

$$NaHCO_{3(s)} + HCl_{(aq)}$$
$$\rightarrow NaCl_{(aq)} + CO_2 + H_2O_{(l)}$$

m = ?   75 mL

84.01 g/mol   110 mol/L

$$n_{HCl} = 75 \text{ mL} \times \frac{0.110 \text{ mol}}{L} = 8.3 \text{ mmol}$$

$$n_{NaHCO_3} = \frac{1}{1} n_{HCl} = \frac{1}{1} \times 8.3 \text{ mmol}$$

$$= 8.3 \text{ mmol}$$

$$m_{NaHCO_3} = 8.3 \text{ mmol} \times \frac{84.01 \text{ g}}{\text{mol}}$$

$$= 6.9 \times 10^2 \text{ mg}$$

$$\text{or } 0.69 \text{ g}$$

NR2. 11.5

The volume of titrant added = final burette volume – initial burette volume

In this case

$$V_{NaOH} = 40.2 \text{ mL} - 28.7 \text{ mL}$$
$$= 11.5 \text{ mL}$$

24. C

A stoichiometric calculation is used to solve most acid-base titration problems. First write the balanced equation

$$C_6H_5COOH_{(aq)} + NaOH_{(aq)}$$
$$\rightarrow C_6H_5COONa_{(aq)} + HOH_{(l)}$$

100 mL   11.5 mL

$\left[C_6H_5COOH_{(aq)}\right]$ $\dfrac{0.015\,5\text{ mol}}{L}$

The number of moles of $NaOH_{(aq)}$ used was

$$n_{NaOH} = 11.5\text{ mL} \times \dfrac{0.015\,5\text{ mol}}{L}$$
$$= 0.178\text{ mmol}$$

Based on the molar ratio, the number of moles of $C_6H_5COOH_{(aq)}$ used was

$$n_{C_6H_5COOH} = \dfrac{1}{1}n_{NaOH} = \dfrac{1}{1} \times 0.178\text{ mmol}$$
$$= 0.178\text{ mmol}$$

Therefore,

$$\left[C_6H_5COOH_{(aq)}\right] = \dfrac{0.178\text{ mmol}}{100\text{ mL}}$$
$$= 1.78 \times 10^{-3}\text{ mol/L}$$

(this may also be stated as 1.78 mmol/L) The benzoic acid molar concentration is 1.78×10^{-3} mol/L.

25. A

Employ the stoichiometric method to answer this acid-base titration problem. Write the balanced equation
$$KOH_{(aq)} + HCl_{(aq)} \rightarrow KCl_{(aq)} + HOH_{(l)}$$

15 mL   8.5 mL

$\left[KOH_{(aq)}\right]$ 0.190 mol/L

The base concentration is 0.11 mol/L

$$n_{HCl} = 8.5\text{ mL} \times \dfrac{0.190\text{ mol}}{L} = 1.6\text{ mmol}$$

Based on the molar ratio, the number of moles of $KOH_{(aq)} : HCl_{(aq)}$ (1:1), the number of moles of $KOH_{(aq)}$ used was

$$n_{KOH} = \dfrac{1}{1}n_{HCl}\dfrac{1}{1} \times 1.6\text{ mmol} = 1.6\text{ mmol}$$

Therefore,

$$\left[KOH_{(aq)}\right] = \dfrac{1.6\text{ mmol}}{15\text{ mL}} = 0.11\text{ mol/L}.$$

The base concentration is 0.11 mol/L.

26. D

The net ionic equation for the reaction is
$$Pb^{2+}_{(aq)} + SO_4^{2-}_{(aq)} \rightarrow Pb(SO_4)_{(aq)}.$$
Since the molar ratios of the two ions are 1:1, the limiting reagent is the reactant with less molar quantity.

$$0.020(0.50\text{ M}) = 0.010\text{ mol of } Pb(NO_3)$$
$$0.015(0.55\text{ M}) = 0.008\,25\text{ mol } Na_2SO_4$$

$$n_{Na_2SO_4} = \dfrac{1}{1}n_{Pb(SO_4)}$$
$$= \dfrac{1}{1} \times 0.008\,25\text{ mol}$$
$$= 0.008\,25\text{ mol}$$

$$0.008\,25\text{ mol} \times \dfrac{303.26\text{ g}}{\text{mol}} = 2.5\text{ g}$$

27. C

Using stoichiometry, write a balanced equation.

$$2K_3PO_{4(aq)} + 3Sn^{2+}_{(aq)}$$
$$\rightarrow Sn_3(PO_4)_{2(s)} + 6K^+_{(aq)}$$

2.00 L	0.689 mg
$[Sn^{2+}_{(aq)}]$	546.82 g/mol

$$n_{Sn_3PO_4} = 0.689 \text{ mg} \times \frac{mol}{546.82 \text{ g}}$$

$$= 0.001\,26 \text{ mmol}$$

Based on the molar ratios of the equation

$$n_{Sn^{2+}} = \frac{3}{1}n_{Sn_3PO_4} = \frac{3}{1} \times 0.001\,26 \text{ mmol}$$

$$= 0.003\,78 \text{ mmol}$$

Therefore,

$$\left[Sn^{2+}_{(aq)}\right] = \frac{3.78 \times 10^{-6} \text{ mol}}{2.00 \text{ L}}$$

$$= 1.89 \times 10^{-6} \text{ mol/L}$$

(may also be stated as 1.89 μmol/L)
The $Sn^{2+}_{(aq)}$ molar concentration is 1.89×10^{-6} mol/L.

28. D

Use the stoichiometric method calculation.

$$BaCl_{2(aq)} + K_2SO_{4(aq)}$$
$$\rightarrow BaSO_{4(s)} + 2KCl_{(aq)}$$

0.700 mol/L	10.0 g
$V_{BaCl2} = ?$	233.39 g/mol

$$n_{BaSO_4} = 10.0 \text{ g} \times \frac{mol}{233.39 \text{ g}} = 0.042\,8 \text{ mol}$$

$$n_{BaCl_2} = \frac{1}{1}n_{BaSO_4} = \frac{1}{1} \times 0.042\,8 \text{ mol}$$

$$= 0.042\,8 \text{ mol}$$

$$V_{BaCl_2} = 0.042\,8 \text{ mol} \times \frac{L}{0.700 \text{ mol}}$$

$$= 0.061\,2 \text{ L}$$

The volume of 0.700 mol/L $BaCl_{2(aq)}$ required is 0.061 2 L or 61.2 mL.

29. D

A stoichiometric calculation is what is needed here (the Na^+ spectator ions are retained for ease of understanding). Write a balanced equation.

$$Mg^{2+}_{(aq)} + Na_2CO_{3(aq)}$$
$$\rightarrow MgCO_{3(s)} + 2Na^+_{(aq)}$$

100 mL	m = ?
0.45 0 mol/L	84.32 g/mol

$$n_{Na_2CO_3} = 0.100 \text{ L} \times \frac{0.450 \text{ mol}}{L}$$

$$= 0.045\,0 \text{ mol}$$

Based on the molar ratio of the equation

$$n_{MgCO_3} = \frac{1}{1}n_{Na_2CO_3} = \frac{1}{1} \times 0.045\,0 \text{ mol}$$

$$= 0.045\,0 \text{ mol}$$

Therefore,
$$m_{MgCO_3} = 0.045\,0 \text{ mol} \times 84.32 \text{ g/mol}$$

$$= 3.79 \text{ g}$$

The mass of precipitate is 3.79 g.

Copyright Protected

30. B

A version of the stoichiometric method gives the answer to this problem. Initially, if 300 g of $CaSO_{4(s)}$ is 85% of the mass of predicted product then the predicted yield of $CaSO_{4(aq)}$ would be,

$$m_{CaSO_4} = \frac{100}{85} \times 300 \text{ g} = 0.35 \text{ kg}$$

Write the balanced equation.

$$CaCl_{2(aq)} + Na_2SO_{4(aq)}$$
$$\rightarrow CaSO_{4(aq)} + 2NaCl_{(aq)}$$

V = ?   0.35 kg
2.33 mol/L   136.14 kg/mol

$$n_{CaSO_4} = 0.35 \text{ kg} \times \frac{\text{mol}}{136.14 \text{ kg}} = 2.6 \text{ mol}$$

Based on the molar ratios of the equation.

$$n_{CaCl_2} = \frac{1}{1} n_{CaSO_4} = \frac{1}{1} \times 2.6 \text{ mol} = 2.6 \text{ mol}$$

Therefore,

$$V_{CaCl_2} = 2.6 \text{ mol} \times \frac{L}{2.33 \text{ mol}} = 1.1 \text{ L}$$

The volume of 2.33 mol/L $CaCl_{2(aq)}$ required is 1.1 L.

NR3.   4.19

The stoichiometric method is the most efficient means of calculating the $AgNO_{3(aq)}$ molar concentration — often written as $\left[AgNO_{3(aq)} \right]$.

Write a balanced equation.
$$AgNO_{3(aq)} + KCl_{(aq)}$$
$$\rightarrow AgCl_{(s)} + KNO_{3(aq)}$$

250 mL   15.0 g
$\left[AgNO_{3(aq)} \right]$ 143.32 g/mol

$$n_{AgCl_{(s)}} = 15.0 \text{ g} \times \frac{\text{mol}}{143.32 \text{ g}} = 0.105 \text{ mol}$$

Based on the ratios of the equation

$$n_{AgNO_3} = \frac{1}{1} n_{AgCl} = 1 \times 0.105 \text{ mol}$$
$$= 0.105 \text{ mol}$$

$$\left[AgNO_{3(aq)} \right] = \frac{0.105 \text{ mol}}{0.250 \text{ L}} = 0.419 \text{ mol/L}$$

The molar concentration of the $AgNO_{3(aq)}$ is 0.419 mol/L or 4.19×10^{-1} mol/L.

31. B

An excess-limiting stoichiometric calculation is required when the quantities of two or more reactants are provided. The limiting reagent is that compound/element present in insufficient quantities to react completely after considering the appropriate mole ratio of reactants.
The predicted reaction of $BaCl_{2(aq)}$ and $Na_2CO_{3(aq)}$ is
$$BaCl_{2(aq)} + Na_2CO_{3(aq)}$$
$$\rightarrow BaCO_{3(s)} + 2NaCl_{(aq)}$$

With a 1:1 mole ratio of reactants, the species present in **least** amount is the limiting reagent.

$$n_{BaCl_2} = 300 \text{ mL} \times \frac{0.100 \text{ mol}}{L}$$
$$= 30.0 \text{ mmol}$$

$$n_{Na_2CO_3} = 200 \text{ mL} \times \frac{0.110 \text{ mol}}{L}$$
$$= 22.0 \text{ mmol}$$

The $Na_2CO_{3(aq)}$ is the limiting reagent.

32. D

An excess limiting stoichiometric calculation must be undertaken.

$$BaCl_{2(aq)} + Na_2CO_{3(aq)}$$
$$\rightarrow BaCO_{3(s)} + 2NaCl_{(aq)}$$

300 mL   200 mL   m =
0.100 mol/L   0.110 mol/L
       197.34 g/mol

We have

$$n_{BaCl_2} = 300 \text{ mL} \times \frac{0.100 \text{ mol}}{L}$$
$$= 30.0 \text{ mmol}$$

We need

$$n_{Na_2CO_3} = \frac{1}{1} n_{BaCl_2} = \frac{1}{1} \times 30.0 \text{ mmol}$$
$$= 30.0 \text{ mmol}$$

Based on previous information we actually have

$$n_{Na_2CO_3} = 200 \text{ mL} \times \frac{0.110 \text{ mol}}{L}$$
$$= 22.0 \text{ mmol}$$

Clearly, we have less $Na_2CO_{3(aq)}$ than is required for complete reaction with the $BaCl_{2(aq)}$. Thus, $Na_2CO_{3(aq)}$, the limiting reagent, determines the mass of product obtained. Based on the molar ratios of the equation

$$n_{BaCl_2} = \frac{1}{1} n_{Na_2CO_3} = \frac{1}{1} \times 22.0 \text{ mmol}$$
$$= 22.0 \text{ mmol}$$

Therefore,

$$m_{BaCl_2} = 22.0 \text{ mmol} \times \frac{197.34 \text{ g}}{\text{mol}}$$
$$= 4.34 \times 10^3 \text{ mg}$$
$$= 4.34 \text{ g}$$

The mass of $BaCO_{3(s)}$ predicted is 4.34 g.

33. D

In simple terms,

$$\% \text{ yield} = \frac{\text{quantity obtained}}{\text{quantity predicted}} \times 100\%$$

Where the yield is 78%, the mass of product from the previous question is

$$m_{BaCl_2} = \frac{78}{100} \times 4.34 \text{ g} = 3.4 \text{ g}$$

34. D

The excess limiting method, in part, must be employed here.

$$2H_{2(g)} + CO_{(g)} \rightarrow CH_3OH_{(l)}$$

We have

$$n_{H_2} = 9.00 \text{ kg} \times \frac{\text{mol}}{2.02 \text{ g}} = 4.46 \text{ kmol}$$

Based on the molar ratio of equation we need

$$n_{CO} = \frac{1}{2} n_{H_2} = \frac{1}{2} \times 4.46 \text{ kmol} = 2.23 \text{ kmol}$$

We actually have

$$n_{CO} = 70.0 \text{ kg} \times \frac{\text{mol}}{28.01 \text{ g}} = 2.50 \text{ kmol}$$

Thus, have more $CO_{(g)}$ than is needed, which makes $CO_{(g)}$ the excess reagent and $H_{2(g)}$ the limiting reagent.

35. A

$$\% \text{yield} = \frac{\text{mass obtained}}{\text{mass predicted}} \times 100\%$$

In the case of the methanol,

$$\% \text{ yield} = \frac{59.2 \text{ kg}}{71.4 \text{ kg}} \times 100\% = 82.9\%$$

(The answer is no different when either rounded off values or those kept in the calculator are used.)
The % yield of methanol is 82.9%.

36. C

$$2NH_{3(g)} + H_2SO_{4(aq)} \rightarrow (NH_4)_2 SO_{4(aq)}$$

1.11 kg   3.20 kg
17.04 g/mol 98.08 g/mol

We have,

$$n_{NH_3} = 1.11 \text{ kg} \times \frac{\text{mol}}{17.04 \text{ g}} = 0.065\,1 \text{ mol}$$

We need,

$$n_{H_2SO_4} = \frac{1}{2} n_{NH_3}$$

$$= \frac{1}{2} \times 0.065\,1 \text{ mol}$$

$$= 0.032\,6 \text{ mol}$$

We actually have

$$n_{H_2SO_4} = 3.20 \text{ kg} \times \frac{\text{mol}}{98.08 \text{ g}}$$

$$= 0.032\,6 \text{ mol}$$

There is marginally more $H_2SO_{4(aq)}$ (about 0.17%) than is required,
but this is so small as to be insignificant. The Law of Conservation of Mass says, simply, the mass of the reactants equals the mass of the products.

In this case.
$m_{products}$ = 1.11 kg + 3.20 kg = 4.31 kg

37. D

The Law of Conservation of Mass states that the mass of the products of a chemical reaction equals the mass of the reactants. Though you may not have realized it, when you balance a chemical reaction by ensuring equal numbers of atoms on both sides of a chemical equation you are applying the Law of Conservation of Mass.

NR4.   14.3

Once again it is possible to use any suitable balanced chemical equation.

$$Cl^-_{(aq)} + AgNO_{3(aq)}$$

$$\rightarrow AgCl_{(s)} + NO_3^-{}_{(aq)}$$

100 mL   m = ?
0.001 0 mol/L   143.32 g/mol

$$n_{Cl^-} = 100 \text{ mL} \times 0.001\,0 \frac{\text{mol}}{\text{L}} = 0.10 \text{ mmol}$$

$$n_{AgCl} = \frac{1}{1} n_{Cl} = \frac{1}{1} \times 0.10 \text{ mmol} = 0.10 \text{ mmol}$$

$$m_{AgCl} = 0.10 \text{ mmol} \times 143.32 \frac{\text{g}}{\text{mol}}$$

$$= 14.3 \text{ mg or } 0.014\,3 \text{ g}$$

14.3 mg of precipitate is predicted for this reaction.

Written Response

1. *Describe the stoichiometric method (your response should include a simple reaction equation and an explanation of excess and limiting reagents).* **(8 marks)**

Step 1. Balance the equation and all the relevant chemical data.

For example

$$2H_{2(g)} + O_{(g)} \rightarrow 2H_2O_{(l)}$$
$$\begin{array}{ll} 2.02 \text{ g} & m = ? \\ 2.02 \text{ g/mol} & 18.02 \text{ g/mol} \end{array}$$

Step 2. A calculation of the number of moles of the given species.

e.g.

$$n_{H_2} = 2.02 \text{ g} \times \frac{\text{mol}}{2.02 \text{ g}} = 1.00 \text{ mol of } H_{2(g)}$$

Step 3. A calculation of the number of moles, of the required entity that incorporates a suitable mol ratio.

$$n_{H_2O} = \frac{2}{2}n_{H_2} = \frac{2}{2} \times 1.00 \text{ mol} = 1.00 \text{ mol}$$

Step 4. A calculation of the answer for the problem is

$$m_{H_2O} = 1.00 \text{ mol} \times \frac{18.02 \text{ g}}{\text{mol}} = 18.0 \text{ g}$$

Step 5. A statement of the answer to the problem, 18.0 g of $H_2O_{(l)}$ are predicted for the reaction of 2.02 g of $H_{2(g)}$.

A total of **5 marks** is given for steps 1–5.

The *limiting reagent* is so called because it limits the mass/volume/concentration of the products in a chemicals reaction. The excess reagent, as its name suggest, reacts only partially and some of it remains once reaction is complete.

(3 marks)

2. A man is found dead in a limestone cave (primarily $CaCO_{3(s)}$). The man bears no bruise, wound, or mark on his body. You are asked to solve the mystery of how the man died. Upon searching the scene, you discover a deep hole in the limestone floor that contains traces of acetic acid. Some bubbling is still occurring.

a) *Write a balanced equation for the reaction of acetic acid with limestone.*
(1 mark)

$$CaCO_{3(s)} + 2CH_3COOH_{(aq)}$$
$$\rightarrow Ca(CH_3COO)_{2(aq)} + H_2CO_{3(aq)}$$

b) *What might be causing the bubbling to occur?*
(Hint: consider carbonated water.)
(1 mark)

$$H_2CO_3 \rightarrow H_2O + CO_{2(g)}$$
The $CO_{2(g)}$ is causing the bubbling.

c) *If the room has an 11.0 kL capacity, and 1 mole of gas occupies 24.8 L, how many litres of a 1.25 mol/L acetic acid would be needed to cause the room to completely fill with gas?*
(5 marks)

$$2CH_3COOH_{(aq)} + CaCO_{3(s)}$$
$$\rightarrow Ca(CH_3COO)_{2(aq)} + H_2CO_{3(aq)}$$

and

$$H_2CO_{3(aq)} \rightarrow H_2O_{(l)} + CO_{2(g)}$$

When combined, these reactions produce an equation suitable for a stoichiometric calculation.

$$2CH_3COOH_{(aq)} + CaCO_{3(s)}$$
$$\rightarrow Ca(CH_3COO)_{2(aq)} + H_2O_{(g)} + CO_{2(g)}$$

$$V = ? \qquad V = 11.0 \text{ kL}$$
$$1.25 \text{ mol/L} \qquad 24.8 \text{ L/mol}$$

$$n_{CO_2} = 11.0 \text{ kL} \times \frac{\text{mol}}{24.8 \text{ L}} = 0.444 \text{ kmol}$$

$$n_{CH_3COOH} = \frac{2}{1} n_{CO_2}$$
$$= \frac{2}{1} \times 0.444 \text{ kmol}$$
$$= 0.887 \text{ kmol}$$

$$V_{CH_3COOH} = 0.887 \text{ kmol} \times \frac{\text{L}}{1.25 \text{ mol}}$$
$$= 0.710 \text{ kL}$$
$$V_{CH_3COOH} = 710 \text{ L}$$

Approximately, 710 L of 1.25 mol/L acetic acid are required.

d) *How might the man have died?*

(1 mark)

The man likely suffocated to death from the $CO_{2(s)}$ that completely filled the room.

38. A

Formula equation:
$$HCl_{(aq)} + NaOH_{(aq)} \rightarrow NaCl_{(aq)} + H_2O_{(l)}$$
Complete ionic equation:

$$H^+{}_{(aq)} + Cl^-{}_{(aq)} + Na^+{}_{(aq)} + OH^-{}_{(aq)}$$
$$\rightarrow Na^+{}_{(aq)} + Cl^-{}_{(aq)} + H_2O_{(l)}$$

Net-ionic equation:
$$H^+{}_{(aq)} + OH^-{}_{(aq)} \rightarrow H_2O_{(l)}$$
[The ions that are unchanged on either side of the equation (called spectator ions) are usually taken out of the ionic equation]

39. A

The formula equation for the reaction is:
$$Ca(NO_3)_{2(aq)} + Na_2CO_{3(aq)}$$
$$\rightleftharpoons CaCO_{3(s)} + 2NaNO_{3(aq)}$$

The complete-ionic equation is:
$$Ca^{2+}{}_{(aq)} + 2NO_3^-{}_{(aq)} + 2Na^+{}_{(aq)} + CO_3^{2-}{}_{(aq)}$$
$$\rightleftharpoons CaCO_{3(s)} + 2Na^+{}_{(aq)} + 2NO_3^-{}_{(aq)}$$

The net-ionic equation is:
$$Ca2^+{}_{(aq)} + CO_3^{2-}{}_{(aq)} \rightleftharpoons CaCO_{3(s)}$$
(Spectator ions are removed from the net ionic equation.)

40. D

The formula equation for the reaction between $Pb(NO_3)_{2(aq)}$ and $NaCl_{(aq)}$ is:
$$Pb(NO_3)_{2(aq)} + 2NaCl_{(aq)}$$
$$\rightarrow PbCl_{2(s)} + 2NaNO_{3(aq)}$$

41. A

A precipitate is formed if the compound formed after the reaction is denoted by a 's' as its sub-script because a precipitate is solid. Among all the given alternatives, only alternative **A** forms a solid compound $[Sr_3(PO_4)_2]$.

42. A

The formula equation for the reaction is:
$$2H_3PO_{4(aq)} + 3Sr(OH)_{2(aq)}$$
$$\rightarrow Sr_3(PO_4)_{2(s)} + 6H_2O_{(l)}$$

The complete ionic equation is:

$$2H_3PO_{4(aq)} + 3Sr^{2+}{}_{(aq)} + 6OH^-{}_{(aq)}$$
$$\rightarrow Sr_3(PO_4)_{2(s)} + 6H_2O_{(l)}$$

Here the net-ionic equation and the complete ionic equation are the same since there are no spectators (ions which do not change during the reaction).

43. D

The formula equation for the given reaction is:

$$CaCl_{2(aq)} + Na_2SO_{4(aq)}$$
$$\rightarrow 2NaCl_{(aq)} + CaSO_{4(s)}$$

The complete ionic equation is:

$$Ca^{2+}_{(aq)} + 2Cl^-_{(aq)} + 2Na^+_{(aq)} + SO_4^{2-}_{(aq)}$$
$$\rightarrow 2Na^+_{(aq)} + 2Cl^-_{(aq)} + CaSO_{4(s)}$$

The net-ionic equation is:
$$Ca^{2+}_{(aq)} + SO_4^{2-}_{(aq)} \rightarrow CaSO_{4(s)}$$
[Because the ions which do not change during the reaction (spectator ions), are cancelled from the complete ionic equation to obtain the net-ionic equation.]

44. B

In a complete ionic equation, the aqueous ionic compounds are represented in ionic form, free ions, in aqueous state and precipitates, in solid state. The complete ionic equation is:

$$Ba^{2+}_{(aq)} + S^{2-}_{(aq)} + Sr^{2+}_{(aq)}$$
$$\rightarrow Sr^{2+}_{(aq)} + S^2_{(aq)} + Ba(OH)_{2(s)}$$

45. D

The total mass of the reactants is 45.9 g + 70.90, which is 116.8 g. The mass of the products is also 116.8 g. Since there is no loss nor gain of mass, mass is conserved.

46. D

Since the molar mass is the number of grams/mol, M = m/n, the experimenter needs to know the number of moles. The Ideal Gas Law is $PV = nRT$. Consisting of 4 variables and one constant, R. If mass, temperature and pressure are known, that still leaves a volume measurement required for substitution into the formula.

47. D

The theoretical yield is the quantity of a product that is predicted as a result of a stoichiometric calculation known as the mass of the products that is expected from the reaction.

48. A

Actual yield is the mass of product obtained from the reaction.

49. C

(Measured yield)/(predicted yield) × 100%,
(11.7 /14.3 g) × 100% = 81.8%

50. D

Impurities in the reactants will mean the assumed amounts of reactants are incorrect; very fine precipitate particles may not be trapped on the filter paper if the pores are too large. The theoretical yield will depend on the number of moles, therefore the mass, of the reactants.

51. A

A titration curve has a steep section (a rapid pH decrease) when a strong base is added to a strong acid sample. This is because the graph is logarithmic, based on powers of ten, not a straight line, or linear.

52.

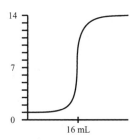

Bromothymol blue would be a suitable indicator, because the midpoint of the rapid rise in the curve, at pH 7, is in the middle of the range of the colour change for bromothymol blue (6.0 to 7.6).
The equivalence point should be marked where the volume is 16 mL and pH is 7.0

53. B

Bromothymol blue would be a suitable indicator, because the midpoint of the rapid rise in the curve, at pH 7, is in the middle of the range of the colour change for bromothymol blue (6.0 to 7.6).

54. B

If the end point occurs at pH = 3.5, the experimenter needs to choose an indicator whose colour change occurs in the middle of the second rapid pH change.
Methyl orange is yellow at pH 4.4 and red at pH 3.2. It will turn from yellow to a pale peach colour at the end point.

55. A

A) In the balanced equation, there is one mole of base for every mole of acid, so at the endpoint, equal numbers of moles must have reacted.

B) Since the end point of a strong acid/strong base reaction will be at pH 7, the numbers of H^+ and OH^- ions must be equal.

C) The original sample is basic, and will become acidic (litmus will turn red) when the endpoint is reached.

D) Sodium chloride is highly soluble.

56. B

Endpoint is the midpoint of the rapid rise on the pH curve

KEY STRATEGIES

FOR

SUCCESS ON EXAMS

NOTES

KEY STRATEGIES FOR SUCCESS ON EXAMS

There are many different ways to assess your knowledge and understanding of course concepts. Depending on the subject, your knowledge and skills are most often assessed through a combination of methods which may include performances, demonstrations, projects, products, and oral and written tests. Written exams are one of the most common methods currently used in schools. Just as there are some study strategies that help you to improve your academic performance, there are also some test writing strategies that may help you to do better on unit test and year-end exams. To do your best on any test, you need to be well prepared. You must know the course content and be as familiar as possible with the manner in which it is usually tested. Applying test writing strategies may help you to become more successful on exams, improve your grades, and achieve your potential.

📖 STUDY OPTIONS FOR EXAM PREPARATION

Studying and preparing for exams requires a strong sense of self-discipline. Sometimes having a study buddy or joining a study group

- helps you to stick to your study schedule
- ensures you have others with whom you can practice making and answering sample questions
- clarifies information and provides peer support

It may be helpful to use a combination of individual study, working with a study buddy, or joining a study group to prepare for your unit test or year-end exam. Be sure that the study buddy or group you choose to work with is positive, knowledgeable, motivated, and supportive. Working with a study buddy or a study group usually means you have to begin your exam preparation earlier than you would if you are studying independently.

Tutorial classes are often helpful in preparing for exams. You can ask a knowledgeable student to tutor you or you can hire a private tutor. Sometimes school jurisdictions or individual schools may offer tutorials and study sessions to assist students in preparing for exams. Tutorial services are also offered by companies that specialize in preparing students for exams. Information regarding tutorial services is usually available from school counsellors, local telephone directories, and on-line search engines.

📖 EXAM QUESTION FORMATS

There is no substitute for knowing the course content. To do well in your course you need to combine your subject knowledge and understanding with effective test writing skills. Being familiar with question formats may help you in preparing for quizzes, unit tests or year-end exams. The most typical question formats include multiple choice, numerical response, written response, and essay. The following provides a brief description of each format and suggestions for how you might consider responding to each of the formats.

MULTIPLE CHOICE

A multiple choice question provides some information for you to consider and then requires you to select a response from four choices, often referred to as distractors. The distractors may complete a statement, be a logical extension or application of the information. When preparing for multiple choice questions, you may wish to focus on:

- studying concepts, theories, groups of facts or ideas that are similar in meaning; **compare and contrast their similarities and differences**; ask yourself "How do the concepts differ?", "Why is the difference important?", "What does each fact or concept mean or include?" "What are the exceptions?"

- **identifying main ideas, key information**, formulas, concepts, and theories, where they apply and what the **exceptions** are

- memorizing important definitions, examples, and applications of key concepts

- learning to **recognize *distractors*** that may lead you to apply plausible but incorrect solutions, and *three and one splits* where one answer is obviously incorrect and the others are very similar in meaning or wording

- **using active reading techniques** such as underlining, highlighting, numbering, and circling important facts, dates, basic points

- making up your own multiple choice questions for practice

NUMERICAL RESPONSE

A numerical response question provides information and requires you to use a calculation to arrive at the response. When preparing for numerical response questions, you may wish to focus on:

- memorizing formulas and their applications
- completing chapter questions or making up your own for practice
- making a habit of **estimating the answer** prior to completing the calculation
- paying special **attention to accuracy** in computing and the use of significant digits where applicable

WRITTEN RESPONSE

A written response question requires you to respond to a question or directive such as "explain," "compare," contrast." When preparing for written response questions, you may wish to focus on:

- ensuring your response **answers the question**
- recognizing **directing words** such as "list," "explain," "define"
- providing **concise answers** within the time limit you are devoting to the written response section of the exam
- identifying subject content that lends itself to short answer questions

ESSAY

An essay is a lengthier written response requiring you to identify your position on an issue and provide logical thinking or evidence that supports the basis of your argument. When preparing for an essay, you may wish to focus on:

- examining **issues** that are relevant or related to the subject area or **application of the concept**
- comparing and contrasting two points of view, articles, or theories
- considering the merits of the opposite point of view
- identifying **key concepts**, principles or ideas
- providing **evidence**, examples, and **supporting information** for your viewpoint
- preparing two or three essays on probable topics
- **writing an outline** and essay within the defined period of time you will have for the exam
- understanding the "marker's expectations"

📖 *KEY* TIPS FOR ANSWERING COMMON EXAM QUESTION FORMATS

Most exams use a variety of question formats to test your understanding. You must provide responses to questions ranging from lower level, information recall types to higher level, critical thinking types. The following information provides you with some suggestions on how to prepare for answering multiple choice, written response and essay questions.

MULTIPLE CHOICE

Multiple choice questions often require you to make fine distinctions between correct and nearly correct answers, so it is imperative that you:

- begin by answering only the questions for which you are certain of the correct answer
- read the question stem and formulate your own response before you read the choices available
- read the directions carefully paying close attention to words such as "mark *all* correct," "choose the *most* correct" and "choose the *one best* answer"
- use active reading techniques such as underlining, circling, or highlighting critical words and phrases
- watch for superlatives such as "all," "every," "none," "always" which indicate that the correct response must be an undisputed fact
- watch for negatives such as "none," "never," "neither," "not" which indicate that the correct response must be an undisputed fact
- examine all of the alternatives in questions which include "all of the above" or "none of the above" as responses to ensure that "all" or "none" of the statements apply *totally*
- be aware of distractors that may lead you to apply plausible but incorrect solutions, and 'three and one splits' where one answer is obviously incorrect and the others are very similar in meaning or wording
- use information from other questions to help you
- eliminate the responses you know are wrong and then assess the remaining alternatives and choose the best one
- guess if you are not certain

WRITTEN RESPONSE

Written response questions usually require a very specific answer. When answering these questions, you should:

- underline key words or phrases that indicate what is required in your answer such as "three reasons," "list," or "give an example"
- write down rough, point-form notes regarding the information you want to include in your answer
- be brief and only answer what is asked
- reread your response to ensure you have answered the question
- use the appropriate subject vocabulary and terminology in your response
- use point form to complete as many questions as possible if you are running out of time

ESSAY

Essay questions often give you the opportunity to demonstrate the breadth and depth of your learning regarding a given topic. When responding to these questions, it may be helpful to:

- read the question carefully and underline key words and phrases
- make a brief outline to organize the flow of the information and ideas you want to include in your response
- ensure you have an introduction, body, and conclusion
- begin with a clear statement of your view, position, or interpretation of the question
- address only one main point or key idea in each paragraph and include relevant supporting information and examples
- assume the reader has no prior knowledge of your topic
- conclude with a strong summary statement
- use appropriate subject vocabulary and terminology when and where it is applicable
- review your essay for clarity of thought, logic, grammar, punctuation, and spelling
- write as legibly as you can
- double space your work in case you need to edit it when you proof read your essay
- complete the essay in point form if you run short of time

📖 KEY TIPS FOR RESPONDING TO COMMON 'DIRECTING' WORDS

There are some commonly used words in exam questions that require you to respond in a predetermined or expected manner. The following provides you with a brief summary of how you may wish to plan your response to exam questions that contain these words.

♦ **EVALUATE** (to assess the worth of something)
  ‣ Determine the use, goal, or ideal from which you can judge something's worth
  ‣ Make a value judgment or judgments on something
  ‣ Make a list of reasons for the judgment
  ‣ Develop examples, evidence, contrasts, and details to support your judgments and clarify your reasoning

♦ **DISCUSS** (usually to give pros and cons regarding an assertion, quotation, or policy)
  ‣ Make a list of bases for comparing and contrasting
  ‣ Develop details and examples to support or clarify each pro and con
  ‣ On the basis of your lists, conclude your response by stating the extent to which you agree or disagree with what is asserted

♦ **COMPARE AND CONTRAST** (to give similarities and differences of two or more objects, beliefs, or positions)
  ‣ Make a list of bases for comparing and contrasting
  ‣ For each basis, judge similarities and differences
  ‣ Supply details, evidence, and examples that support and clarify your judgment
  ‣ Assess the overall similarity or difference
  ‣ Determine the significance of similarity or difference in connection with the purpose of the comparison

♦ **EXPLAIN** (to show causes of or reasons for something)
  ‣ In Science, usually show the process that occurs in moving from one state or phase in a process to the next, thoroughly presenting details of each step
  ‣ In Humanities and often in Social Sciences, make a list of factors that influence something, developing evidence for each factor's potential influence

- ◆ **ANALYZE** (to break into parts)
  - ▸ Break the topic, process, procedure, or object of the essay into its major parts
  - ▸ Connect and write about the parts according to the direction of the question: describe, explain, criticize

- ◆ **CRITICIZE** (to judge strong and weak points of something)
  - ▸ Make a list of the strong points and weak points
  - ▸ Develop details, examples, and contrasts to support judgments
  - ▸ Make an overall judgment of quality

- ◆ **DESCRIBE** (to give major features of something)
  - ▸ Pick out highlights or major aspects of something
  - ▸ Develop details and illustrations to give a clear picture

- ◆ **ARGUE** (to give reasons for one position and against another)
  - ▸ Make a list of reasons for the position
  - ▸ Make a list of reasons against the position
  - ▸ Refute objections to your reasons for and defend against objections to your reasons opposing the position
  - ▸ Fill out reasons, objections, and replies with details, examples, consequences, and logical connections

- ◆ **COMMENT** (to make statements about something)
  - ▸ Calls for a position, discussion, explanation, judgment, or evaluation regardir g a subject, idea, or situation
  - ▸ Is strengthened by providing supporting evidence, information, and examples

- ◆ **DEMONSTRATE** (to show something)
  - ▸ Depending upon the nature of the subject matter, provide evidence, clarify the logical basis of something, appeal to principles or laws as in an explanation, supply a range of opinion and examples

- ◆ **SYNTHESIZE** (to invent a new or different version)
  - ▸ Construct your own meaning based upon your knowledge and experiences
  - ▸ Support your assertion with examples, references to literature and research studies

(Source: http://www.counc.ivic.ca/learn/program/hndouts/simple.html)

📖 TEST ANXIETY

Do you get test anxiety? Most students feel some level of stress, worry, or anxiety before an exam. Feeling a little tension or anxiety before or during an exam is normal for most students. A little stress or tension may help you rise to the challenge but too much stress or anxiety interferes with your ability to do well on the exam. Test anxiety may cause you to experience some of the following in a mild or more severe form:

- "butterflies" in your stomach, sweating, shortness of breath, or a quickened pulse
- disturbed sleep or eating patterns
- increased nervousness, fear, or irritability
- sense of hopelessness or panic
- drawing a "blank" during the exam

If you experience extreme forms of test anxiety you need to consult your family physician. For milder forms of anxiety you may find some of the following strategies effective in helping you to remain calm and focused during your unit tests or year-end exams.

- Acknowledge that you are feeling some stress or test anxiety and that this is normal
- Focus upon your breathing, taking several deep breaths
- Concentrate upon a single object for a few moments
- Tense and relax the muscles in areas of your body where you feel tension
- Break your exam into smaller, manageable, achievable parts
- Use positive self-talk to calm and motivate yourself. Tell yourself, "I can do this if I read carefully/start with the easy questions/focus on what I know/stick with it/. . ." instead of saying, "I can't do this."
- Visualize your successful completion of your review or the exam
- Recall a time in the past when you felt calm, relaxed, and content. Replay this experience in your mind experiencing it as fully as possible.

KEY STRATEGIES FOR SUCCESS BEFORE AN EXAM – A CHECKLIST

Review, review, review. That's a huge part of your exam preparation. Here's a quick review checklist for you to see how many strategies for success you are using as you prepare to write your unit tests and year-end exams.

KEY Strategies for Success Before an Exam	Yes	No
Have you been attending classes?		
Have you determined your learning style?		
Have you organized a quiet study area for yourself?		
Have you developed a long-term study schedule?		
Have you developed a short-term study schedule?		
Are you working with a study buddy or study group?		
Is your study buddy/group positive, knowledgeable, motivated and supportive?		
Have you registered in tutorial classes?		
Have you developed your exam study notes?		
Have you reviewed previously administered exams?		
Have you practiced answering multiple choice, numerical response, written response, and essay questions?		
Have you analyzed the most common errors students make on each subject exam?		
Have you practiced strategies for controlling your exam anxiety?		
Have you maintained a healthy diet and sleep routine?		
Have you participated in regular physical activity?		

📖 *KEY* STRATEGIES FOR SUCCESS DURING AN EXAM

Doing well on any exam requires that you prepare in advance by reviewing your subject material and then using your knowledge to respond effectively to the exam questions during the test session. Combining subject knowledge with effective test writing skills gives you the best opportunity for success. The following are some strategies you may find useful in writing your exam.

- ◆ Managing Test Anxiety
  - ▸ Be as prepared as possible to increase your self-confidence.
  - ▸ Arrive at the exam on time and bring whatever materials you need to complete the exam such as pens, pencils, erasers, and calculators if they are allowed.
  - ▸ Drink enough water before you begin the exam so you are hydrated.
  - ▸ Associate with positive, calm individuals until you enter the exam room.
  - ▸ Use positive self-talk to calm yourself.
  - ▸ Remind yourself that it is normal to feel anxious about the exam.
  - ▸ Visualize your successful completion of the exam.
  - ▸ Breathe deeply several times.
  - ▸ Rotate your head, shrug your shoulders, and change positions to relax.

- ◆ While the information from your crib notes is still fresh in your memory, write down the key words, concepts, definitions, theories or formulas on the back of the test paper before you look at the exam questions.
  - ▸ Review the entire exam.
  - ▸ Budget your time.
  - ▸ Begin with the easiest question or the question that you know you can answer correctly rather than following the numerical question order of the exam.
  - ▸ Be aware of linked questions and use the clues to help you with other questions or in other parts of the exam.

If you "blank" on the exam, try repeating the deep breathing and physical relaxation activities first. Then move to visualization and positive self-talk to get you going. You can also try to open the 'information flow' by writing down anything that you remember about the subject on the reverse side of your exam paper. This activity sometimes helps you to remind yourself that you <u>do</u> know something and you are capable of writing the exam.

📖 GETTING STARTED

MANAGING YOUR TIME

- Plan on staying in the exam room for the full time that is available to you.

- Review the entire exam and calculate how much time you can spend on each section. Write your time schedule on the top of your paper and stick as closely as possible to the time you have allotted for each section of the exam.

- Be strategic and use your time where you will get the most marks. Avoid spending too much time on challenging questions that are not worth more marks than other questions that may be easier and are worth the same number of marks.

- If you are running short of time, switch to point form and write as much as you can for written response and essay questions so you have a chance of receiving partial marks.

- Leave time to review your paper asking yourself, "Did I do all of the questions I was supposed to do?", "Can I answer any questions now that I skipped over before?", "Are there any questions that I misinterpreted or misread?"

USING THE FIVE PASS METHOD

- **BROWSING STAGE** – Scan the entire exam noting the format, the specific instructions and marks allotted for each section, which questions you will complete and which ones you will omit if there is a choice.

- **THE FIRST ANSWERING PASS** – To gain confidence and momentum, answer only the questions you are confident you can answer correctly and quickly. These questions are most often found in the multiple choice or numerical response sections of the exam. Maintain a brisk pace; if a question is taking too long to answer, leave it for the Second or Third Pass.

- **THE SECOND ANSWERING PASS** – This Pass addresses questions which require more effort per mark. Answer as many of the remaining questions as possible while maintaining steady progress toward a solution. As soon as it becomes evident the question is too difficult or is tasking an inordinate amount of time, leave it for the Third Answering Pass.

- **THE THIRD ANSWERING PASS** – During the Third Answering Pass, you should complete all partial solutions from the first two Passes. Marks are produced at a slower rate during this stage. At the end of this stage, all questions should have full or partial answers. Guess at any multiple choice questions that you have not yet answered.

- **THE FINAL REVIEW STAGE** – Use the remaining time to review the entire exam, making sure that no questions have been overlooked. Check answers and calculations as time permits.

USING THE THREE PASS METHOD

- **OVERVIEW** – Begin with an overview of the exam to see what it contains. Look for 'easy' questions and questions on topics that you know thoroughly.

- **SECOND PASS** – Answer all the questions that you can complete without too much trouble. These questions help to build your confidence and establish a positive start.

- **LAST PASS** – Now go through and answer the questions that are left. This is when you begin to try solving the questions you find particularly challenging.

📖 *KEY* EXAM TIPS FOR SELECTED SUBJECT AREAS

The following are a few additional suggestions you may wish to consider when writing exams in any of the selected subject areas.

ENGLISH LANGUAGE ARTS

Exams in English Language Arts usually have two components, writing and reading. Sometimes students are allowed to bring approved reference books such as a dictionary, thesaurus, and writing handbook into the exam. If you have not used these references on a regular basis, you may find them more of a hindrance than a help in an exam situation. When completing the written section of an English Language Arts exam:

- plan your essay
- focus on the issue presented
- establish a clear position using a thesis statement to direct and unify your writing
- organize your writing in a manner that logically presents your views
- support your viewpoint with specific examples
- edit and proof read your writing

When completing the reading section of an English Language Arts exam:

- read the entire selection before responding
- use titles, dates, footnotes, pictures, introductions, and notes on the author to assist you in developing an understanding of the piece presented
- when using line references, read a few lines before and after the identified section

MATHEMATICS

In some instances, the use of calculators is permitted (or required) to complete complex calculations, modeling, simulations, or to demonstrate your use of technology. It is imperative that you are familiar with the approved calculator and the modes you may be using during your exam. When writing exams in mathematics:

- use appropriate mathematical notation and symbols
- clearly show or explain all the steps involved in solving the problem
- check to be sure you have included the correct units of measurement and have rounded to the appropriate significant digit
- use appropriate labelling and equal increments on graphs

SCIENCES

In the Sciences written response and open-ended questions usually require a clear, organized, and detailed explanation of the science involved in the question. You may find it helpful to use the acronym **STEEPLES** to organize your response to these types of questions. STEEPLES stands for **S**cience, **T**echnological, **E**cological, **E**thical, **P**olitical, **L**egal, **E**conomical, and **S**ocial aspects of the issue presented. When writing exams in the sciences:

- use scientific vocabulary to clearly explain your understanding of the processes or issues
- state your position in an objective manner
- demonstrate your understanding of both sides of the issue
- clearly label graphs, diagrams, tables, and charts using accepted conventions
- provide all formulas and equations

SOCIAL STUDIES, HISTORY, GEOGRAPHY

Exams in these courses of study often require you to take a position on an issue and defend your point of view. Your response should demonstrate your understanding of both the positive and negative aspects of the issue and be supported by well-considered arguments and evidence. When writing exams in Social Studies, History or Geography, the following acronyms may be helpful to you in organizing your approach.

- **SEE** – stands for **S**tatement, **E**xplanation, **E**xample. This acronym reminds you to couple your statement regarding your position with an explanation and then an example.

- **PERMS** – stands for **P**olitical, **E**conomic, **R**eligious or moral, **M**ilitary, and **S**ocietal values. Your position statement may be derived from or based upon any of these points of view. Your argument is more credible if you can show that recognized authorities such as leaders, theorists, writers or scientists back your position.

📖 SUMMARY

Writing exams involves a certain amount of stress and anxiety. If you want to do your best on the exam, *there is no substitute for being well prepared.* Being well prepared helps you to feel more confident about your ability to succeed and less anxious about writing tests.

When preparing for unit or year-end exams, remember to:

- use as many senses as possible in preparing for exams
- start as early as possible set realistic goals and targets
- take advantage of study buddies, study groups, and tutorials
- review previously used exams
- study with positive, knowledgeable, motivated, and supportive individuals
- practice the material in the format in which you are to be tested
- try to simulate the test situation as much as possible
- keep a positive attitude
- end your study time with a quick review and then do something different before you try to go to sleep on the night before the exam
- drink a sufficient amount of water prior to an exam
- stay in the exam room for the full amount of time available
- try to relax by focusing on your breathing

If you combine your best study habits with some of the strategies presented here, you may increase your chances of writing a strong exam and maximizing your potential to do well.

PRACTICE EXAMINATIONS

A GUIDE TO PREPARING FOR AN EXAMINATION

The questions presented here are distinct from those in the Unit Review section. **THE KEY** contains detailed answers that illustrate the problem-solving process for every question in this section.

Students are encouraged to write this practice exam under conditions similar to those they will encounter when writing their final exam. This will make students:

- *aware of the mental and physical stamina required to sit through an entire exam*
- *familiar with the exam format and how the course content is tested*
- *aware of any units or concepts that are troublesome or require additional study*
- *more successful in managing their review effectively*

To simulate the exam conditions, students should:

- *use an alarm clock or other timer to monitor the time allowed for the exam*
- *select a quiet writing spot away from all distractions*
- *assemble the appropriate materials that are allowed for writing the exam such as pens, HB pencils, calculator, dictionary*
- *use "test wiseness" skills*
- *complete as much of the exam as possible within the allowable time*

When writing the practice exam, students should:

- *read instructions, directions, and questions carefully*
- *organize writing time according to the exam emphasis on each section*
- *highlight key words*
- *think about what is being asked*
- *plan their writing; once complete, proof for errors in content, spelling, grammar*
- *watch for bolded words such as most, least, best*
- *in Multiple Choice questions, cross out any choices students know are incorrect*
- *if possible, review all responses upon completion of the exam*

NOTES

PRACTICE EXAMINATION 1

Use the following information to answer the next three questions.

Almost all refrigeration and air conditioning devices contain CFCs. The ozone depleting effects of chlorofluorocarbons (CFCs) are well known. In the search for "ozone friendly" alternatives to CFCs, the most promising candidates include hydro-fluorocarbons, HFCs. The compound 1, 1, 1, 2-tetrafluoroethane, CH_2FCF_3, is one alternative currently being used in home refrigeration and automobile air conditioning units.

1. If dissolved in water, CH_2FCF_3 would

  A. conduct electricity

  B. dissociate into ions

  C. behave as a non-electrolyte

  D. behave as an electrolyte

2. The intramolecular bonding in CH_2FCF_3 results from

  A. a simultaneous attraction of neutrons by the atomic nuclei

  B. an exchange of alpha particles between atoms

  C. a mutual attraction of protons by electrons

  D. a mutual attraction of electrons by atomic nuclei

Use this additional information to answer the next question.

Earth's atmosphere consists of nitrogen (78.08%), oxygen (20.95%), argon (0.93%), water vapour (1%) and various trace gases (0.04%). Anthropogenic (man-made) emissions have significantly affected the concentration or composition of these trace gases. Arguably, the most notorious of these trace gases are the CFCs, which now account for some 3 ppb (parts per billion by volume) of the atmosphere.

3. Measuring the CFC concentration in the atmosphere is a

  A. diagnostic test

  B. qualitative analysis

  C. logical test

  D. quantitative analysis

Use the following information to answer the next question.

Phosgene, $COCl_{2(g)}$, is a toxic, volatile liquid that smells like hay. It is primarily used in the manufacture of urethane foams, plastics, and coatings, but has also been used as a military chemical weapon. Air containing 0.500 mg of phosgene gas per litre can be fatal.

Numerical Response

1. The molar concentration in air containing this lethal dose of phosgene is_____ $\times 10^{-6}$ mol/L

(Record your answer to three digits.)

Use the following information to answer the next question.

Modern photography uses silver bromide to form images on paper. Silver bromide is slightly soluble in water and when saturated the solution is described by the equation

$$AgBr_{(s)} \rightleftharpoons Ag^+_{(aq)} + Br^-_{(aq)}$$

4. In this equilibrium equation, the rate of dissolution is

   A. equal to the rate of crystallization

   B. greater than the rate of crystallization

   C. less than the rate of crystallization

   D. independent of the rate of crystallization

Use the following information to answer the next two questions.

Kimchi is a popular Korean appetizer made by fermenting a combination of radishes, turnips, onions, and Chinese cabbages.

Numerical Response

2. If the salt in kimchi has a 3.00% concentration by mass, the mass of salt contained in a 500 g portion of kimchi is _____ g.
(Record your answer to three digits.)

Numerical Response

3. The salt concentration of a 48.0 mL sample of kimchi juice is 0.400 mol/L.
If this sample is diluted to a new final volume of 100 mL, then the molar concentration of the salt in the kimchi juice would be _____ mol/L.
(Record your answer to three significant digits.)

Use the following information to answer the next question.

Svante Arrhenius' doctoral thesis centred on the electrical conductivity of liquid solutions. Arrhenius theorized that only those solutions that contained solvated ions were electrically conductive. Moreover, the solvated ions were produced by ionic dissociation, a process influenced greatly by the nature of the solvent and the solute being mixed.

5. According to Arrhenian theory, aqueous solutions of

   A. weak acids conduct electricity well

   B. strong acids conduct electricity poorly

   C. strong acids conduct electricity well

   D. weak acids conduct electricity poorly

6. Coffee, bananas, spinach, and squash all have a hydrogen ion concentration of about 10^{-5} mol/L. This hydrogen ion concentration corresponds to a pH of

   A. 4

   B. 3

   C. –5

   D. 5

Use the following information to answer the next two questions.

Whitening and de-acidifying old papers can be done with sodium borohydride.
This can be useful in preserving valuable historical documents.

7. If the pH values before and after sodium borohydride bleaching are 5 and 8, respectively, then the corresponding hydrogen ion concentrations before and after de-acidifying are, respectively,

   A. 10^{-5} and 10^{-8} mol/L

   B. 10^{-8} and 10^{-11} mol/L

   C. 10^{5} and 10^{8} mol/L

   D. -10^{5} and -10^{8} mol/L

8. The change in the hydrogen ion concentration after addition of sodium borohydride corresponds to a

   A. 100 fold decrease

   B. 100 fold increase

   C. 1 000 fold decrease

   D. 1 000 fold increase

Use the following information to answer the next question.

The ideal gas law equation is $PV = nRT$.
It can be rearranged to show that pressure and volume are inversely proportional for a fixed amount of gas at a constant temperature. i.e.

$$V = \frac{nRT}{P} \text{ or } V\ \alpha\ \frac{1}{P}$$

9. The law that summarizes the relationship between the volume and pressure of a fixed quantity of gas at constant temperature is

   A. Boyle's Law

   B. Charles' Law

   C. Avogadro's Law

   D. Henry's Law

Use the following information to answer the next question.

Gas exchange in the lungs occurs across the membranes of tiny sacs called alveoli.
Upon inhalation, the alveoli fill with air, of which approximately 20% is oxygen.
(Assume that the air behaves as an ideal gas at body temperature, 37°C; absolute pressure of alveolus = 100 kPa;
Avogadro's number = 6.022×10^{23} particles/mol.)

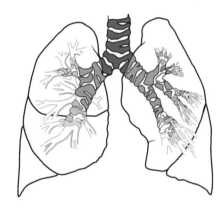

10. If the volume of an alveolus is approximately 8.00×10^{-6} mL, what number of oxygen molecules occupy one alveolus?

   A. 2.67×10^{14} **B.** 2.24×10^{15}

   C. 4.44×10^{-10} **D.** 3.74×10^{13}

Use the following information to answer the next question.

The demand valve on a diver's mouthpiece continually adjusts the pressure of the air released into the diver's mouth. At 10 m underwater, air will only cross the demand valve if the air pressure in the lungs is roughly twice the air pressure on the surface.

11. At this pressure, the alveoli in a diver's lungs will contain

   A. twice the amount of oxygen as they would at the surface

   B. the same amount of oxygen as they would at the surface

   C. one-half the amount of oxygen as they would at the surface

   D. one-quarter the amount of oxygen as they would at the surface

Use the following information to answer the next question.

Normal blood pressure in a young adult is about 120 mm Hg when the ventricles of the heart are contracting (systolic blood pressure) and 80 mm Hg when the ventricles are relaxed (diastolic pressure). This is normally reported as 120/80.

12. In kPa, this blood pressure would be stated as

   A. 16.0/10.7

   B. 91.3/53.2

   C. 158/92.1

   D. 900/525

13. A balanced equation for the reaction of Milk of Magnesia (magnesium hydroxide) with excess stomach acid (hydrochloric acid) is

   A.
   $$HCl_{(aq)} + Mg(OH)_{2(s)} \rightarrow HOH_{(l)} + MgCl_{2(aq)}$$

   B.
   $$HCl_{(aq)} + Mg(OH)_{2(s)} \rightarrow H_2O_{(l)} + MgCl_{(l)}$$

   C.
   $$2HCl_{(aq)} + Mg(OH)_{2(s)} \rightarrow 2HOH_{(l)} + MgCl_{2(aq)}$$

   D.
   $$2HCl_{(aq)} + 2Mg(OH)_{2(s)} \rightarrow HOH_{(l)} + 2MgCl_{(aq)}$$

Numerical Response

4. The volume of 0.110 mol/L HCl that would be neutralized by 0.236 g of magnesium hydroxide in a dose of Milk of Magnesia is _____ mL.
(Record your answer to three digits.)

Use the following information to answer the next two questions.

Potassium chromate and lead acetate can be combined to form lead chromate as shown by the following reaction.

$K_2CrO_{4(aq)} + Pb(CH_3COO)_{2(aq)}$
$\rightarrow PbCrO_{4(s)} + 2KCH_3COO_{(aq)}$

Because of its resistance to mechanical wear, light, and heat, lead chromate (or chrome yellow), is the pigment used for the yellow lane markers on highways.
Lead, however, is toxic and oxidized chromium is carcinogenic, so alternative pigments are preferable.

Numerical Response

5. If 200 kg of lead (II) chromate are produced from the reaction of 1 000 L of $K_2CrO_{4(aq)}$ and excess lead (II) acetate, the concentration of potassium chromate is
_____ $\times 10^{-b}$ mol/L.
Therefore, *b* is an integer.
(Record your answer to three significant digits.)

14. The spectator ions in the reaction of potassium chromate and lead (II) acetate in aqueous solution are

A. Pb^{2+} and K^+

B. Pb^{2+} and CH_3COO^-

C. K^+ and CrO_4^{2-}

D. K^+ and CH_3COO^-

Use the following information to answer the next three questions.

Methanol is used as a fuel in race cars and has the potential to replace gasoline in regular automobiles. Methanol can be manufactured from carbon monoxide and hydrogen as shown.
$$2H_{2(g)} + CO_{(g)} \rightarrow CH_3OH_{(l)}$$

15. If 70.0 kg of $CO_{(g)}$ are combined with 9.00 kg of $H_{2(g)}$ the limiting reagent is

A. $CO_{(g)}$ and $H_{2(g)}$

B. $CH_3OH_{(l)}$

C. $CO_{(g)}$

D. $H_{2(g)}$

Numerical Response

6. The mass of methanol predicted to form from the reactant amounts in the previous question is _____ kg.
(Record your answer to three digits.)

Use the following information to answer the next four questions.

Acetylene is commercially used for welding and cutting steel and other materials because it burns with a very hot flame. Prior to 1955, the sole means of producing acetylene ($C_2H_{2(g)}$) was from the following reaction.
$$CaC_{2(s)} + 2H_2O_{(l)} \rightarrow C_2H_{2(g)} + Ca(OH)_{2(s)}$$

Numerical Response

7. If 4.30 kg of calcium carbide are used, the mass of acetylene expected is _____ kg.
(Record your answer to three digits.)

Numerical Response

8. The mass of $Ca(OH)_2$ that forms in the same reaction is _____ kg.
(Record your answer to three digits.)

Numerical Response

9. The solubility of the calcium hydroxide (lime water) produced is 0.185 g/100 mL at 0°C. Expressed as a molar solubility, this concentration is _____ mmol/L. (Record your answer to three digits.)

Use this additional information to answer the next question.

The unbalanced equation for complete combustion of acetylene is

$$\_C_2H_{2(g)} + \_O_{2(g)} \rightarrow \_CO_{2(g)} + \_H_2O_{(g)}$$

Numerical Response

10. The four digit number created by reading the coefficients from left to right in the balanced equation is ____ ____ ____ ____. (Record your answer as a four digit number.)

Use the following information to answer the next two questions.

The U.S. space shuttles use a fuel that consists mainly of ammonium perchlorate (aluminum powder and an organic polymer are also used).  This ammonium perchlorate-based propellant is also used for sidewinder air to air missiles and Tomahawk cruise missiles. The effectiveness of ammonium perchlorate as a propellant is due to its rapid rate of decomposition. The partial simple decomposition reaction is shown below.

$$NH_4ClO_{4(s)} \rightarrow H_2O_{(g)} + ???$$

16. The additional products in the balanced chemical equation are

A. $2O_{2(g)}$, $Cl_{(g)}$, $N_{(g)}$

B. $3O_{(g)}$, $Cl_{(g)}$, $N_{(g)}$

C. $O_{2(g)}$, $Cl_{2(g)}$, and $N_{2(g)}$

D. $2O_{2(g)}$, $Cl_{2(g)}$, and $N_{2(g)}$

Use this additional information to answer the next question.

Aluminum powder improves the propellants' efficiency by engaging in formation reactions with the oxygen and chlorine produced by the decomposition of $NH_4ClO_{4(s)}$. This formation reaction releases vast quantities of heat energy.

17. The product of these reactions involving $Al_{(s)}$ are

A. $AlO_{(s)}$ and $AlCl_{(s)}$

B. $Al_2O_{2(s)}$ and $Al_2Cl_{4(g)}$

C. $Al_2O_{3(s)}$ and $AlCl_{3(g)}$

D. $AlO_{2(s)}$ and $AlCl_{3(g)}$

Use the following information to answer the next three questions.

Acuras have been designed to reduce the amount of nitric oxide emitted by their engines. In automobile engines, nitric oxide is the product of the reaction of nitrogen and oxygen at high temperature.

$$N_{2(g)} + O_{2(g)} \rightarrow 2NO_{(g)}$$

18. Nitrogen monoxide formation requires heat because it is

A. an exothermic process

B. an endothermic process

C. a spontaneous process

D. a heat losing process

Although $NO_{(g)}$ is involved in the production of photochemical smog leading to the depletion of the ozone layer, it is also extremely useful in the production of nitric acid, fertilizers, and explosives. It is also a key compound in certain biology processes.

19. The type of bonding prevalent within molecules of $NO_{(g)}$ is

   A. ionic

   B. hydrogen bonding

   C. covalent

   D. electronegative

Use this additional information to answer the next question.

Nitrous oxide, also known as laughing gas, is also a by-product of nitrogen assimilation in bacteria and algae. Similar to $NO_{(g)}$, $N_2O_{(g)}$ is also a greenhouse gas that can damage the stratospheric ozone layer.

20. The types of bonding interactions that an individual N_2O molecule, are likely experience

   A. London dispersion forces and dipole-dipole attractions

   B. hydrogen bonds and dispersion forces

   C. ionic bonds and dipole-dipole attractions

   D. network covalent bonds and dispersion forces

Use the following information to answer the next question.

Guncotton is a smokeless powder that was invented in 1845 as a cheap substitute for gunpowder. Guncotton, like nitro-glycerine and other explosive chemicals, contains nitro groups (NO_2) bound to carbon.

21. Based on the electronegativities of N and O, the bonded atom(s) with a slight positive charge would be

   A. O

   B. neither N nor O

   C. both N and O

   D. N

Use the following information to answer the next question.

Explosions such as the one that rocked Guadalajara, Mexico in 1992 can happen when natural gas and hydrocarbon vapours mix with air in city's sewer system.

22. This is a dramatic example of a situation in which

   A. the energy required to break bonds in the reactants was **greater** than the energy released in forming new bonds in the products

   B. the energy required to break bonds in the reactants was **less** than the energy released in forming new bonds in the products

   C. an endothermic reaction occurred rapidly

   D. the energies of bond breaking and bond formation were equal

23. The boiling point of diethyl ether is 34.6°C, while that of 1-butanol is 117°C.
Which of the following statements correctly explains the difference in boiling points?

   A. 1-butanol has a higher molar mass than diethyl ether, therefore, it experiences stronger London dispersion forces.

   B. 1-butanol is polar while diethylether is not, therefore, stronger dipole-dipole forces elevate 1-butanol's boiling point.

   C. Both compounds are polar and have the same molar mass but hydrogen bonding between 1-butanol molecules elevate that compound's boiling point.

   D. Diethyl ether molecules as well as 1-butanol molecules hydrogen-bond in the liquid state but 1-butanol hydrogen-bonds more effectively.

Use the following information to answer the next question.

Sodium chloride is needed to maintain essential body functions. Abnormally low levels of sodium and chloride ions may result in muscular weakness, spasms, dizziness, headaches and even comas. In the laboratory, $NaCl_{(s)}$ can be formed from the direct action of $Cl_{2(s)}$ on $Na_{(s)}$ as shown below.

$$2Na_{(s)} + Cl_{2(g)} \rightarrow 2NaCl_{(s)}$$

24. The bonding between Na and Cl in $NaCl_{(s)}$ is a result of

   A. a transfer of electrons from Cl to Na

   B. equal sharing of valence electrons

   C. reduction of the non-metal and oxidation of the metal

   D. reduction of the metal and oxidation of the non-metal

Use the following information to answer the next two questions.

The hypervalent molecule CLi_6 was observed for the first time in the gas phase in 1992. This observation was significant because of the unusual bonding within the molecule.

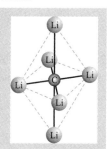

25. According to Lewis bonding theory, how many electrons does carbon appear to have surrounding it?

   A. 6   B. 8

   C. 10   D. 12

26. The number of electrons surrounding the carbon atom

    A. shows that CLi_6 is very unstable

    B. appears to violate the octet rule

    C. conforms to the octet rule

    D. shows that Lithium has no valence electrons

Use the following information to answer the next three questions.

The entertainment that sparklers provide is due to oxidation or reduction reactions. Redox reactions provide the eruptive force necessary to cast metal fragments into the air. These small fragments of metal then react with oxygen to create sparks. One such reaction might be
$$2Mg_{(s)} + O_{2(g)} \rightarrow 2MgO_{(s)}$$

27. In the above reaction, the reduced element is

    A. $Mg_{(s)}$

    B. $O_{2(g)}$

    C. $MgO_{(s)}$

    D. neither $Mg_{(s)}$ nor $O_{2(g)}$

28. The element that is the source of the electrons in the sparkler reaction is

    A. $Mg_{(s)}$

    B. $O_{2(g)}$

    C. both $Mg_{(s)}$ and $O_{2(g)}$

    D. neither $Mg_{(s)}$ nor $O_{2(g)}$

29. The oxidation half-reaction occurring in sparklers is

    A. $Mg_{(s)} \rightarrow Mg^+ + e^-$

    B. $Mg_{(s)} \rightarrow Mg^{2+} + 2e^-$

    C. $O_{2(g)} \rightarrow 2O^+ + 2e^-$

    D. $O_{2(g)} \rightarrow 2O^{2+} + 4e^-$

Use the following information to answer the next question.

Juglone ($C_{10}H_6O_3$) is a compound produced from the husks of black walnuts. It acts as a natural herbicide that destroys competitive plants growing around it. Juglone also has a long history of use as a dye.

30. Juglone would be considered an

    A. inorganic compound with covalent bonds

    B. organic compound with ionic bonds

    C. inorganic compound with ionic bonds

    D. organic compound with covalent bonds

Written Response

1. Provide a laboratory procedure that would allow you to precipitate all the Pb^{2+} from 500 mL of a contaminated waste solution that also contains $Ag^+_{(aq)}$ ions.
Your procedure must allow you to obtain information useful for calculating the $Pb^{2+}_{(aq)}$ ion concentration.
(For full credit you must correctly specify the chemicals and materials used.)

    (8 marks)

NOTES

PRACTICE EXAMINATION 2

Use the following information to answer the next question.

Alka-Seltzer® sold in tablet form is a complex mix of sodium bicarbonate, citric acid, and acetylsalicylic acid (Aspirin).
The tablets, which have a long shelf life in sealed foil packets, dissolve in water within minutes with a characteristic fizz.

1. Due to the $CO_{2(g)}$ that is released as the acids neutralize the bicarbonate ions, it is clear that

   A. the acids react more rapidly with bicarbonate ions in aqueous solution than in solid phase

   B. the acids react less rapidly with bicarbonate ions in aqueous solutions than in solid phase

   C. the reaction of the acids with bicarbonate ions is rapid in the solid phase and, therefore, requires a sealed foil package

   D. the reaction of the acids with bicarbonate ions is rapid in the solid phase leading to the long shelf life of Alka-Seltzer

Use the following information to answer the next question.

Sulfuric acid, $H_2SO_{4(aq)}$ has been the most utilized chemical for most of the twentieth century. This is understandable given that sulphuric acid is used to manufacture fertilizers, plastics, pharmaceuticals, metals, paints, and numerous other commodities. The use of sulfuric acid is so extensive that economists use the tonnage consumed by a country as a measure of its economic health.

2. Sulfuric acid is

   A. a good conductor of electricity

   B. a poor conductor of electricity

   C. a non-electrolyte

   D. a weak electrolyte

Use the following information to answer the next question.

Acetic acid can be found in many foods and drinks including wine and vinegar. It is present as 5% aqueous solution in vinegar and is responsible for the sour taste of spoiled wine.

3. If a suitable electric current were applied to an acetic acid solution, then the acetic acid would

   A. conduct the electric current efficiently

   B. not conduct the electric current

   C. not conduct the electric current as well as distilled water

   D. conduct the electric current inefficiently but better than distilled water

Use the following information to answer the next question.

Margarine is manufactured by hydrogenating a hot mixture of fats and oils. The various varieties of margarine differ largely in the amount of air and moisture they contain. The following observations were recorded in the analysis of two margarine varieties that separate into distinct oil and water layers upon heating.

Analysis of two 14.0 g of margarine samples.

Margarine	Mass of $H_2O_{(g)}$	Mass of Oil
Regular	3.0 g	11.0 g
Light	6.0 g	8.0 g

Numerical Response

1. The percentage difference in water content, as measured by mass, between the two varieties is _____%.
(Record your answer to three digits.)

Use the following information to answer the next question.

Phospholipids are the special fatty acid esters that constitute most cell membranes. One of the most abundant fatty acid residues in mammalian cells is derived from palmitic acid $(CH_3(CH_2)_{14}COOH)$.

4. The approximate mass percentage of each element in palmitic acid as measured by mass is

A. 77% C, 6% H, and 7% O

B. 75% C, 13% H, and 12% O

C. 79% C, 8% H, and 13% O

D. 75% C, 12% H, and 13% O

Use the following information to answer the next two questions.

A 235 mL (8 fluid oz.) cup of Lipton's tea contains 40.0 mg of caffeine, almost 60% less than the same volume of coffee.

Numerical Response

2. The concentration of caffeine in tea expressed as a percentage weight per volume is _____
(Record your answer to four digits.)

Numerical Response

3. If the tea contains 40 mg of caffeine (molar mass 194.19 g/mol) per 8 fluid ounce (235 mL) serving, the molar concentration of caffeine in tea, expressed in scientific notation, is
$a . b \times 10^{-c}$ mol/L.
The value for a, b, and c are respectively, ____, ____, and ____.
(a, b, and c are integers.)

Use the following diagram to answer the next question.

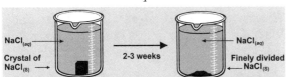

After a few weeks, large salt crystals immersed in a saturated salt solution tend to "break up" into many smaller "powdery" crystals.

5. The best explanation for the above observation is that

   A. solid salt particles from the crystal are continually dissolving, while at the same rate, dissolved salt in the saturated solution is continually precipitating

   B. some of the salt in the crystal dissolves and this makes the salt crystal structurally weak – so weak that it breaks apart

   C. the constant bombardment of the crystal by water molecules and ions in the saturated solution causes it to break down easily

   D. the pressure of water above the salt crystals forces the Na^+ and Cl^- ions apart and causes the crystal to break up

6. Which of the following is the best method of preparing 100 mL of a 0.100 mol/L $Na_2CO_{3(aq)}$ solution?

   A. Obtain 10.6 g of $Na_2CO_{3(s)}$ in a 50 mL beaker. Dissolve it in 40 mL of distilled water. Transfer this to a 100 mL Erlenmeyer flask with the washings of all the apparatus before topping off the solution volume to the 100 mL mark. Lastly, swirl the solution in the flask to ensure thorough mixing.

   B. Obtain 1.06 g of $Na_2CO_{3(s)}$ in a 50 mL beaker. Dissolve it in a 40 mL volumetric flask with the washings of all the apparatus. Top off the solution volume with distilled water to the 100 mL calibration mark. Invert the stoppered flask several times to mix the contents thoroughly.

   C. Obtain 1.06 g of $Na_2CO_{3(s)}$ in a 100 mL graduated cylinder and add sufficient distilled water to make a 100 mL aqueous solution.

   D. Pipette 10.6 g of $Na_2CO_{3(s)}$ into a 100 mL volumetric flask and add sufficient distilled water to make a 100 mL solution. Invert the stoppered flask and solution several times to mix the solution thoroughly.

7. A 2.0 mol/L solution of sulphuric acid is best described as a

   A. concentrated strong acid

   B. dilute strong acid

   C. dilute weak acid

   D. concentrated weak acid

Use the following information to answer the next question.

An ulcer occurs when the mucous cell membrane lining the stomach's inner wall develops a lesion.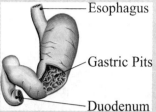

Esophagus

Gastric Pits

Duodenum

The highly acidic gastric juices can cause an acid burn to the exposed soft tissue of the stomach wall, otherwise known as an ulcer. This is not surprising given that the stomach's pH can approach 1.00, which is strong enough to dissolve zinc.

Numerical Response

4. The $H^+_{(aq)}$ ion concentration of gastric juice at a pH of 1.00 would be
_____ mol/L.
(Record your answer to two significant digits.)

Use the following information to answer the next question.

Uric acid, the white component of bird droppings (actually urine), was the first purine to be discovered.

8. In an aqueous solution of uric acid, there will likely be

A. more dissociated than undissociated molecules

B. less dissociated than undissociated molecules

C. equal numbers of dissociated and undissociated molecules

D. equal concentrations of $(H^+_{(aq)})$ and uric acid molecules

Use the following information to answer the next question.

Household bleach, if mixed with sufficient acid to reduce its pH below 8, will release chlorine gas. This is a significant household hazard.

9. A pH of 8 corresponds to a

A. hydrogen ion concentration of 10^8 mol/L

B. hydrogen ion concentration of 10^{-8} mol/L

C. hydroxide ion concentration of 10^8 mol/L

D. hydroxide ion concentration of 10^{-8} mol/L

Numerical Response

5. The pH of a 1.0 mol/L solution of $HCl_{(aq)}$ is
_____.
(Record your answer to two significant digits.)

Use the following information to answer the next two questions.

Buckminsterfullerene, $C_{60(s)}$ is a newly discovered form of the element carbon comprised of carbon atoms in an arrangement identical to the corners of each panel on a World Cup soccer ball. It is possible to fill the cavity of a $C_{60(s)}$ molecule with $He_{(g)}$ or $Ne_{(g)}$ (one atom) at 600°C and at a pressure of 3.00 atmospheres. These are, arguably, the first compounds containing helium and neon.

10. 3.00 atmospheres, stated in units of mm of Hg and kPa, respectively, are

A. 253 mm of Hg and 33.8 kPa

B. 760 mm of Hg and 101 kPa

C. 2.28×10^3 mm of Hg and 304 kPa

D. 304 mm of Hg and 2.28×103 kPa

Numerical Response

6. Expressed as an absolute temperature, 600°C is _____ K
(Record your answer to three digits.)

Use the following information to answer the next question.

Although still controversial, the hyperbaric chamber, used by more and more hockey teams to treat their injured players, seems to speed up the healing process. The reason for quicker healing of injuries may have to do with the extra supply of oxygen to injured cells.

11. Taking into account that standard pressure is about 100 kPa, what would happen to the volume of oxygen available to cells if the chamber pressure was 120 kPa?

A. The oxygen level in the cells would decrease by about 20% because the same amount of oxygen would take up 20% more space.

B. The oxygen level in the cells would increase by about 20% because the same amount of oxygen would take up 20% more space.

C. The oxygen level in the cells would decrease by about 20% because the same amount of oxygen would take up 20% less space.

D. The oxygen level in the cells would increase by about 20% because the same amount of oxygen would take up 20% less space.

Use the following information to answer the next question.

Visiting hockey teams have to cope with the lack of oxygen when playing the Colorado Avalanche at home. This is because atmospheric pressure is much lower in Denver, which is at a higher altitude. One way coaches deal with the lack of oxygen in Denver is to shorten players' shifts.

Numerical Response

7. The volume occupied by 1.00 mol of oxygen in Denver (average pressure 90.0 kPa at a temperature of 25°C) is _____ L.
(Record your answer to three digits.)

Use the following information to answer the next question.

The gas that fills the airbags in most modern cars during a crash comes from the simple decomposition of sodium azide.

$$2NaN_{3(s)} \rightarrow 2Na_{(s)} + 3N_{2(g)}$$

Specifications dictate that 80 L of gas must inflate the bag at temperatures as low as −60°C at a pressure of 1.0 atm.

Numerical Response

8. The mass of sodium azide that must decompose to provide this volume of gas is _____ kg.
(Record your answer to three digits.)

Numerical Response

9. If the temperature inside a 16 L freezer is –20°C and if the pressure is 1.00 atm, then the amount of oxygen in the freezer is _____ mol/L.
(Record your answer to three digits.)

Use this additional information to answer the next question.

Citric acid is completely neutralized by aqueous sodium hydroxide as follows.

Numerical Response

10. If 24.2 mL of 0.100 mol/L NaOH$_{(aq)}$ are required to completely neutralize a 25.0 mL aqueous solution of citric acid, then the acid concentration is _____ mmol/L.
(Record your answer to three digits.)

Use the following information to answer the next question.

Acid rain affects lakes, rivers, and soil as well as the wildlife that live in these environments. The acidity of rain develops primarily from reactions of SO$_2$ and NO$_2$ in the atmosphere. A titration was performed to measure the concentration of acid in rainwater using KOH$_{(aq)}$. (Assume H$_2$SO$_{4(aq)}$ is the acid present in the rainwater sample.)

12. The reaction of KOH$_{(aq)}$ with H$_2$SO$_{4(aq)}$ is

A. KOH$_{(aq)}$ + H$_2$SO$_{4(aq)}$
$$\rightarrow KSO_{4(aq)} + H_2O_{(l)}$$

B. 2KOH$_{(aq)}$ + H$_2$SO$_{4(aq)}$
$$\rightarrow K_2SO_{4(aq)} + 2H_2O_{(l)}$$

C. KOH$_{(aq)}$ + H$_2$SO$_{4(aq)}$
$$\rightarrow H_2S_{(aq)} + KO_{5(aq)}$$

D. 2KOH$_{(aq)}$ + H$_2$SO$_{4(aq)}$
$$\rightarrow K_2S_{(aq)} + 2H_2O_{(l)} + 2O_{2(g)}$$

Numerical Response

11. 2.45 g of calcium carbonate precipitates from 1.00 L of a hard water solution when it is treated with excess sodium carbonate. The Ca^{2+} ion concentration of the hard water is _____ mmol/L.
(Record your answer to three digits.)

Use the following information to answer the next question.

Diabetes mellitus is a group of disorders that all lead to the elevation of glucose in the blood. It is usually characterized by excess glucose excretion in the urine. Urinalysis is often performed on those suspected of having diabetes mellitus. Colorimetric strip tests are used to assay urinary glucose. Like litmus, in some ways, the glucose test strips become a specific colour if abnormal amounts of glucoseare present.

13. The colorimetric strip tests are used to analyze the urine sample

    A. gravimetrically

    B. quantitatively

    C. physically

    D. qualitatively

Use the following information to answer the next question.

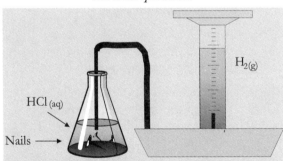

Sufficient 6 mol/L $HCl_{(aq)}$ is added to cover the nails. The $H_{2(g)}$ formed can be trapped and its pressure and volume determined.

Numerical Response

12. If, after 5 minutes, the reaction of 10 g of galvanized nails yielded 0.325 L of H_2 and measured at 20.0°C
(pressure due to $PH_{2(g)}$ = 720 torr), the mass of zinc that dissolved was

_____ g.
(Record your answer to two digits.)

Use the following information to answer the next two questions.

Alkaloids, such as nicotine (M = 162.26 g/mol), can react with acids to produce salts.

Nicotine   **Nicotine Salt**

14. If 60.0 mg of nicotine (a lethal dose) reacted with 10.0 mL of 1.00×10^{-3} mol/L $HCl_{(aq)}$ the limiting reagent of this reaction would be

    A. HCl   **B.** nicotine

    C. nicotine salt   **D.** alkaloid

Numerical Response

13. The mass of the nicotine salt that would form is _____ mg.
(Record your answer to three digits.)

Use the following chart to answer the next three questions.

Three pairs of test tubes, each labelled either A or B, contain solutions according to following chart.

Pair	Test tube A contains	Test tube B contains excess
1.	3.50 g silver nitrate	potassium carbonate
2.	5.00 g lead (II) nitrate	sodium sulphide
3.	4.50 g barium chloride	sodium sulfate

15. What precipitate would result if test tubes A and B of pair 1 were combined?

    A. $Ag_2CO_{3(s)}$ **B.** $AgCO_{3(s)}$

    C. $KNO_{(s)}$ **D.** $K_2NO_{3(s)}$

16. If the contents of test tubes A and B (pair 3) are combined, the expected products are

   A. $PbS_{(s)}$ and $NaNO_{3(aq)}$

   B. $Ba(SO_4)_{2(aq)}$ and $NaCl_{(aq)}$

   C. $BaSO_{4(s)}$ and $NaCl_{(aq)}$

   D. $BaCP_2$ and $NaCl_{(aq)}$

17. The type of reaction that would be expected to occur between each pair of reactants is

   A. electron transfer

   B. simple decomposition

   C. formation

   D. precipitation

Use the following information to answer the next two questions.

Chlorine (Cl_2) is used in great quantity as a bleach for the pulp and paper industry and as a disinfectant for municipal water supplies. Iodine is another chemical commonly used for water disinfection on a smaller scale. The boiling point of chlorine is –34.6°C while the boiling point of iodine is 184°C.

18. The difference in boiling points between chlorine and iodine can be attributed to

   A. covalent bonds

   B. intramolecular bonds

   C. ionic bonds

   D. London dispersion forces

19. The electrons involved in the bonding within chlorine molecules are

   A. completely transferred from one atom to another

   B. equally shared

   C. unequally shared

   D. the inner shell electrons only

Use the following information to answer the next question.

It takes about 7 times as much energy to split 1.00 mole of water into hydrogen and oxygen as is required to vaporize 1.00 mole of water at its boiling point.

20. The forces or bonds overcome in vaporizing water are

   A. ionic bonds

   B. covalent bonds

   C. intermolecular bonds

   D. intramolecular bonds

Use the following information to answer the next question.

The mineral magnetite (Fe_3O_4) is a natural occurring black metal oxide. Its formation (at high temperatures) can be represented by the equation

$$3Fe_{(s)} + 2O_{2(g)} \rightarrow Fe_3O_{4(s)}$$

21. The bonding between the iron and oxygen ions is a result of a

   A. loss of electrons by Fe and a gain of electrons by O

   B. gain of electrons by Fe and a loss of electrons by O

   C. loss of electrons by Fe and a loss of electrons by O

   D. gain of electrons by Fe and a gain of electrons by O

Use the following information to answer the next two questions.

When certain fruits or potatoes are cut, the cut surface turns brown upon exposure to air. This is known as the enzymatic browning reaction.

These dark brown chemical products are known collectively as melanins. Sodium sulfite is often used as a food additive because it prevents this enzymatic browning reaction. Sodium sulfite is a member of a class of compounds called antioxidants.

22. Based on the information, sodium sulfite would

    A. prevent the loss of electrons in food that would normally turn brown

    B. facilitate the loss of electrons in food that would normally turn brown

    C. gain electrons from food that would normally turn brown

    D. help to oxidize foods

Use the following information to answer the next question.

Newspaper clippings tend to brown with age. This is due to the formation of chromophores during degradation of the

paper. Newspapers with a lignin concentration of 40% or greater are particularly susceptible to browning, since lignin is oxidized quite easily.

23. Based on the information, when lignin turns brown, it

    A. undergoes no change in its number of electrons

    B. loses electrons

    C. gains electrons

    D. neither loses nor gains electrons

Use the following information to answer the next question.

The steroid cholesterol, although it has been implicated in atherosclerosis, is an essential component of cell membranes and is a building block for many other essential steroids.

24. If cholesterol is a non-polar molecular substance, it must

    A. be highly soluble in water

    B. have of low solubility in water

    C. be highly reactive in water

    D. dissociate in water

Use the following diagram to answer the next question.

$$\underset{\text{I}}{\overset{\displaystyle H}{\underset{\displaystyle H}{F-C-F}}} \qquad \underset{\text{II}}{\overset{\displaystyle F}{\underset{\displaystyle F}{F-C-F}}} \qquad \underset{\text{III}}{\overset{\displaystyle S}{\underset{\displaystyle S}{C}}} \qquad \underset{\text{IV}}{\overset{\displaystyle}{\underset{\displaystyle H}{H-P-H}}}$$

25. The polar molecule is

    A. I

    B. II

    C. III

    D. IV

Use the following information to answer the next question.

Household bleach can be a dangerous substance. A significant hazard may result from the mixing of bleach with ammonia cleansers. The initial product of this reaction is the toxic and volatile gas chloramine ($NH_2Cl_{(g)}$) It is formed as follows.

$$NH_{3(aq)} + ClO^-_{(aq)} \rightarrow NH_2Cl_{(g)} + OH^-_{(aq)}$$

26. If this reaction is exothermic, then the best definition of this process is that the energy

   A. needed to break bonds in the reactants is greater than the energy released from bond formation in the products

   B. needed to break bonds in the reactants is equal to the energy released from bond formation in the products

   C. needed to break bonds in the reactants is less than the energy released from bond formation in the products

   D. is being created in the form of heat

Use the following information to answer the next question.

Chloral hydrate, better known as "knockout drops" or "Mickey Finn," was often slipped into people's drinks in old detective movies. It is a sedative with the structure:

$$\begin{array}{c} \text{Cl} \quad \text{OH} \\ | \quad\quad | \\ \text{Cl}-\text{C}-\text{C}-\text{OH} \\ | \quad\quad | \\ \text{Cl} \quad \text{OH} \end{array}$$

27. The bonding that occurs within chloral hydrate could best be described as involving

   A. a complete transfer of electrons

   B. equal sharing of electrons

   C. unequal sharing of electrons

   D. unequal sharing of protons

Use the following information to answer the next question.

Commercial glass is hard and generally quite chemically resistant. The predominant constituent of glass is silicon dioxide, SiO_2. Hydrofluoric acid, $HF_{(aq)}$, is one substance that can dissolve glass, as fluorine forms a stronger bond to silicon than oxygen.

28. The most plausible explanation as to why fluorine is able to form a stronger bond with silicon than oxygen can is because

   A. fluorine is a halogen

   B. a fluorine-silicon bond is non-polar

   C. fluorine has a greater electronegativity than oxygen, and is able to "out-compete" oxygen for the silicon electrons

   D. fluorine has fewer lone pairs of electrons than oxygen does

Use the following information to answer the next question.

Isopentyl acetate ($C_7H_{14}O_2$) is the compound responsible for the scent of bananas.
Bees also release a small quantity of this compound when they sting, signalling other bees to join the attack.

29. Isopentyl acetate is an organic compound because it

   A. contains oxygen

   B. occurs naturally

   C. is a molecular compound of carbon

   D. is produced by bees

Use the following information to answer the next question.

Carvone is a compound whose molecules have two structures with the same formula ($C_{10}H_{14}O$). One geometric arrangement provides the characteristic odour of caraway seeds, while the other form gives the pleasant aroma of spearmint oil.

30. These two forms of carvone can best be described as

   A. inorganic compounds

   B. monomers

   C. polymers

   D. isomers

Use the following information to answer the next question.

The use of gasohol (ethyl alcohol plus gasoline) has become more prominent over the last two decades, as a search for alternative energy sources to fossil fuels continues. Corn is often used for the production of ethyl alcohol through fermentation reactions.

31. The complete combustion of ethyl alcohol proceeds according to the equation

   A. $C_2H_5OH + 3O_2 \rightarrow 2CO_2 + 3H_2O$

   B. $2C_2H_5OH + 6O_2 \rightarrow 4CO_2 + 6H_2O$

   C. $2C_2H_5OH + 3\frac{1}{2}O_2 \rightarrow 2CO_2 + 3H_2O$

   D. $C_2H_5OH + 3\frac{1}{2}O_2 \rightarrow 2CO_2 + 4H_2O$

Written Response

DNA, or deoxyribonucleic acid, is found in the form of long chain-like molecules. Two strands of DNA usually run in opposite directions and associate with each other to form a twisted structure called a double helix.

1. Explain the nature of the bonding within guanine and cytosine and the interaction occurring between them. Which type of bonds would be harder to break?

2. The boiling point of a molecular compound is a measure of the type and extent of bonding between molecules of that compound.

    a) Construct a table that summarizes the total number of electrons, polarity and type(s) of intermolecular bonding for the compounds $CH_3CH_2CH_3$, CH_2CH_2OH, $CH_3CH_2NH_3$ and CH_3CH_2F

    b) With appropriate reasoning, list the compounds in **(a)** from lowest to highest boiling point.

ANSWERS AND SOLUTIONS — PRACTICE EXAMINATION 1

1. C	5. C	12. A	NR7. 1.75	19. C	26. B
2. D	6. D	13. C	NR8. 4.97	20. A	27. B
3. D	7. A	NR4. 73.6	NR9. 25.0	21. D	28. A
NR1. 5.06	8. C	NR5. 6.19	NR10. 2 5 4 2	22. B	29. B
4. A	9. A	14. D	16. D	23. C	30. D
NR2. 15.0	10. D	15. D	17. C	24. C	WR1.*
NR3. 0.192	11. A	NR6. 71.4	18. B	25. D	

*for written response, see solutions

1. C

Though CH_2FCF_3, a molecular compound held together by strong C–H, C–F and C–C (intramolecular) bonds, might be soluble in water (it is polar), it will not dissociate into aqueous ions. According to Arrhenius' dissociation theory, a solution containing dissolved ions conducts electricity. The dissolved entity and solution are both called an electrolyte. CH_2FCF_3 will, therefore, behave as a non-electrolyte.

2. D

Intermolecular bonding describes the weak forces of interaction between molecules in the liquid and solid state.
Intramolecular bonding describes the covalent bonds that bind atoms together within molecules. The atoms in molecules of CH_2FCF_3 are held together by covalent bonds. The electrons that form a covalent bond between two atoms are shared between the bound nuclei (shared between means "mutually attracted to") by the overlap of partially filled valence atomic orbitals.

3. D

Measuring the concentration of a chemical entity in a solution is a quantitative analysis (e.g., measuring the mass of acetylsalicylic acid in an Aspirin tablet by acid base titration, measuring the molar volume of hydrogen by collecting a sample over water and measure its P, V and T).
A qualitative analysis
(e.g., starch test for iodine) only detects the presence of a chemical entity.

NR1.   5.06

$$\left[COCl_{2(g)}\right] = \frac{0.000\,500\ g \times \dfrac{mol}{98.91\ g}}{L}$$
$$= 5.06 \times 10^{-6}\ mol/L$$

Note: $[COCl_{2(g)}]$, denotes the concentration of $COCl_{2(g)}$

4. **A**

In all solutions where a saturated aqueous solution and undissolved solid solute occupy the same vessel the following dynamic solubility equilibrium occurs.

$$solute_{(s)} \rightleftharpoons solute_{(aq)}$$

Equilibria like this occur when the rate of the forward process
$$solute_{(s)} \rightarrow solute_{(aq)}(dissolution)$$
Is equal to rate of reverse process
$$solute_{(aq)} \rightarrow solute_{(s)} (crystallization)$$
For the solubility equilibrium

$$AgBr_{(s)} \rightleftharpoons Ag^+_{(aq)} + Br^-_{(aq)}$$

the solute dissociates, as do all ionic compounds, when it dissolves.

NR2. **15.0**

$$M_{salt} = 3.00\% \times 500 \text{ g} = \frac{3.00}{100} \times 500 \text{ g} = 15.0 \text{ g}$$

There are 15.0 g of salt in a 500 g kimchi portion.

NR3. **0.192**

For dilution purposes, the formula $C_1V_1 = C_2V_2$ is used where 1 and 2 refer to the initial and final states and C and V refer to the concentration and volume of the manipulated solutions.

$$\left.\begin{array}{l} C_1 = 0.400 \text{ mol/L} \\ V_1 = 48.0 \text{ mL} \\ C_2 = ? \\ V_2 = 100 \text{ mL} \end{array}\right\} \begin{array}{l} C_2 = \dfrac{C_1V_1}{V_2} \\[2ex] = \dfrac{0.400 \text{ mol/L} \times 48.0\text{mL}}{100 \text{ ml}} \\[2ex] = 0.192 \text{ mol/L} \end{array}$$

The final kimchi salt concentration is 0.192 mol/L.

5. **C**

Generally speaking, molecular acids are weak electrolytes and thus poor conductors of electricity. Without exception, all strong acids are strong electrolytes — they conduct electricity well.

6. **D**

The pH of an aqueous solution indirectly measures the $H^+_{(aq)}$ ion concentration of that solution using a small range of numbers (from about −1 to 15). In fact, pH is a function of $[H^+_{(aq)}]$ defined as pH= −log$[H^+_{(aq)}]$, where $[H^+_{(aq)}]$ is the molar concentration of the hydrogen ions and log is the function logarithm to the base 10. The following table will help to illustrate this.

$[H^+_{(aq)}]$(mol/L)	pH	$[H^+_{(aq)}]$(mol/L)	pH
10^1	−1	10^{-7}	7
10^0	0	10^{-8}	8
10^{-1}	1	10^{-9}	9
10^{-2}	2	10^{-10}	10
10^{-3}	3	10^{-11}	11
10^{-4}	4	10^{-12}	12
10^{-5}	5	10^{-13}	13
10^{-6}	6	10^{-14}	14
10^{-7}	7	10^{-15}	15

Note:
(1) The pH for these concentrations is simply the negative of the exponent.
(2) A 10 fold increase in the $[H^+_{(aq)}]$ decreases the pH by one.
(3) A 10 fold decrease in the $[H^+_{(aq)}]$ increases the pH by one.
(4) pH has no units.

7. **A**

Remember, the pH of a solution with an $H^+_{(aq)}$ concentration of 10^{-x} mol/L is x. By definition,$[H^+_{(aq)}] = 10^{-pH}$. Therefore, at pH = 5, $[H^+_{(aq)}] = 10^{-5}$ mol/L and at a pH = 8, $[H^+_{(aq)}] = 10^{-8}$ mol/L.

8. C

An increase of one in pH corresponds to a 10 fold decrease in $[H^+_{(aq)}]$
An increase of two in pH corresponds to a 100 fold decrease in $[H^+_{(aq)}]$.
An increase of three in pH corresponds to a 1 000 fold decrease $[H^+_{(aq)}]$.
An increase of x in pH corresponds to a decrease in $[H^+_{(aq)}]$.

9. A

The ideal gas law combines

(1) Boyle's law: $V \propto \dfrac{1}{P}$

(2) Charles' Law: $V \propto T$, and

(3) Avogadro's Law: $V \propto n$

to give $V \propto \dfrac{nT}{P}$

The constant of proportionality, R, when included, gives $V = \dfrac{nRT}{P}$, which is usually written as $PV = nRT$

R is known as the Universal Gas Constant, the most commonly used values of which are:

$8.314\,5 \dfrac{L \times kPa}{mol \times K}$ or $0.082\,06 \dfrac{L \times atm}{mol \times K}$

The gas law that summarizes the relationship between gas volume and pressure is

Boyle's Law which states that the volume of a fixed quantity of gas at a constant temperature is inversely proportional to its pressure.

10. D

$$n_{O_2} = \frac{1}{5} n_{AIR}$$

$$n_{O_2} = \frac{1}{5} \times \frac{PV}{RT}$$

$$= \frac{1}{5} \times \frac{100\ kPa \times 8.00 \times 10^{-9}\ L}{8.314 \dfrac{kPa \times L}{mol \times K} \times 310\ K}$$

$$= 6.21 \times 10^{-11}\ mol\ of\ O_{2(g)}$$

$$n_{O_2} = n_{O_2} \times n_A$$

$$= 6.21 \times 10^{-11}\ mol \times 6.022 \times 10^{23} \frac{molecules}{mol}$$

$$= 3.74 \times 10^{13}$$

In each alveoli, there are an estimated 3.74×10^{13} molecules.

11. A

Any container, even an alveolus, containing twice the pressure of the same gas has twice the amount of gas present according to Avogadro's Law. Alternatively, call the amounts and pressure of oxygen at sea level n_0 and P_0 and at 10 m depth n_{10} and P_{10}, respectively.

$$n_0 = \frac{P_0 V}{RT}$$

$$n_{10} = \frac{P_{10} V}{RT}$$

since $P_{10} = 2P_0$

substitute $n_{10} = \dfrac{2 P_{10} V}{RT}$

$$n_0 = \frac{P_0 V}{RT} \therefore P_0 = \frac{n_0 RT}{V}$$

$$n_{10} = \frac{2 n_0 \cancel{RTV}}{\cancel{RTV}}$$

$$n_{10} = 2 n_0$$

There is twice as much gas present in the same alveolus at twice the gas pressure.

12. A

Since 760 mm Hg pressure = 101.325 kPa, a simple conversion is all that is needed.

$$P_{120} = 120 \text{ mm Hg} \times \frac{101.325 \text{ kPa}}{760 \text{ mm Hg}} = 16.0 \text{ kPa}$$

$$P_{80} = 80 \text{ mm Hg} \times \frac{101.325 \text{ kPa}}{760 \text{ mm Hg}} = 10.7 \text{ kPa}$$

(Three significant digits are stated though two would be more appropriate — Physicians would in all likelihood not adhere to the dictates of significant digits in this case.)

13. C

When Arrhenius acids and bases (acids contain H^+ ions and bases contain OH^- ions) react, they do so according to the generic equation

$$acid + base \rightarrow salt + water$$

Following normal balancing rules, which fulfill the law of conservation of mass, we can equate the moles of reactants with those of the products. The correct answer is **C**.

NR4.   73.6

We must use the stoichiometric method the answer this question.

$$2HCl_{(aq)} + Mg(OH)_{2(s)} \rightarrow$$
$$MgCl_{2(aq)} + 2HOH_{(l)}$$

$$m = 0.236 \text{ g}$$

$$0.110 \frac{\text{mol}}{\text{L}} \qquad 58.33 \frac{\text{g}}{\text{mol}}$$

$$n_{Mg(OH_2)} = \frac{m}{N}$$

$$n_{Mg(OH_2)} = \frac{0.236 \text{ g}}{58.33 \frac{\text{g}}{\text{mol}}}$$

$$= 0.004\,05 \text{ mol}$$

$$n_{HCl} = \frac{2}{1} n_{Mg(OH)_2}$$

$$= \frac{2}{1} \times 0.004\,05 \text{ mol}$$

$$= 0.008\,09 \text{ mol}$$

$$V_{HCl} = \frac{0.008\,09 \text{ mol}}{0.110 \frac{\text{mol}}{\text{L}}}$$

$$= 0.073\,6 \text{ L} = 73.6 \text{ mL}$$

The volume of 0.110 mol/L $HCl_{(aq)}$ needed to neutralize 0.236 g of $Mg(OH)_{2(s)}$ is 73.6 mL.

NR5. 6.19

A simple use of the stoichiometric method is required

(**Note:** 1 000 L = 1.000 kL).

$$K_2CrO_{4(aq)} + Pb(CH_3COO)_{2(aq)}$$
$$\rightarrow PbCrO_{4(s)} + 2KCH_3COO_{(aq)}$$

1.000 kL   200 kg

$$\left[K_2CrO_{4(aq)}\right] = ?$$ 323.19 g/mol

$$n_{PbCrO_4} = 200 \text{ kg} \times \frac{\text{mol}}{323.19 \text{ g}}$$
$$= 0.619 \text{ kmol}$$

$$n_{K_2CrO_4} = \frac{1}{1}n_{PbCrO_4}$$
$$= \frac{1}{1} \times 0.619 \text{ mol/L}$$

$$\left[K_2CrO_{4(aq)}\right] = \frac{0.619 \text{ kmol}}{1.000 \text{ kL}}$$
$$= 0.619 \text{ mol/L}$$
$$= 6.19 \times 10^{-1} \text{ mol/L}$$

The molar concentration of $K_2CrO_{4(aq)}$ is 0.619 mol/L.

14. D

Spectator ions are those ions that survive unchanged in a chemical reaction. Spectator ions are removed when a net reaction is written, as shown.

Non-Ionic Equation

$$K_2CrO_{4(aq)} + Pb(CH_3COO)_{2(aq)}$$
$$\rightarrow PbCrO_{4(s)} + 2KCH_3COO_{(aq)}$$

Total Ionic Equation

$$2K^+_{(aq)} + CrO_4^{2-}{}_{(aq)} + Pb^{2+}_{(aq)} + 2CH_3COO^-_{(aq)}$$
$$\rightarrow PbCrO_{4(s)} + 2K^+_{(aq)} + 2CH_3COO^-_{(aq)}$$

Net Ionic Equation

$$CrO_4^{2-}{}_{(aq)} + Pb^{2+}{}_{(aq)} \rightarrow PbCrO_{4(s)}$$

Clearly, the $2K^+_{(aq)}$ and $2CH_3COO^-_{(aq)}$ on both sides of the total ionic equation are the spectator ions since they remain unaltered.

15. D

An excess limiting stoichiometric method, in part, must be used here.
We have

$$n_{H_2} = 9.00 \text{ kg} \times \frac{\text{mol}}{2.02 \text{ g}} = 4.46 \text{ kmol}$$

We need

$$n_{CO} = \frac{1}{2}n_{H_2} = \frac{1}{2} \times 4.46 \text{ kmol} = 2.23 \text{ kmol}$$

We actually have

$$n_{CO} = 70.0 \text{ kg} \times \frac{\text{mol}}{28.01 \text{ g}} = 2.50 \text{ kmol}$$

Thus, we have more $CO_{(g)}$ than is needed, which makes the $CO_{(g)}$ the excess reagent and the $H_{2(g)}$ the limiting reagent.

NR6. 71.4

We need to use an excess limiting stoichiometric method.

$$2H_{2(g)} + CO_{(g)} \rightarrow CH_3OH_{(l)}$$

9.00 kg   70.0 kg $m = ?$

2.02 g/mol 28.01 g/mol 32.05 g/mol

We have

$$n_{H2} = 9.00 \text{ kg} \times \frac{\text{mol}}{2.02 \text{ g}} = 4.46 \text{ kmol}$$

We need

$$n_{CO} = \frac{1}{2}n_{H2} = \frac{1}{2} \times 4.46 \text{ kmol} = 2.23 \text{ kmol}$$

We actually have

$$n_{CO} = 70.0 \text{ kg} \times \frac{\text{mol}}{28.01 \text{ g}} = 2.50 \text{ kmol}$$

The $CO_{(g)}$ is in excess, therefore, $H_{2(g)}$ is the limiting reagent.

$$n_{CH_3OH} = \frac{1}{2}n_{H_2} = \frac{1}{2} \times 4.46 \text{ kmol}$$
$$= 2.23 \text{ kmol}$$

$$m_{CH_3OH} = 2.23 \text{ kmol} \times \frac{32.05 \text{ g}}{\text{mol}} = 71.4 \text{ kg}$$

In this reaction 71.4 kg of methanol are predicted.

NR7. 1.75

A stoichiometric calculation will work here.

(**Note:** there is no need to convert kg to g).

$$CaC_{2(s)} + 2H_2O_{(l)} \rightarrow C_2H_{2(g)} + Ca(OH)_{2(s)}$$

4.30 kg   m = ?
64.10 g/mol   26.04 g/mol

$$n_{CaC_2} = 4.30 \text{ kg} \times \frac{\text{mol}}{64.10 \text{ g}}$$

$$= 0.067\,1 \text{ kmol}$$

$$n_{C_2H_2} = \frac{1}{1}n_{CaC_2}$$

$$= \frac{1}{1} \times 0.067\,1 \text{ kmol}$$

$$= 0.067\,1 \text{ kmol}$$

$$m_{C_2H_2} = 0.067\,1 \text{ kmol} \times \frac{26.04 \text{ g}}{\text{mol}}$$

$$= 1.75 \text{ kg}$$

The mass of acetylene produced is 1.75 kg.

NR8. 4.97

A stoichiometric calculation is necessary here

$$CaC_{2(s)} + 2H_2O_{(l)} \rightarrow C_2H_{2(g)} + Ca(OH)_{2(s)}$$

4.30 kg   m = ?
64.10 g/mol   74.10 g/mol

$$n_{CaC_2} = 4.30 \text{ kg} \times \frac{\text{mol}}{64.10 \text{ g}} = 0.067\,1 \text{ kmol}$$

$$n_{Ca(OH)_2} = \frac{1}{2}n_{CaC_2} = \frac{1}{2} \times 0.067\,1 \text{ kmol}$$

$$= 0.067\,1 \text{ kmol}$$

$$m_{Ca(OH)_2} = 0.067\,1 \text{ kmol} \times \frac{74.10}{\text{mol}}$$

$$= 4.97 \text{ kg}$$

The mass of $Ca(OH)_{2(s)}$ produced by 4.30 kg of calcium carbide is 4.97 kg.

NR9. 25.0

The molar solubility of calcium hydroxide at 0°C is easily calculated from the data given as follows.

$$\left[Ca(OH)_{2(aq)}\right] = \left(\frac{0.185 \text{ g} \times \dfrac{\text{mol}}{74.10 \text{ g}}}{0.100 \text{ L}}\right)$$

$$= 0.025\,0 \text{ mol/L}$$

$$= 25.0 \text{ mmol/L}$$

The molar solubility of $Ca(OH)_{2(aq)}$ is 25.0 mmol/L at 0°C.

NR10. 2, 5, 4, 2

When balancing the complete combustion reaction of $C_2H_{2(g)}$, the number of moles of acetylene is doubled to ensure an equal number of moles of $H_2O_{(g)}$ and an equal numbers of moles of O on both sides of the equation.
This gives

$$\underline{2}C_2H_{2(g)} + \underline{5}O_{2(g)} \rightarrow \underline{4}CO_{2(g)} + \underline{2}H_2O_{(g)}$$

16. D

$$2NH_4ClO_{4(s)}$$
$$\rightarrow 4H_2O_{(g)} + Cl_{2(g)} + N_{2(g)} + 2O_{2(g)}$$

17. C

When aluminum reacts with oxygen and chlorine, it forms the ionic compounds aluminum oxide and aluminum chloride, $Al_2O_{3(s)}$ and $AlCl_{3(g)}$, respectively.

18. B

Endothermic processes or reactions are those that require or absorb heat energy to proceed. Exothermic processes or reactions release or lose heat energy as they progress.

19. C

$NO_{(g)}$ is a molecular species – a form of chemical whose atoms are bound together by covalent bonds.

20. A

All chemical matter contains circulating electrons, so all matter experiences London Dispersion forces (named for Fritz London). Since N_2O is weakly polar, its molecules will also interact through dipole-dipole attractions.

21. D

In polar covalent bonds, a greater share of the bonding electrons, along with a slightly negative charge, goes to the atom of higher electro negativity. Obviously, the atom of lower electro negativity has a slight positive charge. In $NO_{2(g)}$ the nitrogen will have a slight positive charge.

22. B

Explosions are invariably exothermic reactions that generate vast quantities of gaseous products. In all reactions, energy is absorbed in breaking bonds in the reactants and released on forming bonds in the products. For an exothermic reaction, more energy is released forming bonds in the products than is absorbed to break bonds in the reactants.

23. C

Both diethyl ether and 1-butanol are polar molecules so each will experience London Dispersion forces and dipole-dipole attractions. Only 1-butanol has a highly polar $-^{\sigma-}O-H^{\sigma+}$ bond. It will associate with its near neighbours through hydrogens. Though hydrogen bonds are themselves weak, the presence of a great many of them between suitable molecules means that it takes extra energy to break them during vaporization. Ethers, because they lack OH bonds have relatively low boiling points.

24. C

The reaction $2Na_{(s)} + Cl_{2(g)} \rightarrow 2NaCl_{(s)}$ can be broken into two half reactions.

(1) $2Na_{(s)} \rightarrow 2Na^+_{(s)} + 2e^-$

(2) $Cl_{2(g)} + 2e^- \rightarrow 2Cl^-_{(s)}$

Reaction **(1)** shows two moles of sodium atoms losing two moles of electrons – this is oxidation. Reaction **(2)**, on the other hand, shows a mol of chlorine molecules gaining the two moles of electrons lost by the sodium – this is reduction. The metal is oxidized and the non-metal is reduced in the reaction.

25. D

If each atom in the molecule is bonded with a bonding pair of electrons, there ought to be $12e^-$, (6 pairs of bonding e^-) surrounding the carbon.

26. B

The octet rule states that most of the representative elements tend to be most stable when they have eight electrons in their valence shells. Carbon normally obeys this rule but in CLi_6 this may not be the case.

27. B

The redox reaction, $2Mg_{(s)} + O2_{(g)} \rightarrow 2MgO_{(s)}$ can be split into two halves.

(1) $2Mg_{(s)} \rightarrow 2Mg^{2+}_{(s)} + 2e^-$

(2) $O_{2(g)} + 4e^- \rightarrow 2O^{2-}_{(s)}$

Reaction **(1)** is an oxidation of magnesium while reaction **(2)** is the reduction of oxygen. (The mnemonic LEO the Lion say GER reminds us that **L**oss of **E**lectrons is **O**xidation while a **G**ain of **E**lectrons is **R**eduction.) Clearly the $O_{2(g)}$ is the reduced element.

28. A

The element that loses electrons in the sparkler reaction is the source of the electrons that reduce the oxygen.
It is the magnesium that loses the electrons. (In a redox reaction, the oxidized entity is the Reducing Agent and the reduced entity is the Oxidizing Agent.)

29. B

In the reaction, $2Mg_{(s)} + O_{2(g)} \rightarrow 2MgO_{(s)}$ the positive magnesium ions of the product form by the loss of electrons – in this case two moles of electron per mole of magnesium. The oxidation reaction is $Mg_{(s)} \rightarrow Mg^{2+}_{(s)}\ 2e^-$

30. D

Juglone, which is a product of a living organism, contains covalently bonded carbon. Therefore, it must be an organic compound.

Written Response

1. Write up a laboratory procedure that would allow you to precipitate all the Pb^{2+} from 500 mL of a contaminated waste solution that also contains $Ag^+_{(aq)}$ ions.
Your procedure must allow you to obtain information useful for calculating the $Pb^{2+}_{(aq)}$ ion concentration.
(For full credit you must correctly specify the chemicals and materials used.)

(8 marks)

Solution

Key components: a viable procedure should include removal of $Ag^+_{(aq)}$ as $AgCH_3COO_{(s)}$ after adding $NaCH_3COO_{(aq)}$

Precipitate $Pb^{2+}_{(aq)}$ by adding any of the following: $NaCl_{(aq)}$, $NaBr_{(aq)}$, $NaI_{(aq)}$, $Na_2SO_{4(aq)}$, $NaOH_{(aq)}$ or another suitable reagent.

(4 marks)

Support

Obtain the mass of filter paper used to remove the lead containing precipitate.

Allow the filter paper and the lead containing precipitate to dry thoroughly.

Obtain the mass of the dry filter paper and precipitate.

(4 marks)

ANSWERS AND SOLUTIONS — PRACTICE EXAMINATION 2

1. A	6. B	11. D	NR12. 0.84	20 C	27. C
2. A	7. A	NR7. 22.9	14. A	21. A	28. C
3. D	NR4. 0.10	NR8. 0.20	15. A	22. A	29. C
NR1. 21.4	8. C	NR9. 0.77	16. C	23. B	30. D
4. B	9. B	NR10. 32.3	17. D	24. B	31. A
NR2. 0.017	NR5. 0.0	12. B	18. D	25. A	WR1 *
NR3. 8, 8, 4	10. C	NR11. 24.5	19. B	26. C	WR2 *
5. A	NR6. 873	13. D			

*for written response, see solutions

1. A

Alka-Seltzer's non-reactivity in the solid state illustrates that many reactions are faster in the liquid phase than in the solid phase. The reason for this is that in the solution phase the "surface area" of the reactants is increased considerably.

2. A

Because they contain dissolved ions from dissociation, electrolytes are solutions that will conduct an electric current.

The term electrolyte is usually applied directly to dissolved entities that dissociate or ionize in aqueous solution.

Strong electrolytes dissociate or ionize completely and conduct an electric current efficiently. Weak electrolytes dissociate or ionize partially in aqueous solution and conduct an electric current less efficiently than solutions of strong electrolytes.

Strong acids $HClO_{4(aq)}$, $HI_{(aq)}$, $HBr_{(aq)}$ $HCl_{(aq)}$, $H_2SO_{4(aq)}$, $HNO_{3(aq)}$ in water are strong electrolytes.

$H_2SO_{4(aq)}$ dissociates completely as follows:
$$H_2SO_{4(aq)} \rightarrow H^+_{(aq)} + HSO_4^-_{(aq)}$$

3. D

Acetic acid is a weak acid, (i.e., it dissociates partially in aqueous solution at normal concentrations). Weak acids are weak electrolytes, therefore, vinegar would not conduct an electric current efficiently.

Empirical evidence shows that water is a very weak electrolyte.

NR1. 21.4

1. Light margarine: 6.0 g of water in 14.0 g sample
% of mass that is water
$$\frac{6.0\,g}{14.0\,g} \times 100\% = 42.8571\%$$

2. Regular margarine: 3.0 g of water in 14.0 g sample
% of mass that is water
$$\frac{3.0\,g}{14.0\,g} \times 100\% = 21.42857\%$$

3. Differences in % mass
$= 42.8571\% - 21.42857\% = 21.4\%$

4. **B**

Palmitic ($C_{16}H_{32}O_2$) acid has the molar mass of 256.48 g/mol

$$\%C = \frac{(16 \times 12.01)\,g}{256.48\,g} \times 100\% = 74.92\%\,(75\%)$$

$$\%H = \frac{(32 \times 1.01)\,g}{256.48\,g} \times 100\% = 12.6\%\,(13\%)$$

$$\%O = \frac{(2 \times 16.00)\,g}{256.48\,g} \times 100\% = 12.48\%\,(12\%)$$

The approximate mass percent of each element in palmitic acid is 75%C, 13%H and 12%O.

NR2. 0.017

$$\% \text{ caffeine} = \frac{\text{mass of caffeine }(g)}{\text{solution volume }(mL)} \times 100\%$$

$$= \frac{0.040\,g}{235\,ml} \times 100\% = 0.017\%$$

The % caffeine W/V is $1.70 \times 10^{-2}\%$ (0.017%) in this cup of tea.

NR3. 8, 8, 4

$$[\text{caffeine}] = \frac{n_{\text{caffeine}}}{235\,mL}$$

$$= \frac{0.040\,g \times \dfrac{\text{mol}}{194.19\,g}}{235\,mL}$$

$$= 8.8 \times 10^{-4}\,\text{mol/L}$$

The caffeine concentration is 8.8×10^{-4} mol/L.

5. **A**

The excess solid solute in a saturated solution is continually dissolving. At the same time, with the same reaction rate, dissolved solute in the saturated solution is continually precipitating (as small crystals). The result is that over time large crystals are replaced by much smaller crystals.

6. **B**

The important first step in preparing a standard solution from a solid solute is calculating the mass of solute required.

$$n_{Na_2CO_3} = 0.100\,L \times 0.11\,\text{mol/L} = 0.010\,0\,\text{mol}$$

$$m_{Na_2CO_3} = 0.010\,0\,\text{mol} \times 105.99\,\text{g/mol} = 1.06\,g$$

1.06 g of $Na_2CO_{3(s)}$ are required to prepare a 100 mL 0.100 mol/L solution.

7. **A**

Concentrations in excess of about 0.5 mol/L are commonly referred to as concentrated. In water, the acids $HClO_{4(aq)}$, $HI_{(aq)}$, $HBr_{(aq)}$, $HCl_{(aq)}$, $H_2SO_{4(aq)}$, and $HNO_{3(aq)}$ are referred to as strong acids because they dissociate completely. Most other acids in water, other than these six, are called weak acids. A concentrated solution of acetic acid, while it still must be handled with care, contains a solute that is a weak acid – weak because it dissociates partially.

NR4. 0.10

The pH scale is based on the log 10 scale, so to convert a pH of 1.00, use the equation

$$10^{-pH} = \left[H^+_{(aq)}\right] = 10^{-100}\,\text{mol/L} = 0.10\,\text{mol/L}$$

8. **C**

Weak acid aqueous solutions do not conduct electricity well but they do have a pH below 7 that indicates that they produce $H^+_{(aq)}$ ions in aqueous solution.

9. B

If pH = 8 then

$$\left[H^+_{(aq)}\right] = 10^{-pH} = 10^{-8}\,mol/L$$

Since

$$\left[H^+_{(aq)}\right]\left[OH^-_{(aq)}\right] = K_w = 1.0 \times 10^{-14}\,(mol/L)^2$$

then

$$\left[OH^-_{(aq)}\right] = \frac{K_w}{\left[H^+_{(aq)}\right]} = \frac{1.0 \times 10^{-14}\,(mol/L)^2}{10^{-8}\,mol/L}$$

$$= 10^{-6}\,mol/L$$

The hydroxide ion concentration of the solution is 10^{-6} mol/L but its hydrogen ion concentration is 10^{-8} mol/L.

NR5.   0.0

The pH of a 1.0 mol/L $HCl_{(aq)}$ is given by

$$pH = -\log\left[H^+_{(aq)}\right]$$

$$= -\log(1.0\,mol/L) = 0.00$$

The number of decimal places in a pH value is the same as the number of significant digits in the hydrogen ion concentration.

10. C

It is important to know the value of one standard atmosphere in kPa and mmHg
1 atm = 101.325 kPa = 760 mm Hg

$$P_{atm} = 3.00\,atm \times \frac{101.325\,kPa}{atm} = 304\,kPa.$$

$$P_{mmHg} = 3.00\,atm \times \frac{760\,mmHg}{atm}$$

$$= 2.28 \times 10^3\,mmHg$$

NR6.   873

Adding 273.15 to a Celsius temperature (°C) converts it into Kelvin temperature (K).
Thus,
$T = (600 + 273.15)\,K = 873.15\,K = 873\,K$
(Rounded to three digits.)

11. D

When comparing two containers that have the same volume of the same gas at the same temperature, the one that contains the higher pressure contains more of that gas. (Twice the pressure—twice the amount of gas; 20% higher pressure = 20% more gas). It is possible to perform a simple $PV = nRT$ comparison as shown.
Assumed that V, R, and T are the same per both partial pressures, P_1 and P_2, then:
$$P_1V = n_1RT$$
$$P_2V = n_2RT$$

$$n_1 = \frac{P_1V}{RT} \qquad n_2 = \frac{P_2V}{RT}$$

$$n_1 = \frac{1(V)}{RT} \qquad n_2 = \frac{1.20(V)}{RT}$$

Since V, R, and T are the same in both equations we can ignore them.
Therefore, $n_1 = 1$ and $n_2 = 1.20$
Therefore, at a 20% increase in partial pressure (120 kPa vs. 100 kPa) the number of moles of a given gas are 20% as much (1.20 moles vs. 1.00 moles).
Thus, at 120 kPa there are 20% more moles of air (oxygen) available in the same volume.

NR7.   22.9

This question can be answered by applying the ideal gas law
R = 8.314 kPaL/mol K
T = 25°C = 298 K
$$V = \frac{nRT}{P}$$

$$= \frac{1\,mol \times 8.314\,\dfrac{kPa \times L}{mol \times K} \times 298\,K}{90.0\,kPa} = 27.5\,L$$

The volume occupied by a mole of oxygen will be 27.5 L.

NR8. 0.20

A stoichiometric calculation incorporating $PV = nRT$ is all that is needed here.

$$2NaN_{3(s)} \rightarrow 2Na_{(s)} + 3N_{2(g)}$$

$m = ?$ $P = 1.0 \text{ atm}$ $V = 80 \text{ L}$

65.02 g/mol $T = -60°C = 213 \text{ K}$

$$n_{N_2} = \frac{PV}{RT} = \frac{1.0 \text{ atm} \times 80 \text{ L}}{0.082\,06 \dfrac{L \times atm}{mol \times K} \times 213 \text{ K}} = 4.6 \text{ mol}$$

$$n_{NaN_3} = \frac{2}{3} n_{N_2} = \frac{2}{3} \times 4.6 \text{ mol} = 3.1 \text{ mol}$$

$$m_{NaN_3} = 3.1 \text{ mol} \times \frac{65.02 \text{ g}}{mol} = 2.0 \times 10^2 \text{ g} = 0.20 \text{ kg}$$

It is predicted that 0.20 kg of sodium azide are required to meet the specifications necessary for air bag deployment.

NR9. 0.77

This problem can be solved by using the ideal gas equation. Whenever the chemical identity of a gas is specified and a set of fixed conditions
(rather than changes in conditions) is given, the ideal gas equation is required.
Additionally, amount refers to the number of moles of gas, n.

$$n = \frac{PV}{RT}$$

$$= \frac{1.00 \text{ atm} \times 16 \text{ L}}{0.082\,06 \dfrac{L \text{ atm}}{mol \text{ K}} \times 253 \text{ K}}$$

$$= 0.77 \text{ mol}$$

There are 0.77 mol of air in the refrigerator. It is possible to calculate the number of moles of air in the freezer even though it is an 80:20 mix of $N_{2(g)}$ and $O_{2(g)}$.

NR10. 32.3

R - C - H   Alkanes

C = C   Alkenes

R — C ≡ C — R   Alkynes

R —   Arenes

R — X   Haloalkanes (X=F,Cl,Br,I)

R — O — H   Alkanols/Alcohols

R — O — R   Ethers

R — N — R   Amines
    |
    R

R — C — R′   Alkanones/Ketones

R — C — H   Alkanals/Aldehydes

R — C — OH   Alkanoic/ Carboxylic Acids

R — C — O — R   Esters/ Alkyl Alkanoates

R — C — O — NR$_2$ Amides/Alkanamides

The **stoichiometric method** is widely employed to solve for the masses, volumes, and concentrations of reactants and or products in chemical reactions. Most teachers would agree that the stoichiometric method comprises the following four steps.

1) Write a balanced reaction equation that includes all the relevant data (often the most difficult step).
2) Calculate the number of moles of the given reactant or product (n_{given}).
3) Use the appropriate mole ratio to convert n_{given} into the number of moles of required reactant or product, $n_{required}$.
4) Determine the answer by converting the $n_{required}$ into a mass, a volume, or a concentration.

The titration of citric acid often written as $H_3Ct_{(aq)}$ by $NaOH_{(aq)}$ is represented readily by the equation

$$H_3Ct_{(aq)} + 3NaOH_{(aq)} \rightarrow Na_3Ct_{(aq)} + 3HOH_{(l)}$$

$$n_{NaOH} = 24.2 \text{ mL} \times 0.100 \text{ mol/L}$$
$$= 2.42 \text{ mmol}$$

$$n_{Na_3Ct} = \frac{1}{3}n_{NaOH} = \frac{1}{3} \times 2.42 \text{ mmol}$$
$$= 0.807 \text{ mmol}$$

$$\left[H_3Cl_{(aq)}\right] = \frac{0.807 \text{ mmol}}{25.0 \text{ mL}} = 0.032\ 3 \text{ mol/L}$$

The citric acid concentration is 0.032 3 mol/L.
(This can be reported as 32.3 mmol/L.)

12. B

Strong acids and strong bases react completely according to the generic equation: acid + base → salt + water. Thus, "both H^+ ions" in $H_2SO_{4(aq)}$ react completely with the $OH^-_{(aq)}$ ions of $KOH_{(aq)}$. (The precise nature of the "H^+" ions in $H_2SO_{4(aq)}$ is beyond the scope of Chemistry 20.)

NR11. 24.5

A stoichiometric method will suffice here.

$$Ca^{2+}_{(aq)} + CO_3^{2-}_{(aq)} \rightarrow CaCO_{3(s)}$$

1.00 L	2.45 g
$\left[Ca^{2+}_{(aq)}\right] = ?$	100.09 g/mol

$$n_{CaCO_3} = 2.45 \text{ g} \times \frac{\text{mol}}{100.09 \text{ g}} = 0.024\ 5 \text{ mol}$$

$$n_{Ca^{2+}} = \frac{1}{1}n_{CaCO_3} = \frac{1}{1} \times 0.024\ 5 \text{ mol} = 0.024\ 5 \text{ mol}$$

$$\left[Ca^{2+}_{(aq)}\right] = \frac{0.024\ 5 \text{ mol}}{1.00 \text{ L}} = 0.024\ 5 \text{ mol/L}$$

The molar concentration of the $Ca^{2+}_{(aq)}$ is 0.024 5 mol/L or 24.5 mmol/L.

13. D

A test that only detects the **presence** of a chemical entity only is essentially a qualitative analysis.

NR12. 0.84

A stoichiometric calculation involving $PV = nRT$ is needed to solve this problem.

$$Zn_{(s)} + 2HCl_{(aq)} \rightarrow H_{2(g)} + ZnCl_{2(aq)}$$

m = ?	V = 0.325 L
65.38 g/mol	T = 20.0°C 293 K
	P = 96 kPa

$$n_{H_2} = \frac{PV}{RT} = \frac{96 \text{ kPa} \times 0.325 \text{ L}}{8.314\frac{\text{kPa} \times \text{L}}{\text{mol} \times \text{K}} \times 293 \text{ K}} = 0.013 \text{ mol}$$

$$n_{Zn} = \frac{1}{1}n_{H_2} = \frac{1}{1} \times 0.013 \text{ mol} = 0.013 \text{ mol}$$

$$m_{Zn} = 0.013 \text{ mol} \times \frac{65.38 \text{ g}}{\text{mol}} = 0.84 \text{ g}$$

The mass of zinc that reacted is 0.84 g.

14. A

60.0 mg
10.0 mL
m = ?
We have

162.26 g/mol
1.00×10^{-3} mol/L
198.72 g/mol

$$n_{nicotine} = 60.0 \text{ mg} \times \frac{mol}{162.26 \text{ g}} = 0.370 \text{ mmol}$$

According to the balance equation, each mole of nicotine consumes one mole of $HCl_{(aq)}$.

We need $n_{Ha} = \frac{1}{1} n_{nicotine} = \frac{1}{1} \times 0.370$ mmol

$$= 0.370 \text{ mmol}$$

We have $n_{Ha} = 10.0 \text{ mL} \times 100 \times 10^{-3}$ mol/L

$$= 0.010\,0 \text{ mmol}$$

Since there is much less $HCl_{(aq)}$ than is required, $HCl_{(aq)}$ is the limiting reagent.

NR13. 1.99

Continuing from the previous solution,

$$n_{nicotine.HCl} = \frac{1}{1} n_{Ha} = \frac{1}{1} \times 0.010\,0 \text{ mmol}$$

$$= 0.010\,0 \text{ mmol}$$

$$m_{nicotine.HCl} = 0.010\,0 \text{ mmol} \times 198.72 \text{ g/mol}$$

$$= 1.99 \text{ mg}$$

The predicted mass of nicotine hydrochloride salt would be 1.99 mg.

15. A

The reaction of pair 1 is
$$2AgNO_{3(aq)} + K_2CO_{3(aq)}$$
$$\rightarrow Ag_2CO_{3(s)} + 2KNO_{3(aq)}$$

16. C

The reaction of pair 3 is
$$BaCl_{2(aq)} + Na_2SO_{4(aq)}$$
$$\rightarrow BaSO_{4(s)} + 2NaCl_{(aq)}$$

$BaSO_{4(s)}$ and $NaCl_{(aq)}$ are the products of this precipitation or double replacement reaction.

17. D

Each pair of reactant compounds combines to make a low solubility product, (one of $Ag_2CO_{3(aq)}$, $PbS_{(s)}$ and $BaSO_{4(s)}$) in a double replacement or precipitation reaction. The solubility of an ionic compound is easy to ascertain using a solubility chart.

18. D

The strength of London dispersion forces, the only intermolecular attractions available to non-polar Cl_2 and I_2 molecules, is proportional to the total numbers of electrons within their molecules. With over three times as many electrons per molecule as chlorine, iodine molecules experience dispersion forces of greater strength than chlorine. This, in part, explains iodine's much higher boiling point than the boiling point of chlorine.

19. B

Chlorine is a molecular element held together by a single covalent bond. Since each bonded atom has the same electronegativity, the electrons are shared equally.

20. C

Consider the following equations.
$2H_2O_{(l)} \rightarrow 2H_{2(g)} + O_{2(g)}$ water is "split"
$H_2O_{(l)} \rightarrow H_2O_{(g)}$ water is vaporized only
When a molecular compound is vaporized (or melted) only weak intermolecular bonds are broken. However, if a molecular compound is chemically transformed, strong intramolecular (in this case covalent) bonds must be broken. A process that breaks stronger bonds requires more energy.

21. A

$Fe_3O_{4(g)}$ is an ionic compound wherein bonding results from the simultaneous attractions of oppositely charged ions. Metals tend to lose electrons and form positive ions, while non-metals tend to gain electrons and form negative ions during chemical reaction.
(The iron lost e^-, the oxygen gained e^-.)

22. A

The name antioxidant suggests sodium sulfite prevents oxidation, i.e., it prevents the loss of electrons in the food to which it is added.

23. B

Oxidation is a loss of electrons (LEO). Thus, if lignin is easily oxidized it easily loses electrons.

24. B

Polar solvents like water readily accommodate polar solutes (remember the phase **"like dissolves like"**) but a non-polar solute like cholesterol is likely to be of low solubility in water.

25. A

Only molecules that contain polar bonds can be polar and then only if the bond dipoles do not cancel as a consequence of molecular geometry. Thus the V.S.E.P.R. shape of a molecule is necessary to predict that molecule's polarity.

C-H bonds are essentially non-polar. C-F dipoles give an overall polarity to this molecule.

Dipoles cancel

The electronegativities of C and S are the same. Hence, no dipoles exist..

The electronegativities of P and H are the same. Hence, no dipoles exist.

Communicates which atom has the greater share of the bonding electrons.

26. C

The energy change in all chemical reactions has two components. It should come as no surprise that a chemical reaction involves the formation of new bonds in the products after bonds have been broken in the reactants. Now, breaking bonds requires energy while making bonds releases energy. In an endothermic (heat absorbing) reaction, more energy is absorbed to break bonds in the reactants than is released in forming bonds in the products. Conversely, in an exothermic reaction, more energy is released in making bonds in the products than is absorbed to break bonds in the reactants.

In simple terms

(1) Call the energy needed to break reactant bonds E_{in}.
(2) Call the energy released in making product bonds E_{out}.
If $E_{out} > E_{in}$, then the reaction releases energy and is exothermic.

If $E_{in} > E_{out}$, then the reaction **absorbs** energy and is **endothermic.**

27. C

Chloral hydrate is a molecular substance and molecules are held together by covalent bonds. In addition, virtually all the bonds in chloral hydrate are polar.
Polar bonds involve one or more shared electron pairs between two atoms in which the higher electronegativity atom has the greater share. Clearly, the bonding within chloral hydrate molecules involves unequal sharing of electrons.

28. C

Sometimes a multiple-choice question can be answered by eliminating the unlikely answers. In this case: fluorine is a halogen; a Si–F bond will be very polar because of the large difference in electronegativity of Si and F.
Lewis dot structures of fluorine:
and oxygen;

show that the halogen has one more lone pair. Evidently, fluorine with its greater electronegativity is able to out compete oxygen for a share of silicons bonding electrons.

29. C

Organic compounds are molecular compounds of carbon. Isopentyl acetate, the name of which labels it as an ester of acetic acid, is one such compound.

30. D

Isomers are compounds that have the same chemical formula but different chemical structures. More often than not isomers have different chemical and/or physical properties. Without knowing the precise structures of carvone (other than that it is an organic compound), its two forms meet the qualification for isomers.

31. A

When balancing the combustion reactions of hydrocarbons and their derivatives it is important to balance the quantities of H in $H_2O_{(g)}$ and C in $CO_{2(g)}$ before balancing the O as $O_{2(g)}$.

Written Response

DNA, or deoxyribonucleic acid, exists in the form of long chain-like molecules. Two strands of DNA usually run in opposite directions and associate with each other to form a twisted structure called a double helix. **(8 marks)**

1. Explain the nature of the bonding within guanine and cytosine and the interaction occurring between them. Which type of bonds would be harder to break?

The type of bonding occurring within guanine and cytosine is covalent.
This means that there is a simultaneous attraction for the electrons by the nuclei of the constituent atoms.

This attraction results in a sharing of the electrons between the atoms.
In some instances, there is an equal sharing of electrons, as in the carbon-carbon bonds. In other cases, there is an equal sharing of the electrons, as between nitrogen and hydrogen.

The unequal sharing of electrons results from a difference in electronegativities. Nitrogen has a greater electronegativity (pull or attraction from electrons) than does hydrogen. This results in a slight negative charge for nitrogen and a slight positive charge for hydrogen. This unequal sharing of electrons is also known as a polar covalent bond.

Double bonds also exist between some carbons, oxygen and nitrogen in the ring structures. The polar covalent bonds lead to the development of hydrogen bonds (represented by the dashed lines) between opposing hydrogens and nitrogen of cytosine and guanine. Hydrogen bonds are a type of intermolecular force, and in thus case they help DNA maintain its double helix structure.

Of the bonds present, the double bonds would require the greatest energy to be overcome, followed by the single covalent bonds and then the intermolecular bonds.

2. The boiling point of a molecular compound is a measure of the type and extent of bonding between molecules of that compound.

(8 marks)

Construct a table that summarizes the total number of electrons, polarity, and type (*s*) of intermolecular bonding for the compounds $CH_3CH_2CH_3$, $CH_2CH_2OH_1$, $CH_3CH_2NH_3$ and CH_3CH_2F

(5 marks)

	Total # electrons	Polarity	Intermolecular bonding
$CH_3CH_2CH_3$	26	Non-polar	London dispersion forces
CH_3CH_2F	26	polar	London dispersion forces and dipole bond
$CH_3CH_2NH_2$	26	polar	London dispersion forces, dipole bonds and hydrogen bonds
CH_3CH_2OH	26	polar	London dispersion forces, dipole bonds and hydrogen bonds

With appropriate reasoning, list the compounds in (a) from lowest to highest boiling point. **(3 marks)**

Boiling Point	Certified Values
$CH_3CH_2CH_3$	–42.1°C
CH_3CH_2F	–2.5°C
$CH_3CH_2NH_2$	47.9°C
CH_3CH_2OH	97.2°C

The compound with the fewest intermolecular bonds will have the lowest boiling point – propane. The compound with two types of intermolecular bonds only will have the second lowest boiling point – fluoroethane. The boiling point of ethanol exceeds that of ethanamine because –OH functional groups tend to be stronger hydrogen bonded than N–H functional groups: the –OH bond is more polar. Both ethanol and ethanamine will have boiling points higher than that of flouroethane.

NOTES

NOTES

Chemistry 20 – Data Sheets

Common Formulas and Units of Measurement

- *STP conditions:* 0°C (273.15 K) and 1 atm (101.325 kPa) pressure.

- *SATP conditions:* 25°C (298.15 K) and 100 kPa pressure.

- *Molar Volumes*: $V_{STP} = 22.4$ L and $V_{SATP} = 24.8$ L

- 1 atm = 101.325 kPa = 760 mm Hg = 760 torr

- $T(K) = T(°C) + 273.15$

- *Ideal Gas Law*: $PV = nRT$

- *Combined Gas Law*: $\dfrac{P_1 V_1}{T_1} = \dfrac{P_2 V_2}{T_2}$

- *The Gas Constant*: $R = 8.314 \dfrac{L \times kPa}{mol \times K}$ or $0.082\,06 \dfrac{L \times atm}{mol \times K}$

- *Avogadro's Number*: $N_A = 6.022 \times 10^{23}$

- $K_W = 1.0 \times 10^{-14} \left(\dfrac{mol}{L}\right)^2$ at 25°C

- $pH = -\log\left[H^+_{(aq)}\right]$ *note:* $\left(\left[H^+_{(aq)}\right] \text{ in } \dfrac{mol}{L}\right)$

- $\left[H^+_{(aq)}\right] = 10^{-pH}$

- $C_1 V_1 = C_2 V_2$ (for dilution only)

Titration Indicator Chart

Indicator	Acid Form	Neutralized	Basic Form
Thymol blue	pH < 1.2 red	pH from 1.2–2.8 orange	pH > 2.8 yellow
Methyl orange	pH < 3.2 red	pH from 3.2–4.4 orange	pH > 4.4 yellow
Bromocresol green	pH < 4.0 yellow	pH from 4.0–5.6 green	pH > 5.6 blue
Bromocresol purple	pH < 5.2 yellow	pH from 5.2–6.8 green	pH > 6.8 purple
Bromothymol blue	pH < 6.0 yellow	pH from 6.0–7.6 green	pH > 7.6 blue
Cresol red	pH < 7.2 yellow	pH from 7.2–8.8 orange	pH > 8.8 red
Phenolphthalein	pH < 8.0 colourless	pH from 8.0–10.0 pink	pH > 10.0 red
Alizarin yellow	pH < 10.0 yellow	pH from 10.0–12.0 orange	pH > 12.0 red
Trinitrobenzoic acid	pH < 12.0 colourless	pH from 12.0–13.4 pink	pH > 13.4 orange-red

SOLUBILITY OF SOME COMMON IONIC COMPOUNDS IN WATER AT 298.15 K (25°C)

ION	Group IA NH_4^+ $H^+(H_3O^+)$	ClO_3^- NO_3^- ClO_4^-	CH_3COO^-	Cl^- Br^- I^-	SO_4^{2-}	S^{2-}	OH^-	PO_4^{3-} SO_3^{2-} CO_3^{2-}
Solubility greater than or equal to 0.1 mol/L (very soluble)	all	all	most	most	most	Group IA Group IIA NH_4^+	Group IA NH_4^+ Sr^{2+} Ba^{2+} Tl^+	Group IA NH_4^+
Solubility less than 0.1 mol/L (slightly soluble)	none	none	Ag^+ Hg^+	Ag^+ Pb^{2+} Hg^+ Cu^+ Tl^+	Ca^{2+} Sr^{2+} Ba^{2+} Ra^{2+} Pb^{2+} Ag^+	most	most	most

COLOR CHART OF COMMON AQUEOUS IONS

ION	SYMBOL	COLOR
chromate	CrO_4^{2-}	yellow
chromium(III)	Cr^{3+}	green
chromium(II)	Cr^{2+}	blue
cobalt(II)	Co^{2+}	pink
copper(I)	Cu^+	green
copper(II)	Cu^{2+}	blue
dichromate	$Cr_2O_7^{2-}$	orange
iron(II)	Fe^{2+}	pale green
iron(III)	Fe^{3+}	pale yellow
manganese(II)	Mn^{2+}	pale pink
permanganate	MnO_4^-	purple

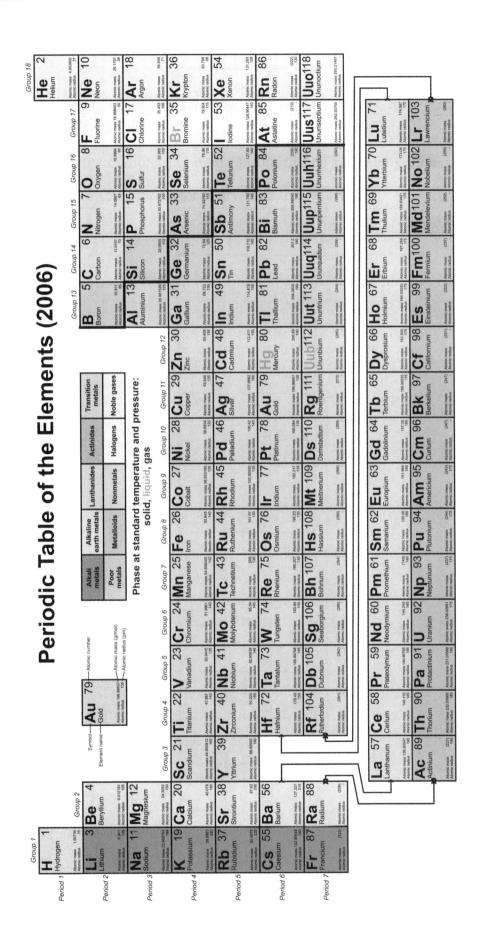

Periodic Table of the Elements (2006)

PERIODIC CHART OF IONS

TABLE OF POLYATOMIC IONS

acetate	CH_3COO^-	dihydrogen phosphate	$H_2PO_4^-$
ammonium	NH_4^+	silicate	SiO_3^{2-}
benzoate	$C_6H_5COO^-$	sulphate	SO_4^{2-}
borate	BO_3^{3-}	sulphite	SO_3^{2-}
carbonate	CO_3^{2-}	hydrogen sulphide	HS^-
hydrogen carbonate	HCO_3^-	hydrogen sulphate	HSO_4^-
chlorate	ClO_3^-	hydrogen sulphite	HSO_3^-
hypochlorite	ClO^-	thiocyanate	SCN^-
chromate	CrO_4^{2-}	thiosulphate	$S_2O_3^{2-}$
dichromate	$Cr_2O_7^{2-}$		
cyanide	CN^-		
hydroxide	OH^-		
iodate	IO_3^-		
nitrate	NO_3^-		
nitrite	NO_2^-		
oxalate	$OOCCOO^{2-}$		
permanganate	MnO_4^-		
phosphate	PO_4^{3-}		
hydrogen phosphate	HPO_4^{2-}		

Main chart:

1 H$^+$ hydrogen

3 Li$^+$ lithium
4 Be^{2+} beryllium

11 Na$^+$ sodium
12 Mg^{2+} magnesium

19 K$^+$ potassium
20 Ca^{2+} calcium
21 Sc^{3+} scandium

37 Rb$^+$ rubidium
38 Sr^{2+} strontium
39 Y^{3+} yttrium

55 Cs$^+$ cesium
56 Ba^{2+} barium
57-71

87 Fr$^+$ francium
88 Ra^{2+} radium
89-103

22 Ti titanium(V) Ti^{4+} / titanium(III) Ti^{3+}
23 V vanadium(V) V^{5+} / vanadium(IV) V^{4+}
24 Cr chromium(III) Cr^{3+} / chromium(II) Cr^{2+}
25 Mn manganese(II) Mn^{2+} / manganese(V) Mn^{4+}
26 Fe iron(III) Fe^{3+} / iron(II) Fe^{2+}
27 Co cobalt(II) Co^{2+} / cobalt(III) Co^{3+}
28 Ni nickel(II) Ni^{2+} / nickel(III) Ni^{3+}
29 Cu copper(II) Cu^{2+} / copper(I) Cu$^+$
30 Zn^{2+} zinc

40 Zr^{4+} zirconium
41 Nb niobium(V) Nb^{5+} / niobium(III) Nb^{3+}
42 Mo^{6+} molybdenum
43 Tc^{7+} technetium
44 Ru ruthenium(III) Ru^{3+} / ruthenium(IV) Ru^{4+}
45 Rh^{3+} rhodium
46 Pd palladium(II) Pd^{2+} / palladium(IV) Pd^{4+}
47 Ag$^+$ silver
48 Cd^{2+} cadmium

72 Hf^{4+} hafnium
73 Ta^{5+} tantalum
74 W^{6+} tungsten
75 Re^{7+} rhenium
76 Os^{4+} osmium
77 Ir^{4+} iridium
78 Pt platinum(IV) Pt^{4+} / platinum(II) Pt^{2+}
79 Au gold(III) Au^{3+} / gold(I) Au$^+$
80 Hg mercury(II) Hg^{2+} / mercury(I) Hg$^+$

5 B boron
13 Al^{3+} aluminum
31 Ga^{3+} gallium
49 In^{3+} indium
81 Tl thallium(I) Tl$^+$ / thallium(III) Tl^{3+}

6 C carbon
14 Si silicon
32 Ge^{4+} germanium
50 Sn tin(IV) Sn^{4+} / tin(II) Sn^{2+}
82 Pb lead(II) Pb^{2+} / lead(IV) Pb^{4+}

7 N^{3-} nitride
15 P^{3-} phosphide
33 As^{3-} arsenide
51 Sb antimony(III) Sb^{3+} / antimony(V) Sb^{5+}
83 Bi bismuth(III) Bi^{3+} / bismuth(V) Bi^{5+}

8 O^{2-} oxide
16 S^{2-} sulphide
34 Se^{2-} selenide
52 Te^{2-} telluride
84 Po polonium(II) Po^{2+} / polonium(IV) Po^{4+}

1 H$^-$ hydride
9 F$^-$ fluoride
17 Cl$^-$ chloride
35 Br$^-$ bromide
53 I$^-$ iodide
85 At astatide

2 He helium
10 Ne neon
18 Ar argon
36 Kr krypton
54 Xe xenon
86 Rn radon

Lanthanides:

57 La^{3+} lanthanum
58 Ce^{3+} cerium
59 Pr^{3+} praseodymium
60 Nd^{3+} neodymium
61 Pm^{3+} promethium
62 Sm samarium(III) Sm^{3+} / samarium(II) Sm^{2+}
63 Eu europium(III) Eu^{3+} / europium(II) Eu^{2+}
64 Gd^{3+} gadolinium
65 Tb^{3+} terbium
66 Dy^{3+} dysprosium
67 Ho^{3+} holmium
68 Er^{3+} erbium
69 Tm^{3+} thulium
70 Yb ytterbium(III) Yb^{3+} / ytterbium(II) Yb^{2+}
71 Lu^{2+} lutetium

Actinides:

89 Ac^{3+} actinium
90 Th^{4+} thorium
91 Pa protactinium(V) Pa^{5+} / protactinium(IV) Pa^{4+}
92 U uranium(VI) U^{6+} / uranium(IV) U^{4+}
93 Np^{5+} neptunium
94 Pu plutonium(IV) Pu^{4+} / plutonium(VI) Pu^{6+}
95 Am americium(III) Am^{3+} / americium(IV) Am^{4+}
96 Cm^{3+} curium
97 Bk berkelium(III) Bk^{3+} / berkelium(IV) Bk^{4+}
98 Cf^{3+} californium
99 Es^{3+} einsteinium
100 Fm^{3+} fermium
101 Md mendelevium(II) Md^{2+} / mendelevium(III) Md^{3+}
102 No nobelium(II) No^{2+} / nobelium(III) No^{3+}
103 Lr^{3+} lawrencium

KEY

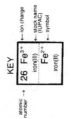

atomic number → 26 Fe^{3+} ← ion charge
iron(III) ← stock name (IUPAC)
Fe^{2+} ← symbol
iron(II)

Periodic Table of Electronegativity
Using the Pauling Scale

→ **Atomic radius decreases** → **Ionization energy increases** → **Electronegativity increases** →

Group (vertical)

| 1 | 2 | 3 | 4 | 5 | 6 | 7 | 8 | 9 | 10 | 11 | 12 | 13 | 14 | 15 | 16 | 17 | 18 |

Period (horizontal)

Period	1	2	3	4	5	6	7	8	9	10	11	12	13	14	15	16	17	18
1	H 2.20																	He
2	Li 0.98	Be 1.57											B 2.04	C 2.55	N 3.04	O 3.44	F 3.98	Ne
3	Na 0.93	Mg 1.31											Al 1.61	Si 1.90	P 2.19	S 2.58	Cl 3.16	Ar
4	K 0.82	Ca 1.00	Sc 1.36	Ti 1.54	V 1.63	Cr 1.66	Mn 1.55	Fe 1.83	Co 1.88	Ni 1.91	Cu 1.90	Zn 1.65	Ga 1.81	Ge 2.01	As 2.18	Se 2.55	Br 2.96	Kr 3.00
5	Rb 0.82	Sr 0.95	Y 1.22	Zr 1.33	Nb 1.6	Mo 2.16	Tc 1.9	Ru 2.2	Rh 2.28	Pd 2.20	Ag 1.93	Cd 1.69	In 1.78	Sn 1.96	Sb 2.05	Te 2.1	I 2.66	Xe 2.67
6	Cs 0.79	Ba 0.89	*	Hf 1.3	Ta 1.5	W 2.36	Re 1.9	Os 2.2	Ir 2.20	Pt 2.28	Au 2.54	Hg 2.00	Tl 1.62	Pb 2.33	Bi 2.02	Po 2.0	At 2.2	Rn
7	Fr 0.7	Ra 0.9	**	Rf	Db	Sg	Bh	Hs	Mt	Ds	Rg	Uub	Uut	Uuq	Uup	Uuh	Uus	Uuo

Lanthanides	*	La 1.1	Ce 1.12	Pr 1.13	Nd 1.14	Pm 1.13	Sm 1.17	Eu 1.2	Gd 1.2	Tb 1.1	Dy 1.22	Ho 1.23	Er 1.24	Tm 1.25	Yb 1.1	Lu 1.27
Actinides	**	Ac 1.1	Th 1.3	Pa 1.5	U 1.38	Np 1.36	Pu 1.28	Am 1.13	Cm 1.28	Bk 1.3	Cf 1.3	Es 1.3	Fm 1.3	Md 1.3	No 1.3	Lr

Credits

ORDERING INFORMATION

All School Orders

School Authorities are eligible to purchase these resources by applying the Learning Resource Credit Allocation (LRCA – 25% school discount) on their purchase through the Learning Resources Centre (LRC). Call LRC for details.

THE KEY *Study Guides* are specifically designed to assist students in preparing for unit tests, final exams, and provincial examinations.

KEY *Study Guides* – $29.95 each plus G.S.T.

SENIOR HIGH		JUNIOR HIGH	ELEMENTARY
Biology 30 Chemistry 30 English 30-1 English 30-2 Math 30 (Pure) Math 30 (Applied) Physics 30 Social Studies 30 Social Studies 33	Biology 20 Chemistry 20 English 20-1 Math 20 (Pure) Physics 20 Social Studies 20 English 10-1 Math 10 (Pure) Science 10 Social Studies 10	Language Arts 9 Math 9 Science 9 Social Studies 9 Math 8 Math 7	Language Arts 6 Math 6 Science 6 Social Studies 6 Math 4 Language Arts 3 Math 3

Student Notes and Problems (SNAP) Workbooks contain complete explanations of curriculum concepts, examples, and exercise questions.

SNAP Workbooks – $29.95 each plus G.S.T.

SENIOR HIGH		JUNIOR HIGH	ELEMENTARY
Chemistry 30 Math 30 Pure Math 30 Applied Math 31 Physics 30	Chemistry 20 Math 20 Pure Math 20 Applied Physics 20 Math 10 Pure Math 10 Applied Science 10	Math 9 Science 9 Math 8 Math 7	Math 6 Math 5 Math 4 Math 3

Visit our website for a "tour" of resource content and features at
www.castlerockresearch.com

#2340, 10180 – 101 Street Edmonton, AB Canada T5J 3S4 e-mail: learn@castlerockresearch.com	Phone: 780.448.9619 Toll-free: 1.800.840.6224 Fax: 780.426.3917

SCHOOL ORDER FORM

Castle Rock Research Corp

THE KEY	QUANTITY
Biology 30	
Chemistry 30	
English 30-1	
English 30-2	
Math30 (Pure)	
Math 30 (Applied)	
Physics 30	
Social Studies 30	
Social Studies 33	
Biology 20	
Chemistry 20	
English 20-1	
Math 20 (Pure)	
Physics 20	
Social Studies 20	
English 10-1	
Math 10 (Pure)	
Science 10	
Social Studies 10	
Science 9	
Language Arts 9	
Math 9	
Science 9	
Social Studies 9	
Math 8	
Math 7	
Language Arts 6	
Math 6	
Science 6	
Social Studies 6	
Math 4	
Math 3	
Language Arts 3	

SNAP WORKBOOKS Notes and Problems/ Student Notes and Problems	QUANTITY	
	Workbooks	Solutions Manuals
Chemistry 30		
Chemistry 20		
Physics 30		
Physics 20		
Math 31		
Math 30 Pure		
Math 30 Applied		
Math 20 Pure		
Math 20 Applied		
Math 10 Pure		
Math 10 Applied		
Science 10		
Science 9		
Math 9		
Math 8		
Math 7		
Math 6		
Math 5		
Math 4		
Math 3		

TOTALS

KEYS

WORKBOOKS

SOLUTION MANUALS

Learning Resources Centre

Castle Rock Research is pleased to announce an exclusive distribution arrangement with the Learning Resources Centre (LRC). Under this agreement, schools can now place all their orders with LRC for order fulfillment. As well, these resources are eligible for applying the Learning Resource Credit Allocation (LRCA), which gives schools a 25% discount off LRC's selling price. Call LRC for details.

**Orders may be placed with LRC by
telephone:** (780) 427-5775
fax: (780) 422-9750
internet: www.lrc.learning.gov.ab.ca
or mail: 12360 - 142 Street NW
Edmonton, AB T5L 4X9

Learning Resources Centre

PAYMENT AND SHIPPING INFORMATION

Name:

School Telephone:

SHIP TO

School:

Address:

City: _____ Postal Code: _____

PAYMENT

☐ by credit card

VISA/MC Number:

Name on Card:

☐ enclosed cheque _____ Expiry Date: _____

☐ invoice school   P.O. number:

#2340, 10180 – 101 Street, Edmonton, AB T5J 3S4   Tel: 780.448.9619   Fax: 780.426.3917
email: learn@castlerockresearch.com   Toll-free: 1.800.840.6224

www.castlerockresearch.com

2006 (4)